APR   2005

No Such Thing as Over-Exposure

Inside the Life and Celebrity of Donald Trump

ADVANCE PRAISE FOR
NO SUCH THING AS OVER-EXPOSURE

"The Donald Trump that I have come to know over the years is not easy to capture in a book. It was a pleasure to read Robert Slater's well-researched, fascinating look at what makes Trump tick. Other than reading Trump's own books, there is no better way to find out why Donald is so successful."

—Alan "Ace" Greenberg, Chairman of the Executive Committee,
Bear Stearns

"There is no bigger ego that ever walked this earth than Mr. Trump. Beyond his success as the world's preeminent developer, he's built THE power brand that stands for wealth and success around the world. Slater's book takes us farther inside the Trump mind and modus operandi than anything else to date. I should know. I have worked closely with Donald Trump for years."

—Barbara Corcoran, Chairman and Founder, The Corcoran Group,
Author of *If You Don't Have Big Breasts, Put Ribbons On Your Pigtails*

"The audacious genius of Donald Trump is fully revealed in Robert Slater's latest book, *No Such Thing as Over-Exposure*. I've worked for a lot of business titans in my career, including The Donald, and no one understands the power of publicity and the value of a brand better than Mr. Trump. Whether it's a 70-story tower, a reality show, or a bottle of water, when Trump affixes his name to a project it turns to gold. This is a must read for all those who want to understand fully the brilliance of our era's best entrepreneurial promoter."

—Howard J. Rubenstein, President, Rubenstein Associates, Inc.

"When I was asked if I would consider writing a brief—100 words or less—endorsement for *No Such Thing as Over-Exposure: Inside the Life and Celebrity of Donald Trump*, it immediately occurred to me that I could write an endorsement for the book in one word—mastery.

Donald Trump is a "master" at everything he does, everything he says, and everything he thinks. That is not to say that he hasn't made mistakes or gone through challenging periods in his personal and professional life—he has. However he has brilliantly developed his own personal mastery over it all—the good, the bad, and the ugly.

You'll read all about his true genius of mastery in Robert Slater's *No Such Thing as Over-Exposure: Inside the Life and Celebrity of Donald Trump*, who I would also like to add, has mastered the art of writing business biographies."

—George M. Steinbrenner, III, Principal Owner, New York Yankees

"A refreshing antidote to the mumbling modesty that bedevils much of our culture. Trump understands that self-promotion and fame is the best insurance of power already attained. Slater captures this lesson beautifully in this fast-paced, punchy book, packed with interviews, savvy, and insight into one of the phenomena of our age."

—Paul Levinson, Professor of Communication and Media Studies, Fordham University; Author of *Cellphone: The Story of the World's Most Mobile Medium*

"Donald Trump is a master of the game. Robert Slater's entertaining book provides an enticing behind-the-scenes look into Donald's unique world. The complete access Donald gave Slater enabled the writer to capture the strategies and thinking behind the key deals and business moves which contributed to Donald's impressive rise. I really enjoyed reading *No Such Thing as Over-Exposure*—and I think it will be appreciated by those fascinated by Donald's incredible career."

—Preston Robert Tisch, Chairman, Loews Corporation, Chairman and Co-CEO, New York Football Giants

"This is a fascinating look at one of today's more interesting and unusual personalities."

—Steve Wynn, Owner of Wynn Las Vegas

"Much has been said and much has been written about and by Donald Trump. As a friend for over 35 years and as a fellow real-estate developer, I can say without reservation that this book provides unique perspectives on Donald's character and methods that reveal why he is a billionaire. The book is so insightful that I have insisted that my own sons read it so they can begin to understand the Trump Magic."

—Richard S. Lefrak, The Lefrak Organization

"Donald Trump is one of the most interesting personalities in modern times and Robert Slater is, without question, unparalleled at capturing the essence of our captains of industry.

The combination is a fascinating behind-the-scenes look at Donald's charm, his business intuition, and the richness of his character. A must-read."

—Alex Yemenidjian, Chairman of the Board, Chief Executive Officer, Metro-Goldwyn-Mayer Studios Inc.

No Such Thing as Over-Exposure

Inside the Life and Celebrity of Donald Trump

Robert Slater

Library of Congress Number: 2004116294

Publisher: Tim Moore
Editorial Assistant: Richard Winkler
Development Editor: Russ Hall
Marketing Manager: Martin Litkowski
International Marketing Manager: Tim Galligan
Cover Designer: Chuti Prasertsith
Managing Editor: Gina Kanouse
Senior Project Editor: Kristy Hart
Copy Editor: Krista Hansing
Proofreader: Sheri Cain
Senior Indexer: Cheryl Lenser
Interior Designer and Composition: Gloria Schurick
Manufacturing Buyer: Dan Uhrig

© 2005 by Pearson Education, Inc.
Publishing as Prentice Hall
Upper Saddle River, New Jersey 07458

**Prentice Hall offers excellent discounts on this book when ordered in quantity for bulk
purchases or special sales. For more information, please contact U.S. Corporate and
Government Sales, 1-800-382-3419, corpsales@pearsontechgroup.com.
For sales outside the U.S., please contact International Sales, 1-317-581-3793,
international@pearsontechgroup.com.**

Company and product names mentioned herein are the trademarks or registered trademarks of
their respective owners.

Printed in the United States of America

First Printing, February 2005

ISBN 0-13-149734-0

Pearson Education LTD.
Pearson Education Australia PTY, Limited.
Pearson Education Singapore, Pte. Ltd.
Pearson Education North Asia, Ltd.
Pearson Education Canada, Ltd.
Pearson Educatión de Mexico, S.A. de C.V.
Pearson Education—Japan
Pearson Education Malaysia, Pte. Ltd.

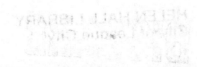

For my wife, Elinor
with love and gratitude.

CONTENTS

Preface: The Letter and the Phone Call   XIII

Part I   Forging an Image   **1**
    Chapter 1   Have You Seen My Ratings?   3
    Chapter 2   Behind Open Doors   19

Part II   Seizing an Island   **41**
    Chapter 3   Marching Up Fifth Avenue   43
    Chapter 4   Changing a Skyline   57

Part III   The Value of Celebrity   **75**
    Chapter 5   Conquering a Boardwalk   77
    Chapter 6   Fall and Comeback   99

Part IV   The Nurturing of a Name   **117**
    Chapter 7   Student of the Media   119
    Chapter 8   Branding a Name   145

Part V   Suddenly, a Household Name   **167**
    Chapter 9   The Perfect Match   169
    Chapter 10   Heightened Demand, Persistent Debt   193
    Chapter 11   No Such Thing as Over-Exposure   209

Acknowledgments   227

Endnotes   231

Index   241

ABOUT THE AUTHOR

Robert Slater was born in New York City on October 1, 1943, and grew up in South Orange, New Jersey. He graduated from Columbia High School in 1962 and graduated with honors from the University of Pennsylvania in 1966, where he majored in political science. He received a masters of science degree in international relations from the London School of Economics in 1967. He worked for UPI and *Time Magazine* for many years, in both the United States and the Middle East.

Slater wrote 16 books about major business personalities before his new book on Donald Trump:

- *The Titans of Takeover* (Englewood Cliffs, NJ: Prentice Hall, 1987).
- *Portraits in Silicon* (Cambridge, MA: MIT Press, 1987).
- *This ... .Is CBS: A Chronicle of 60 Years* (Englewood Cliffs, NJ: Prentice Hall, 1988).
- *The New GE: How Jack Welch Revived an American Institution* (Homewood, IL: Business One Irwin, 1993).
- *Get Better or Get Beaten! 31 Leadership Secrets from GE's Jack Welch* (Burr Ridge, IL: Irwin Professional Publishing, 1994). This book made the business best-seller list in Japan.
- *SOROS: The Life, Times, and Trading Secrets of the World's Greatest Investor* (Chicago, IL: Irwin Professional Publishing, 1996). This book profiles superinvestor George Soros, and it appeared on the *Business Week* best-seller list.
- *Invest First, Investigate Later: And 23 Other Trading Secrets of George Soros, the Legendary Investor* (Chicago, IL: Irwin Professional Publishing, 1996).

- *John Bogle and the Vanguard Experiment: One Man's Quest to Transform the Mutual Fund Industry* (Chicago, IL: Irwin Professional Publishing, 1996). This book profiles the most important business figure in the mutual fund field.

- *Ovitz: The Inside Story of Hollywood's Most Controversial Power Broker* (New York, NY: McGraw-Hill, 1997). This book made the *Los Angeles Times* and the *New York Times* business best-seller lists.

- *Jack Welch and the GE Way: Management Insights and Leadership Secrets of the Legendary CEO* (New York, NY: McGraw-Hill, 1998). This is an updated look at the business secrets of General Electric's chairman and chief executive officer. It made the *Business Week* and *The Wall Street Journal* best-seller lists.

- *Saving Big Blue: Leadership Lessons & Turnaround Tactics of IBM's Lou Gerstner* (New York, NY: McGraw-Hill, 1999).

- *The GE Way Fieldbook: Jack Welch's Battle Plan for Corporate Revolution* (New York, NY: McGraw Hill, 1999).

- *The Eye of the Storm: How John Chambers Steered Cisco Systems Through the Technology Collapse* (New York, NY: HarperBusiness, 2003).

- *Magic Cancer Bullet: How a Tiny Orange Capsule May Rewrite Medical History* (New York, NY: HarperBusiness, 2003), co-authored with Novartis CEO, Dan Vasella.

- *The Wal-Mart Decade: How a New Generation of Leaders Turned Sam Walton's Legacy into the World's #1 Company* (New York, NY: Portfolio, 2003). A paperback version was published in June 2004.

- *Microsoft Rebooted: How Bill Gates and Steve Ballmer Re-Invented Their Company* (New York, NY: Portfolio, 2004).

PREFACE

THE LETTER AND THE PHONE CALL

"Be advised that Mr. Trump has instructed me to take such action... which may include, but will not be limited to, bringing an action to enjoin you from publishing and disseminating the book...."

That was the key sentence in the e-mail that I received April 8, 2004.

I had barely begun my research on a book about Donald Trump when a man named Jason D. Greenblatt, vice president and assistant general counsel of the Trump Organization, wrote me that e-mail.

I did not know Trump. Nor did I know Greenblatt. Moreover, I had not written a word of the book at that point. I had conducted a grand total of three interviews. My only contact with Trump's office had been a phone call and a follow-up e-mail, requesting to meet with Trump and/or his staff.

I thought it odd, to say the least, that a Donald Trump attorney was threatening me with a lawsuit long before the book had become a reality—odd and chilling.

The idea of writing a book about Donald Trump came to me upon hearing his name mentioned on television over and over during a 24-hour period early in 2004. Having written books on major business personalities for two decades, I had rejected Trump as a possible book subject until then, deciding that he was a minor business player. Like many others, I had concluded dismissively that he was more showman than serious business leader. Then as his hit reality television series, *The Apprentice*, began to attract a huge audience, and as Donald Trump became a household name, I quickly decided that he would make a great book.

Among the well-known business personalities I have written books about are Jack Welch of General Electric, Wall Street investor George Soros, mutual fund pioneer John Bogle, Hollywood agent Michael Ovitz, IBM's Lou Gerstner, Cisco Systems' John Chambers, Wal-Mart's Lee Scott, and Microsoft's Bill Gates and Steve Ballmer.

Most of these business leaders agreed to be interviewed for my books on them. Only Soros and Gerstner declined. Neither Soros nor Gerstner, however, threatened to enjoin the publication of the book. George Soros passed word through an attorney that I would not be able to interview Soros or anyone who worked for him. Lou Gerstner indicated that neither he nor his fellow IBM executives would have time for interviews, but he did make his public relations staff available for fact-checking.

My routine in starting a book project on a business personality has been to seek a publisher and obtain a contract for the book first, and only then to approach the book's subject and colleagues with a request for interviews. Thus it was that, on March 23, 2004, 16 days before the e-mail arrived and 1 day after obtaining a contract for a book on Trump, I phoned the Trump Organization, requesting to visit with Trump and/or his associates to tell them about the book. Meredith McIver, who co-authored Trump's 2004 book, *How to Become Rich*, came on the line. When I told her that I planned to write a book on Trump, she asked me to send her an e-mail giving more details about the book and me. I did.

AN UNEXPECTED E-MAIL

I wrote that I hoped I might have the chance to tell her in person about the kind of book I planned to write. "The book," I went on, "will take an in-depth look at Mr. Trump's management strategies and techniques, along with his business achievements over the years." I planned to focus the book around such questions as 1) What were Trump's definable business strategies and attitudes toward leadership and management? 2) Why did he, and not a thousand other real-estate developers, become a business celebrity? 3) Why did *The Apprentice* become the surprise hit reality show of the year?

I hoped that Ms. McIver would arrange for me to meet someone within the Trump senior echelons to help me get the book started. During that meeting, I planned to ask for an interview with both Donald Trump and those business colleagues closest to him.

Instead of hearing back from Ms. McIver that such a meeting would be possible, I received the e-mail from Greenblatt.

As I read the opening sentence of his April 8 e-mail, I felt a momentary sense of relief at finally getting a response to my March 23 request of cooperation. But my relief quickly became bemusement as I realized that Trump had assigned an attorney to pen the response.

Here is the e-mail in its entirety:

I am counsel to Donald J. Trump. Your email (sent on March 23, 2004) to Ms. Meredith McIver was referred to me for a response.

You are hereby advised that Mr. Trump does not authorize your proposed book, nor does he wish to contribute to the proposed book in any manner.

You indicate that the proposed book will portray an in-depth look at Mr. Trump's management strategies and techniques, along with his business achievements. Implicit in such portrayal is that you are very familiar with such strategies and techniques, many of which have been developed by Mr. Trump and are, therefore, unique and proprietary to him. Because you have no current or former association with Mr. Trump or any of his business endeavors, it would be virtually impossible for you to write a book that purports to accurately portray Mr. Trump's management strategies and techniques. Since you cannot accurately portray Mr. Trump's management strategies and techniques, you would, of necessity, have to fictionalize such information. Therefore, we believe that this book would be prohibited under Section 51 of the New York Civil Rights Law and constitute an unauthorized exploitation of Mr. Trump's name and/or image for purposes of advertisement and/or trade (see, for example, Warren E. Spahn, Respondent vs. Julian Messner, Inc., et al., Appellants [Court of Appeals of New York; Decided October 27, 1996]).

Be advised that Mr. Trump has instructed me to take such action as may be necessary in the protection of his interests, which may include, but will not be limited to, bringing an action to enjoin you from publishing and disseminating the book, as well as seeking to recover from you and the publisher of the book any damages that Mr. Trump may sustain in connection with the book.

Be advised that Mr. Trump has instructed me to take such action as may be necessary in the protection of his interests, which may include, but will not be limited to, bringing an action to enjoin you from publishing and disseminating the book, as well as seeking to recover from you and the publisher of the book any damages that Mr. Trump may sustain in connection with the book. Please note that the statutes in question expressly authorize the awarding of exemplary (punitive) damages in the event that it is determined that you knowingly violated Mr. Trump's civil rights.

I trust you will be guided accordingly.
Very truly yours,
Jason D. Greenblatt

I was astonished to read this letter.

It had always been my assumption that authors who wish to write a book about a public figure do not require that person' s approval—and Trump certainly qualifies as a public figure.

Accordingly, it was also my assumption that a public figure had no legal ground to enjoin the publication of a book about him or her. A public figure certainly had a right to take action against an author and/or publisher if that figure felt legally injured, but any legal action, by its very nature, had to await the publication of the book. One could not expect a court to enjoin publication over what an author might write.

I had written numerous books on public figures. Never once had any of them even hinted that they had a legal basis for preventing me from writing a book about them. Nor did I know of any other public figure who had sought to prevent an author from writing a book about that person.

I felt on very safe legal ground in proceeding with the book. Happily, my editor, Tim Moore at Financial Times Prentice Hall, agreed, as did the publisher's attorneys. During one long and pleasant lunch in New York City, Tim and I spent a total of five minutes going over the threatening e-mail. We both felt that Trump had no legal grounds that would permit him to prevent the publication of our book, and we would proceed with the book whether or not he brought suit.

My editor and I decided not to respond directly to the e-mail, and to keep it and its threat to prevent publication of the book a secret until much closer to the publication of the book. I was concerned that if at that early stage of my interviewing word got into the newspapers of Trump's legal threat against the book, people would automatically decline to be interviewed. I had been getting positive replies to my requests for interviews from many people who had known Trump at different stages of his career; I wanted my good fortune to continue.

Although I was firm in not wanting to respond to Mr. Greenblatt's e-mail, I did believe that it made sense for me, farther along in my research, to submit a list of questions that arose from my research directly to Donald Trump. I always had accorded the subjects of my books the opportunity to respond to the assertions of others. I saw every reason to act in the same manner toward Donald Trump, despite the substance of that e-mail. I felt an obligation to be fair to him, and the only way to be fair in my view was to offer him the chance to respond to my questions. Given his attorney's e-mail to me, I fully believed that he would not reply, but I planned to ask a series of questions anyway.

As I continued with the research and interviews for this book, I often asked myself: Why does Donald Trump not want me to write this book? I had not come across any evidence that he had tried to quash any other author's book on him. Why, then, was he singling out my book and me? And why was he threatening legal action at this very preliminary stage in my research?

CONTROLLING HIS IMAGE

The more I learned about Donald Trump, the more certain I was that he wanted to control his image fully by controlling as much as he could what was written about him. He was prepared to use whatever resources were available to him, especially the threat of and even the actual use of litigation. I came across newspaper articles that told of his litigious nature. Still, he must have known, I assumed, that it was nearly impossible—even via the threat of litigation—to control his image, given the amount of television and newspaper copy he had been generating.

What, I asked, was he afraid of?

Why did he believe that my book would harm his public image?

Whether I was "business-friendly" (as some book reviewers called me) or not, what legal right did Mr. Trump have to suppress my book?

Whatever his own personal motivation was for having his attorney send me that e-mail, I decided that I would do my best not to let the e-mail influence the way I wrote the book. Even if the e-mail had not been written, I would have sought to portray Donald Trump fairly, objectively, and honestly; I intended to do the same, despite the e-mail. I knew it would be a challenge. It was already having some effect. For instance, I had never written a preface to one of my books that looked anything like this. Despite the legal cloud hanging over the project, I was determined to carry on with the book. I did not know whether Trump would go ahead with his threatened lawsuit. I could not control what he might do. But I could control how I wrote the book.

To be sure, I hoped that Trump would change his mind, withdraw the legal threat, and grant me one or more interviews for the book. Yet, although I hoped for such a change of heart, I had no illusions that he would recant. Once before in my career, a business leader had turned down my bid to interview him for my book on him; but then six weeks later, he changed his mind:

John Chambers, president and CEO of the Internet infrastructure firm Cisco Systems, eventually granted me numerous interviews for my 2003 book *The Eye of the Storm: How John Chambers Steered Cisco Systems Through the Technology Collapse.* Still, just because Chambers had shifted gears was no reason to assume that Donald Trump might.

I wanted Trump to remove the legal threat, not because I felt intimidated by him, but because I genuinely wanted to interview him. As both a journalist and an author, I had been trained to interview the people who loomed large in my story or book so that I could offer the best possible description and analysis of that person. It was the only way a professional writer should behave, so I was taught.

A number of weeks passed. I carried on with the project, interviewing people who had known Donald Trump at one time or another. Some declined to be interviewed or simply did not answer my requests. I assumed correctly that a certain number would accede to my request only after getting a green light from Donald Trump.

On the morning of May 18, nearly six weeks after receiving the e-mail, I wrote a draft of this preface, explaining that Trump had threatened legal action to stop this book from being published. I assumed there might well be new twists and turns in his actions toward the book, and I would simply add them to the draft at a later stage. I had no idea that the strangest twist would come only hours later.

THE PHONE RINGS

That afternoon, my phone rang. A woman identified herself as calling from Donald Trump's office. She said he would like to talk with me. My first reaction was that he probably wanted to launch the lawsuit through this phone call. He must have been getting phone calls from people I wanted to interview, concrete evidence that I was continuing with the book despite his threat of litigation. In truth, I hardly had any time to think carefully about why he was calling. An instant later, he came on the line.

I prepared myself for some screaming, but none came.

Instead, his voice was friendly. His words came fast. He seemed pleased to be talking with me. He began by telling me that he had just spoken with Jack Welch and that Welch had told him "what an amazing guy you are." Trump sounded upbeat, positive about me, not at all like someone who was threatening a lawsuit.

He explained that indeed he had been getting calls from people whom I had wanted to interview for my book. They had asked Trump for his permission before granting the interview. At a certain point, Trump decided that he would check out my credentials. He presumably looked over the e-mail I had sent him and saw that I had written books on Jack Welch. He decided to phone Welch, fully expecting the former GE chairman and CEO to suggest that Trump steer clear of me. Instead, Welch gave me a rave review. "He said you were always fair," Donald Trump reported to me, "and if Jack Welch says that about you, that's good enough for me."

I was, of course, startled—and pleasantly surprised at this turn of events. It had always been my goal to interview Trump, and now it appeared that I would have the opportunity, though at first he said half-pleadingly that he did not have much time for interviews because *The Apprentice* was taking up so much of his time. Eventually, he agreed to meet me in his office at Trump Tower in New York City on the morning of June 3.

He suggested some people he thought I should interview, people whom I was sure he trusted to present him in the most favorable light. I said I would be pleased to talk with them. Trump's executive assistant, Rhona Graff, came on the line and gave me phone numbers for the people Trump wanted me to interview. All I could think of was how the world had turned.

Never in our 20-minute phone conversation did Trump mention the lawyer's letter that he had sent in early April. It was as if the e-mail had never been sent, never even existed. Nor did I mention the letter. Certainly, if he was now willing to be interviewed and to have other acquaintances interviewed for the book, his original threat to enjoin the publication of the book was, it seemed fair to conclude, off the table.

I knew that, at some point, I would want to ask him about why he had sent the lawyer's letter to me. Would he tell me that he had no idea it had been sent? Would he dismiss it as something he did routinely without any intention of actually launching a lawsuit?

What would he say? I was very eager to find out.

But I decided not to raise the subject during our first interview, eager for our first meeting to go smoothly; I was, quite frankly, concerned that the mere mention of the threatened lawsuit might add unnecessary tension between us. Only if he brought up the lawsuit would I ask him why his lawyer had sent the e-mail to me.

On June 3, we met for nearly two hours. He was, as he had been on the phone, friendly, warm, and welcoming. He made it clear almost from the beginning that he was agreeable to meeting a second time. He did not raise the threatened lawsuit, nor did I. I contented myself with knowing that I would try to raise the subject during our second meeting. He did offer hints about why he had been unwilling to meet with me at first: He didn't know my work or me.

All throughout that first session, Trump expressed the utmost respect for my book project and for me.

At one point, he asked me a series of questions about the value of his participating in my book project.

Did I, as the author, like to have the subject of a book participate in that book?

Did the subject's participation impact sales?

Did my interviewing the subject give me a better feel for the person?

Was it correct that five or six years ago (presumably, when he was less in the news than in 2004), I would not have wanted to do the book?

Was I doing a book on him now because he was "hot" (his word)?

I answered each question briefly, trying to get back as quickly as I could to interviewing him. But I appreciated the irony that our relationship had gone from his threatening to bring legal action to a rational discussion of the merits of his participating in the project—after he had agreed to participate!

THE MERCURIAL MAN

The e-mail and the subsequent telephone call serve as the best possible evidence of Donald Trump's mercurial, in-your-face manner of handling personal relationships. Unlike most of the other business leaders I have written books about, Trump is capable of launching a blistering attack against someone, only to turn warm and affectionate when such a change of behavior makes sense to him. He does not feel a need to explain his mercurial nature. It is simply the way he is.

When we met for a second interview on July 27, I decided that it was time to ask Trump why he had sent me the lawyer's letter; I was, I confess, eager to hear what his reaction would be. I also felt that because I planned to write this preface explaining the e-mail and the subsequent phone call, it was only proper that I ask him to explain his threat of legal action.

> *RS: You actually threatened to sue me.*
> *Trump: I did?*
> *RS: You did.*
> *Trump: Oh, Okay.*
> *RS: I assume you knew that.*
> *Trump: I actually think I did.*

I raised the subject as part of a question about how he worked; I noted that he appeared to use the threat of litigation often enough that it seemed to be almost a systematic business strategy for him.

RS: You actually threatened to sue me.

Trump: I did?

RS: You did.

Trump: Oh, Okay.

RS: I assume you knew that.

Trump: I actually think I did. But I didn't think of it then. (It's) hard to believe because you're such a nice guy.

I began to show him the letter.

Trump: That's all right (waving his hand, as if to show he didn't need to see the letter). Well, I heard there was a guy going around doing a book. [I said to myself,] I might as well put him on notice because I have so many false things written about me, it pisses me off.

RS: Is that one of your business strategies? You also talk—in interviews—about being vindictive toward people who deserve your wrath. But that's not a strategy. When you use the threat of litigation, is it because you say, "I'm going to advance my business career with the legal threat"?

Trump replied that, relative to his company's size, which is, he said, much larger than people understand, he is in very little litigation. "I sue people when I get screwed. If people are fair to me, I never do it, but when I get screwed—in your case, we sent you a letter, which isn't a lawsuit; it's a letter.

RS: It's a threat of a lawsuit.

Trump: Yeah, it is, it is a threat because I had heard there was some guy going around talking to people, some of whom were friends of mine, who immediately called me and said, "Donald, there's a guy writing a book about you, and this and that. [I asked my friends,] 'Well, what kind of questions?' Well, he doesn't sound so friendly. Well, he doesn't sound this and that. So, I say, 'All right, fuck him. Let's write him a letter and say we're going to sue your ass off if you write false statements.'"

RS: Was this the first time you have threatened to sue an author?

At first, he said he rarely sued authors, and then he went on: "Except I was getting all these calls. And the only one you hadn't called that I knew of was me."

RS: I did [contact you]. You were the first.

Trump: See, I wasn't told.

RS: You were the first.

Trump: Okay, see, I wasn't told. Usually, when a guy is going around talking to a lot of people and writing a book, there's usually an agenda.

I said that I had no agenda in any of my books and that I had simply wanted to interview him and others for the book.

He said he did not normally write such letters to authors, but he was getting calls from everyone that I was talking to. "And," he repeated, "you hadn't spoken to me. I respect Jack Welch a lot; I called Jack Welch. He said you're really a good guy, a fair guy, you're a great guy."

I noted neutrally that I had written four books on Welch.

Trump: He said you're a great guy. "Really?" [Trump replied to Welch]. I was shocked. Then I called you after that and I said, "Come on in, let's talk." Because usually when that happens, the people are up to no good. It's like I say, Robert, there are times in my life when a bad book can be written in all fairness. In the early '90s, and again, I never went bankrupt like a lot of other people, but people went bankrupt, the fucking world was collapsing, the real-estate market was collapsing; in the early '90s, I could have had a bad book written about me. At that point in my life, I wasn't exactly doing great, but today, I have the number one show on television. I am the biggest developer in New York, by far. I do the best job. I'm building buildings all over the place.

I noted to Trump that I understood his feeling that he did not want bad books written about him because they would form part of the literature that would become his legacy.

Trump: It's true. It's very important, books like you're writing. I think it's going to sell very well because right now, I'm selling.

It was August 16, 2004. I was again in Donald Trump's office for a brief interview. Some people arrived, people who had organized a daily radio broadcast for him over hundreds of stations. He introduced me to them and then, in encapsulated form, told them the whole story, the threatened lawsuit ("we were going to sue his ass off"), the call to Jack Welch, the cooperation since then. Again, I thought about how the world had turned.

But the true irony for me in my roller coaster of a relationship with Donald Trump came when he asked my advice on whether to include balconies on the new condominium tower he was building in Las Vegas and on whether the Trump Hotels & Casino Resorts Inc.'s prenegotiated bankruptcy in the summer of 2004 might weaken the ratings of *The Apprentice*. Trump points out that the company has nothing to do with him on a personal basis. Trying to avoid giving my opinion, I was amazed at how the relationship had evolved from that bizarre e-mail at the start of my writing this book to those moments when Donald Trump was seeking my advice!

The challenge in writing a book about Donald Trump in 2004 is the fact that he is such a public figure; he is so visible, so accessible, and such a pervasive figure that I knew I had to go behind the scenes of his business life for the book to work. I wanted not just new material on Trump, but the chance to probe deeply into his multifaceted business and personal existence to try to understand why he functioned the way he did.

For that, I did not want to rely simply on his books, interviews, and speeches. Above all else, I wanted to sit down with him for a series of interviews. He agreed, and starting in early June and running through mid-October 2004, I interviewed him on a regular basis. Some interviews lasted several hours; some were only 15 or 20 minutes long. The shorter ones afforded me the chance to engage in fact-checking.

Because Donald Trump does his own public relations and has no real spokesperson, it became clear to me that the only way to do the routine checking and clarifying of information arising from our interviews was to go back to Donald Trump himself. Every other business leader would have sent me to some public relations executive to field the fact-checking questions. He was happy to field them himself. I was not used to such a practice, but after a while, I came to realize that if I wanted answers to a whole set of queries, I had to go directly to the main subject of the book.

Apart from the interviews, I wanted to look carefully into the private moments of his business career.

Happily, when I began interviewing him in early June, he became comfortable enough to give me glimpses into the less public sides of his business life. Accordingly, I attended a number of private meetings at which he and his construction executives held "buy-out sessions." At these sessions, Trump telephoned various bidders to decide who would get a certain contract for lockers at a golf course, floors, and so on.

I also attended a casting call for the third season of *The Apprentice*, held on the basement floor at Trump Tower. I was able to "eavesdrop" near the tables where Trump and his associates interviewed candidates for the show, watching candidate after candidate try to make the right impression that would land a slot on the series.

I asked Trump to let me tag along when he made a visit to one of his properties, and he acquiesced: One summer afternoon, the two of us walked the few blocks from Trump Tower to Trump Park Avenue at Park Avenue and 59th Street. There for an hour or so, we moved from one part of the building to another as Trump issued orders to fix this or fix that.

Finally, I wanted to get a sense of the various projects he has embarked upon in the wake of *The Apprentice*: One evening, I flew with him in his helicopter from a heliport along the Hudson River to West Chester, Pennsylvania, where he was a guest on the QVC shopping channel, promoting his latest book, *Trump: Think Like a Billionaire: Everything You Need to Know About Success, Real Estate, and Life*, published in October 2004. In late October 2004, I flew on Trump's plane with him from New York to Chicago and back, and was on hand for a demolition party of his new Chicago property.

While I was talking to Trump, his business associates, colleagues in the real-estate and casino hotel industries, and other acquaintances, I spoke as well to a long list of people who have not worked for him directly but who had contact with him on various occasions. I wanted to present as full a view as possible of the man.

This book begins with an in-depth look at Donald Trump in 2004 and at the various themes that run through this book.

PART

I

FORGING AN IMAGE

CHAPTER

1

HAVE YOU SEEN MY RATINGS?

Donald J. Trump's spacious office in Trump Tower on 57th Street and Fifth Avenue in Manhattan is chock-a-block full of collector's items, action figures, building designs, and a movie poster parodying his hit television show, *The Apprentice*. It is a roomful of memories, an ode to the large-framed (6 foot, 3 inches) titan with the swept-backed blond mane seated behind his oversize rectangular desk. Surrounding him are ceiling-high glass windows, through which appears a Manhattan skyline on which Trump has placed an indelible stamp by erecting high-end residential towers bearing his name.

On the walls hang glass-covered magazine covers, all adorned with Trump's face, another ode to the man of superlatives, the real-estate developer cum casino owner cum television star who audaciously engages in "truthful hyperbole" (his phrase), one of his numerous techniques for attracting public attention.

Many business leaders seek such attention, but few receive it. Trump receives it in plentitude because millions of people delight in getting a peek into a billionaire's life—and he is very accommodating: Cheerfully, willingly, boastfully, he opens up his fantasy world of gilded mansions, sleek helicopters, lavishly accoutered jet planes, and beautiful women to friends and business acquaintances (often the same), with stunning disregard for his own privacy. Trump is certainly not the wealthiest American; Microsoft's co-founder Bill Gates is. But few are interested in how the multibillionaire Bill Gates lives, other than to be curious about what high-tech gadgets he has in his ultramodern home near Seattle. By contrast, millions of people are interested in how Trump makes and spends money—and on whom.

Trump attracts attention because, even when he exaggerates, which is often, he is not far from the mark. He wants to be known as the best and the smartest—and, most important, the most popular. He often *is* the best and the smartest. And that very fact gives him his special charm and makes him an object of intense curiosity. Normally, one would not be curious about a man who openly engages in "truthful hyperbole," who constantly says he is the best in his field, and whose stadium-size ego dwarfs the egos of so many humbler business leaders. But one forgives the exaggeration, knowing that he *is* the most important real-estate developer in New York, he *is* one of the major players in the gaming industry, and he *is* a television star.

Unlike so many other business leaders, Donald Trump is comfortable seeking and attracting personal publicity; he has no trouble letting millions of people into the seemingly private aspects of his life. Speaking to a jewelry convention in October 2004, a group of total strangers to him, he spoke candidly of the problems of being engaged to a much younger women. He told the jewelers that when his newly affianced Slovenian-born Melania Knauss, 33 years old, asked him when he graduated from college, he replied, "Next question." Of his ex-wife Marla, he said, "She cost me a lot of money, but she's a wonderful woman." And of his newly engaged son, Donald Trump Jr., he noted, "He wants to give his fiancée a ring that will cost $65,000. That seems cheap to me." The audience loved the family disclosures, and Trump did not seem to mind divulging them.

He insists that he does not pursue celebrity, that celebrity pursues him. Yet, better than anyone else in the business world, he shrewdly understands the business value of bathing his persona in the klieg lights.

He is careful not to unveil every aspect of his business and personal life. He happily puts his assets at $6 billion but offers few specifics on how he arrives at that figure. To document his holdings with too much precision, he feels, would be tantamount to handing over a treasure trove of intelligence to others who could then exact larger sums from Trump in real-estate deals.

Whereas most business leaders detest personal publicity, Donald Trump thrives on it and is superb at knowing how to attract it. He is so good at what he does that some colleagues call him the greatest marketer around, or the greatest salesman in the world; but unlike others, who sell toothpaste and aircraft engines and software, Donald Trump sells himself as much as he sells his products. Therein lies his true uniqueness.

And, oh, how he knows how to sell himself.

Piles of newspaper and magazine articles, some of which Trump personally clips, sit on the desk. When he wants to illustrate a point, to buttress a claim, to cite a statistic, he quickly searches through the piles, like a diver searching for buried treasure. If he cannot find the article he wants, he shouts explosively to an executive assistant outside his door: "Rhona, bring me *The Apprentice* ratings," or, "Robin, bring me the best-seller listings." A clipping service locates articles in which his name appears. He often sends these articles to acquaintances along with a brief handwritten note explaining why he's sending it. Some recipients of these "Trump notes" cherish the thought; others (usually, they are journalists) enjoy tossing the articles into the wastebasket.

With lightning speed, Rhona or Robin appears with the requested article, their efficiency indicating that they know the boss's routine. They keep the often-requested ratings and best-seller listings close at hand because he cannot wait to boast to visitors about his recent successes. Virtually every conversation Trump holds on the phone or in person begins with him asking some variant of "Are you aware how popular I am?"

SEVENTY - THIRD RICHEST IN AMERICA

It is the morning of June 3, 2004, 11 days short of Trump's 58th birthday. He is in an ebullient mood, and why should he not be? He is, according to *Forbes* magazine, the 205th richest person in the world and the 73rd richest person in the United States. He is pleased that, after much persuasion on his part, *Forbes* credits him with a net worth of $2.5 billion. He would like *Forbes* to report that he is worth $6 billion, but unless he spells out all that he owns, the magazine's editors will simply not make that leap. Most of the superwealthy play down their true worth, eager perhaps to ward off kidnappers or tax authorities, but not Trump: He urges *Forbes'* editors to use the highest amount possible. In September 2004, *Forbes* credited Trump with $2.6 billion for 2004, making him the 74th richest man in the United States. For Donald Trump, the *Forbes* designation seems to validate all that he has worked for the past decade even though *Forbes* fell short of what Trump regards as his true net worth.

Never before has his career soared so high. In a few days, he will be the star attraction at the annual Donald Trump "birthday bash" put on at his Trump Taj Mahal casino hotel in Atlantic City to celebrate his 58th birthday, his newly affianced Melania by his side. He has just returned from Ecuador, where his Miss Universe 2004 pageant topped all key television ratings categories in its time slot, garnering 10.5 million viewers. Nothing gives him more pleasure, however, than the surprising popularity of *The Apprentice*, his hit television reality show, which is among the highest-rated entertainment shows of the 2003–2004 television season. Finally, his latest book, *Trump: How to Get Rich*, the fifth one he has penned in the last 17 years, is atop *The New York Times* business best-seller list.

That summer and fall of 2004 Donald Trump appeared to be everywhere. He refused to slow down, to take time off, or to lower his profile. Business colleagues and friends advised him to cool it, insisting that the public would tire of him. But he refused to heed their advice. They might as well have asked him to dive off the roof of Trump Tower.

He knows all too well that he is at the top of his game. He was always widely known and, at least in certain quarters, quite popular. But he has now acquired a degree of fame that shocks him. He genuinely believed that he would do the television show for one season, have some fun doing it, and then go on to the next project. But, as he says about his newly acquired superstardom, "This is ridiculous. This is amazing."

All through the first season of *The Apprentice* (from January to April 2004) and in the months afterward, he chose to live life to the fullest, giddily taking in everything it had to offer. Trump knows that his sudden stardom is prompting all sorts of new possibilities for him. Every day people want to partner with him, offering to provide a product if he would provide his name, his persona, and his fame.

He might have turned them all away, saying he had no time or no wish to have his name exploited so broadly. Instead, he chose to listen to numerous proposals, to digest them, and then decide upon which ones to endorse. He wanted to know the true value of his sudden superstardom—no timeouts for him. He often cited the classic song "Is That All There Is?," wondering what more life had to offer a man who seemingly had already acquired or experienced all that there was.

THE MULTITASKER

All this makes Trump seem like a man juggling a hundred balls in the air at once—and loving every minute of it. At times, he complained that he was overscheduled, that the excessive demands on him kept him on the go far too much. "I've been out 23 nights in a row," he said with some exasperation one October evening in 2004, knowing full well that he could have said no to most, if not all, of the events that required his presence; deep down, he seemed to relish the attention and loved the frenetic pace of his life.

That fall, he was building nine buildings and two golf courses.

He was also laboring to breathe new life into his three Atlantic City casino hotels, trying to ease the financial burden on the casino hotel corporation, which faced a debt payment of $1.3 billion by 2006. Although newspaper accounts gave the impression that once again Trump faced financial trouble, he exuded supreme confidence that he was about to conclude "one of the most amazing deals I've ever done."

He was shooting the third season of *The Apprentice*, appearing in often-daily photo shoots, sometimes in his office at Trump Tower or on the building's roof. He knew that if ratings for the show dropped, his thus far brief adventure in television would end abruptly. He clearly did not want that to happen, finding the whole medium quite "infectious." Already he has agreed to produce a new television series called *Trump Tower*, a *Dynasty*-like soap opera with an actor playing the Donald Trump character ("I want someone very good looking," he volunteered, exhibiting the telltale signs of making a joke.)

From behind his desk, he conducts phone interviews with overseas media, targeting countries where *The Apprentice* opens in the next few months. Shocked and thrilled that he has become a household name in the United States, he now wants to seize the international stage.

He is getting ready to launch his third book of the year, *Trump: Think Like a Billionaire: Everything You Need to Know About Success, Real Estate, and Life*. He has no qualms coming out with so many books in one year, normally taboo in publishing. He argues that the publishers come to him and offer him tons of money. How can he refuse? He is, according to his publisher, Random House, the greatest-selling business author ever; senior executives at the publishing house want Trump to write yet another book. He confesses that he's not sure he has much more to say, but he also admits that he probably will accede to the request. He tells his co-author, Meredith McIver, to start taking notes for yet another book project.

He is putting the finishing touches on his plan to build a Trump Tower in Las Vegas. He has tried to gain a toehold in the gambling mecca for years, but this is his first actual project. He loves the idea of erecting a deluxe condo on the famous Las Vegas strip, but he is wincing at all those New York–Las Vegas trips he will need to make on his 727 jet. Though he flies often in his helicopter and jet plane, he professes no great love of flying. He is a superbillionaire, but he is no jet-setter. He prefers sitting behind his desk, juggling all those balls in the air.

If he has a hobby or an indulgence, it is the game of golf. A three- to five-handicap golfer, he loves playing 18 holes at one of his golf courses, mixing business with pleasure, keeping a watchful eye out for fallen trees and overgrown grass even as he laces into that tiny white object.

Occasionally, he enters a specially designed "studio" at Trump Tower to star in a television commercial, for which he is paid millions of dollars. Though he is a multibillionaire, he relishes the millions of dollars he earns for these commercials, often referencing his father, Fred Trump, who felt that anyone would be crazy to pass up such money. When an unfriendly reporter asked Donald Trump why he alone among the fraternity of American billionaires did television commercials, Trump replied that he did them because he was asked to do them—and they paid a great deal of money. What he didn't say, because he didn't want to say it in public, was that most of those in that exclusive fraternity would not be asked!

To accommodate the seemingly endless demands on his time, Trump has designed a number of board rooms within Trump Tower so that he is only an elevator ride away from the necessary backdrop for the requested events. He is, he proudly proclaims, the most efficient person he knows or knows of. He is efficient because, being Donald Trump, he can command that anyone who wants his involvement has to show up at Trump Tower.

Meeting with a writer one morning, he says he must interrupt the conversation, but only for 15 minutes so he can meet with people seeking his approval to sell a Trump Pillow (he approves). He asks the writer to wait outside his office. Sure enough, 15 minutes later, he emerges from his office, introduces the Trump Pillow people to the writer, and resumes the interview.

By the end of the morning, Donald Trump might well have spoken to 50 people either on the telephone or in person. To each one, he seems on cloud nine because, as he tells each one, he has the number one show on television. "Have you seen my ratings?" he asks, ready to produce an article on a second's notice to read to the phone caller or office guest.

Nothing seems to faze him.

Only media attacks against him, perceived or real, big or small, bother Trump. But there are fewer such assaults today than in the past, he happily reports, and if in the past he had trouble containing his anger, he is now able to move on and cool off after a day or two. He knows now that such attacks do not hurt his business; indeed, by adding to his notoriety, they probably broaden his fame and, as perverse as he finds it, sell more apartments.

But, knowing that even bad publicity might help him in business, he is still a perfectionist; he still wants complete control over his image, so he scrutinizes the media for unfriendly comments the way a young woman might look for new blemishes on her face. He wants no blemishes.

THAT CLOUD-NINE FEELING

The cloud-nine feeling and the personal bruising were part and parcel of Donald Trump's complicated, intriguing persona during the summer and fall of 2004.

For years, he had searched for acceptance as a great builder and developer. In the fall of 2004, he was getting the highest dollar per square foot of any developer in New York. Apartments at his Park Avenue and 59th Street property were getting $4,500 a square foot, the highest of its kind. For years, he attached the name Trump to his buildings, all too aware that it was a high-risk strategy: The financial failure of a building meant a blow to his reputation. Today, he takes great satisfaction in knowing that the strategy is paying off handsomely. Even the most cynical professionals in public relations and marketing congratulate him for being among the best branding machines around.

Over the years, he has sought a kind of peace treaty, or at least a truce, with the media, which tracked his career with a patronizing air, as if Trump were some lesser specimen, worthy of mockery but not of praise. Because he seemed a caricature of how a billionaire behaved, he was covered in the media as if he was indeed a caricature and not a genuine, serious business figure.

Now in the summer and fall of 2004, the media is displaying new, uncharacteristic warmth toward the man. Even when it covered Trump's financial misfortunes in Atlantic City during the summer, it ran straightforward stories, accepting Trump's point that the prepackaged bankruptcy being prepared for his casino hotel corporation meant smoother sailing for the casinos.

In earlier years, the media would have fired one missile after another at Trump.

Cover stories on Donald Trump in 2004 were about the drama and excitement of *The Apprentice*—not, as in the past, about how much he was truly worth. Both *Newsweek* (March 1) and *Fortune* (April 26) put Trump on their covers, focusing on the new television celebrity. "He's never been hotter (just ask him)..." was part of the headline on the April 26, 2004, *Fortune* cover.

Trump did not allow himself to get too smug over the media's sudden adulation. He knew it could be ephemeral. He worried about whether the media coverage of his Atlantic City troubles might affect ratings for the second season of *The Apprentice*, which started in September. He randomly sampled opinions from office visitors and phone callers. The general feeling was that the show's ratings would remain high.

All throughout his career, Trump seemed transfixed by the kind of stardom that came to entertainers or sports heroes or astronauts. But to him, celebrity was a means to an end, not the end itself: He hoped that whatever celebrity he gained would give him a business advantage.

Even before *The Apprentice*, he was well known.

In the spring of 2000, a Gallup Poll noted that 98 percent of Americans knew who he was. (Bill Gates and Ross Perot also scored in the high 90s, but Jack Welch, Warren Buffett, Steve Jobs, and Ted Turner were much further down in the poll.) With *The Apprentice*, however, a whole new slice of America has gotten to know him—especially youngsters 12 years old and below. Trump senses that he is far better liked in 2004 among the public than ever before.

So, what he has now is supercelebrity status with much less of the notoriety that attached itself to his reputation in the past. That stratospheric status has brought him instant recognition whenever he walks along the street. As he makes his way along Fifth Avenue, or anywhere, for that matter, in Manhattan, heads turn, passersby shout greetings, and small crowds gather to stare. The greetings are friendly. "Trump," shouted one African watch-seller, giving Donald Trump a warm feeling and leading him to wonder whether that might be the only English word the man knew.

Trump and stardom have now become synonymous. Not surprisingly, Donald Trump is just where he has always wanted to be: "It's been an amazing five years for me. It's been by far the best five years in business beyond *The Apprentice.*"

What has motivated Donald Trump through the years?

Was it, as some of his earlier critics suggested, greed?

Or perhaps it was the respect of his peers?

Or could it have been public acclaim?

He seems far more motivated by the struggle to build a fortune than by the opportunity to use the accumulated items of wealth. He loves to negotiate. He loves to make deals. He loves running a successful business, trying to expand it wherever possible. But most of all, he is motivated by a desire to nurture the one aspect of his life that is so unique and so characteristic of him: the Trump brand.

If that means appearing in public as much as possible, that is fine with him. If that means promoting all things that bear the name Trump, he is comfortable with that. If it means exploring any idea that might expand the Trump brand and, hence, deepen his fortune, he has time for that.

He is prepared to work zealously at pumping up the Trump brand because he is all too aware of how difficult it was for him to make a genuine comeback. He is all too aware that, even as he showed an incredible resilience in the early 1990s, erasing that huge debt and rebuilding his fortune, he had remained a marginal figure in the business world. He wanted the public to honor his comeback and to treat him with new respect. But even as he attracted attention—because he was, after all, famous, or, perhaps more accurately, infamous—he was still, even in the late 1990s, not taken as seriously as he wished. His face *did* appear on magazine covers, but, as often as not, he made the cover of the tabloids, not the business magazines. Most books written about him were negative. The media stood aloof from Trump, not quite sure what to make of him, not liking his all-too-personal approach to public relations and never really falling in love with him.

So he sought to improve his image, choosing a unique approach that focused on himself.

Dating back to the mid-1970s, when he first entered the real-estate business in Manhattan with a great flourish, attempting to rebuild one of the city's more important but crumbling landmarks, the Commodore Hotel on 42nd Street next to Grand Central Station, Donald Trump sought to build an image for himself that spoke of unalloyed success. He promised efficiently built edifices that spelled high quality and elegance. "I've never seen anything he does that's been second rate as far as money can buy," said developer Lou Cappelli. "He doesn't cut corners. You may not like the brass at Trump Tower because it's too ostentatious, but it's the best that money can buy."

> *"He doesn't cut corners. You may not like the brass at Trump Tower because it's too ostentatious, but it's the best that money can buy."*

He boldly chose to employ his name atop his buildings even as close advisers thought little of the gesture. But for Trump, this kind of high-risk yet monumentally powerful marketing technique represented an in-your-face assertion of self-confidence that was part and parcel of his ego-oriented persona. Even his last name had a Dickensian sound to it. Had the British author created a character of massive wealth that erected skyscrapers and lived in high style, he might have given him the name Trump because it connotes strength and success. Trump loves the name for signifying those qualities.

Other business personalities have sought to brand themselves, but no one has had the temerity to put his or her own name on so many prominent landmarks: hotel casinos, high-priced residential towers, a shuttle airline, a game, a bicycle race. An ad from Trump's early days proclaimed, "Everything does seem to be very Trump these days." And indeed, it was. He had to swallow some ridicule for marketing himself as if he were a bar of soap or a box of Corn Flakes.

But he sought to equate the Trump brand with high quality, and he succeeded in most instances; for years, no business rival tried to emulate his branding technique (in a kind of tribute to Trump's success at personal branding, Steve Wynn planned to open a casino hotel on the Las Vegas strip in April 2005 and call it simply Wynn Las Vegas.)

Because so much of his business success depends on the value attached to the Trump brand, he has had to make sure that the public has only positive thoughts about the brand. To ensure those positive thoughts, Trump has chosen a unique way of dealing with the media—unique for business leaders, that is. He has decided to handle the media himself.

Instead of relying on public-relations specialists either inside or outside his organization, he, in effect, has become his own public-relations agency. Those specialists might from time to time advise him to steer clear of the media, and he did not want to heed such advice. More than any other business leader of his era, he understood the business necessity of whipping up a public-relations storm around his name and his projects. As he wrote in his 2004 book, *How to Get Rich*, "If you don't tell people about your success, they probably won't know about it."

By thrusting himself into the public spotlight, Donald Trump differentiated himself from all other business leaders of his time. Caution and shyness were not part of his DNA. He fervently believed that the burnishing of his ego was critical to his business success. And he burnished it on a regular basis: "Billionaire authors are harder to find ... than millionaire authors," he boasted in his 2004 book, *How to Get Rich.*

> *"...billionaire authors with their own Manhattan skyscrapers and hit prime time TV series are the rarest of all."*

"Billionaire authors with interests in real estate, gaming, sports, and entertainment are rarer still. And billionaire authors with their own Manhattan skyscrapers and hit prime time TV series are the rarest of all."

Most business figures have peanut-size egos—or, if they have large egos, they are eager to conceal them, believing that the very act of parading themselves in public is a flamboyance that might prove bad for business; they also feel that self-glorification is a sin that only distracts from the selling of the company's product. In stark contrast, Donald Trump believes firmly in a nexus between the forging of his ego—his image—and his success in business.

To initially forge his ego, he felt he had to open up to the world, to nurture a persona that was of interest to the public. In doing so, he had to reveal himself in a way that other business figures rarely did. He had to exhibit a good deal of his lifestyle to the public, be accessible to the media, and deliver colorful yet pithy quotes.

Other business leaders exhibited much restraint in their public statements, not wanting to cause even the slightest discomfort to shareholders. Trump, with less than 1 percent of his net worth tied up in a public company (which controlled his casino hotels), had no such concerns, openly calling people idiots and, worse, cursing routinely, exhibiting bouts of anger and fire and passion, making fun of himself.

If most of his business colleagues wanted to avoid the public spotlight, Donald Trump seemed to be perfectly comfortable with it.

The media responded to Trump's openness and flamboyance by covering his business achievements to a certain degree, but by monitoring his personal life far more passionately and aggressively. Because he invited the media to cover him, he seemed to be open game, and almost any aspect of his personal life hit the newspapers. When second wife Marla Maples was quoted in the newspapers as saying that Donald Trump gave her the best sex she ever had, it was a front-page headline.

He had no way of knowing where his self-promotion might lead, only that he wanted to be accepted (by whom was always an open question), to be taken seriously, and to be given full credit for his accomplishments. Thus, the marketing of his persona became a major business strategy for him, a strategy tailor-made for his unrelenting egocentrism. He needed to be seen and heard at every possible time and place. Hence, he saw no value in limiting his exposure.

Trump's operation was small (20,000 employees) in comparison to the large corporations; it was highly segmented and depended entirely on the man at the top. It was no accident that the main business strategies Donald Trump adopted had to do with managing his own persona and building his celebrity.

There are, of course, important business lessons to be gleaned from the way Trump behaves. Because he spends so much time negotiating, many of those lessons have to do with how best to negotiate. And because Trump advertises himself as a highly competent money machine, he has ample advice on "how to get rich" and how to "think like a billionaire" and, when things got tough, how to make a comeback. His most novel business lessons are those that encourage executives to burnish their egos and trumpet their achievements in public; these are not lessons that most business leaders will find easy to adopt. But they have worked for Donald Trump.

What the story of Donald Trump offers to other business executives is a roadmap of how to succeed in business by not being afraid of seeking out and taking advantage of the public spotlight. Most business leaders have an inherent aversion to that spotlight—but by watching Trump in action and understanding the way he turns the quest for publicity and the nurturing of his personal brand into successful business strategies, other business leaders might become a little more willing to make the media and other means of communication work for them in a positive way.

A UNIQUE FIGURE

It is Trump's unabashed willingness to be so public a figure that makes him unique on the business landscape.

Cautious, even mistrustful of the media, other business leaders openly worry that merely granting an interview might arouse jealousy among colleagues. They wince when magazines put their faces on covers. They eschew television. Despite the marketing power inherent in such major media outlets, these leaders think it best to keep low profiles. Even as these people made the magazine lists of the most powerful and most influential, few know their names outside of the business world. When *Fortune* magazine published its "Power 25: The Most Powerful People in Business" on August 9, 2004, the top 10 were, in order of importance, Lee Scott, Warren Buffett, Bill Gates, Jeff Immelt, Rupert Murdoch, Michael Dell, Chuck Prince, Ned and Abby Johnson, Sam Palmisano, and Hank Greenberg. Were any of them to walk down the street, few would recognize them, with the possible exception of Gates.

Donald Trump did not make that list. But when he walked up Fifth Avenue nine days after the *Fortune* list appeared, nearly every passerby recognized him. And he labored hard to attain such a status.

It was no accident that before he embarked on his business career, he toyed with the idea of entering the film world, dreaming of becoming a Hollywood mogul. He abandoned that dream, but he could not stop being a promoter, a marketer, an entertainer. To understand how Donald Trump functions in business, one should think of him not necessarily as an entertainer, but rather as someone with the skills of an entertainer. Neither he nor some of those who work with him on *The Apprentice* like to hear him described as an actor, perhaps because to do so might appear to denigrate his business acumen. Yet he certainly employs the same skills of an entertainer—especially an actor—and he gets very far with those skills.

In promoting his products—his real estate and his casinos—he has as much stage presence and as much self-confidence in front of an audience as many actors in Hollywood. In working out the details of a negotiation, he acts out the role of victim ("Hey, your price is way too high") with skills that seem to be honed in some acting school. He is not at all embarrassed to be called a showman; after all, as he has commented often, he enjoys injecting show business into the real-estate world.

In his own phrase, Donald Trump was "hot" and he did not want to let it go. He was certainly the hottest new star on television, and he got a great kick out of comments that he was helping NBC in the same way that the cast of *Friends* had lifted the network. The surge to the top made him no less immodest: He eagerly told friends that they (the cast of *Friends*) are six people, while he was one person: "They are on for 30 minutes; I'm on for an hour." He relished it when Jeff Zucker, the president of the NBC Universal Television Group, joked in front of thousands attending an NBC publicity gathering that Jennifer Anniston might have better hair than Donald Trump, but he was getting higher ratings.

Oh, how he was enjoying the stardom. When Harvey Weinstein, whom Donald Trump referred to as the biggest producer in Hollywood, told him he was the largest star in Weinstein's town and no one else was even close, Trump repeated the comment to his closest 1,000 friends. He was a true entertainer now, so a little harmless hyperbole would not hurt, he was sure, so rather than note accurately that he was the biggest star of reality television, he took a slight liberty and described himself as the biggest star on television. No one questioned that statement. There seemed little purpose—he was soaring through the heavens, and he loved the altitude.

If anyone required proof that Donald Trump during that summer and fall of 2004 had attained a degree of acceptance and popularity that was, even for him, beyond his wildest dreams, there he was, seated behind his desk suddenly reaching for a copy of the *Palm Beach Post*. He opened the newspaper to a full-page article on him and *The Apprentice*, and then proudly proclaimed that he had made "the bible," as Palm Beach royalty call it. Here was another moment for him to savor: "Now what do you think of all the bluebloods of Palm Beach when they see this (article)? They get sick to their stomachs. They say, 'I can't fuckin' believe this.'"

It was Donald Trump's colorful way of saying, "I made it. I finally made it."

This was Donald Trump in 2004, conscious of how close he had come to the edge of financial disaster in the early 1990s, vowing that he would never let that recur, and thrilled at becoming a superstar.

How had all this happened?

How had so many facets of American society—the business world, the media, the world of society, the entertainment world, and, last but not least, the world of young people—after marginalizing Donald Trump for so long, now have turned him into a household word?

How had Donald Trump gone from that neophyte real-estate guy hoping to make a big splash in Manhattan real-estate to one of the most famous people in the country?

How had he gone from the mainstream media's gossip columns and the tabloids' front pages to nearly iconic status, author of the most famous two-word phase in the America of 2004 ("You're fired")?

Finally, why are so many people from all slices of life—young and old, rich and poor—interested in this man?

This book deals with these questions.

The first part of this book looks at the way Donald Trump works and what he is like personally.

The second part covers his childhood years and his early forays into real estate in Manhattan.

The third part focuses on his conquest of the Atlantic City world, his subsequent fall, and his comeback.

The fourth part takes a careful look at how he employed his skills in promotion and marketing and public relations to burnish his image.

The final chapters examine in some depth Donald Trump's achievement of household name status through *The Apprentice* and his willingness to exploit his new status by embarking on a whole new set of media-oriented initiatives aimed at keeping his name before the public.

We begin with a behind-the-scenes look at the way Donald Trump works.

CHAPTER

2

BEHIND OPEN
DOORS

Donald Trump awakens most days at 5 AM. The newspapers arrive early at his three-story residence atop Trump Tower, and Trump digs into *The New York Times*, *The Wall Street Journal*, the *New York Post*, leafing through *New York Daily News* as well. He is in the office by 7 or 8 AM each day. It is an easy commute: His office is on the 26th floor of the same building. The early arrival at the office is fairly constant except when he schedules a breakfast meeting at a newly opened restaurant in the Trump Tower garden level, one floor below the lobby. Not pleased with the way the previous owners were running the place, he took it over and brought it up to a standard at which he felt he could take business acquaintances for a meal.

He ventures from his office infrequently. In the early days, he traveled to other people's offices for meetings. No longer, for he is Donald Trump, television star, household name. In a form of noblesse oblige, one *always* holds a meeting with him at Trump Tower. He does not like to stray. He even does his daily radio broadcast to 400 radio stations for Clear Channel Communications from his desk. Certain out-of-the-office activities do not require him to go very far; sometimes, he needs only to take an elevator ride: The mock board room for *The Apprentice* was built on one of the lower floors. A "studio" for making commercials was designed elswhere in the building.

"It's a hassle for him to go down the street," says his 26-year-old son, Donald Trump Jr., who works closely with his father as a senior executive at the Trump Organization. So getting him out of the office is, his son says, "sometimes like pulling teeth."

The oldest of his four children, Donald Jr. began working for the Trump Organization in 2001, trying to learn all aspects of the building business. Since then, he has helped to oversee the building of Trump Place along the Hudson River, Trump Park Avenue, and a new Trump residence/hotel tower in Chicago. (Trump's three other children are Ivanka, 23; Eric, 19; and Tiffany, 11.)

When the Cat Is Away

Why does Trump stay so close to the office?

For several reasons: One is that Donald Trump in 2004 feels the need to mind the store, to remain in control. When his career nearly ended in the early 1990s, he did not blame the collapse of the real-estate market nearly as much as he blamed himself for taking his eye off the ball, for losing focus. He had begun to believe his press clippings that suggested he had a Midas touch, so he drifted away from the day-to-day operations of the Trump Organization. He visited fashion shows in Paris, spent hours on the golf course, and generally enjoyed his billionaire's lifestyle: the mansions, the yacht, the fancy restaurants, the jet plane, and the helicopter. Then his world came crashing down: His multifaceted business empire nearly collapsed. He vowed that he would stay more focused on his business.

Now he sits at his desk as if he were glued to it, and the reason, says his son, Donald Jr., is simple: "There's an element of when the cat is away, the mouse will play. He feels he's most effective as a manager and boss when he's here."

Of equal importance in keeping Trump close to his office is the loose, free-wheeling schedule that he keeps. Unlike many other business leaders, who coop themselves up in their offices for hours behind closed doors, Trump eagerly encourages his hundreds of acquaintances to "call me next week" or "drop by any time." And they do. So he feels the need to be on hand when luminaries drop by. One day it is Lawrence Taylor, ex–New York Giants football star; another it is New York Yankee third baseman Alex Rodriguez; still another, it's California Governor Arnold Schwarzenegger.

When a VIP is meeting with Trump, word spreads among the executive ranks at Trump Tower, and within minutes, Trump executives are standing outside his door, waiting to be introduced to the honored guest. "If 'A-Rod' or 'LT' are around," said one star-struck executive, "we all come running." ("A-Rod" and "LT" are the nicknames for Rodriguez and Taylor, respectively.) Cynics have been heard to say that unannounced visitors get to see Trump immediately because he has so little to do. They miss the point. What he does a good part of each day is conduct such spur-of-the-moment encounters with a whole host of people, some superstars, some employees, and some visitors.

The cultivation of celebrities is as much a part of the work style of Donald Trump as is his unstructured schedule and his eagerness to stay close to the office. He enjoys counting celebrities as his friends and acquaintances, and he often boasts that such-and-such a celebrity is a "good friend of mine."

He counts numerous celebrities among his friends and acquaintances, and often he nurtures a relationship without any apparent thought of getting something from that person.

One day early in 1998, he was at the CNN studies in New York about to appear on *Larry King Live* when he bumped into the son of an acquaintance from the real-estate world. The young man's name was Eliot Spitzer, and he was an up-and-coming New York politician. Trump knew that Spitzer was running for the post of Attorney General of the State of New York. "You're great," he said to Spitzer, "but you'll never win because unseating an incumbent attorney general is virtually impossible to do." Spitzer won the election, and some time later Trump sent him a handwritten note saying, "Dear Eliot, I know I told you you wouldn't win, but you proved me wrong. It shows what hard work will do." Spitzer was impressed, noting in 2004: "Most people wouldn't have remembered that first conversation. Not only did he do the graceful thing, but he did it with a sense of humor."

Trump had the advantage of offering celebrities the resources to sit back and enjoy life. Often, upon finding out that some well-known figure was in New York or in Palm Beach, Trump got in touch with the person and asked him to visit. One day Bob Kraft, the owner of the New England Patriots of the National Football League, was at Mar-a-Lago in Palm Beach having drinks in the courtyard. Donald Trump saw Kraft from a distance, came up to him, and began chatting. Trump wanted to know what Kraft had ordered.

"You've got to try the meat loaf," Trump advised him, as if he had been the chef who had personally cooked the item.

Kraft had ordered fish.

Upon hearing this, Trump marched into the kitchen, got an order of meat loaf, and personally brought it out to Kraft's table himself.

"There was no ulterior motive," Kraft said later. "He just believed in the meat loaf" (and cultivating the rich and famous).

There is nothing unusual about someone wanting to hang around famous people. It is, however, quite remarkable when someone who is equally or more famous seeks systematically to pursue such relationships. Trump appears to have several motivations: In his building projects, he seeks to create an atmosphere of luxury and wealth, and anytime celebrities visit one of his buildings, the aura of high-end living is enhanced. Beyond that, Trump believes, perhaps on a subconscious level, that the more celebrities he knows and befriends, the more of a celebrity he becomes. For further evidence of how much he cherishes and nourishes relationships with celebrities, one has only to look at the name-dropping he does at great length throughout his books. Photos of Trump with Bill Clinton, Regis Philbin, Michael Bloomberg, Katie Couric, Arnold Schwarzenegger, and Jay Leno adorn the pages of his books as well.

If his office routine seems chaotic, it is not. To be sure, an unstructured ambiance pervades the place. Some of that has to do with Trump's open-door policy. Anyone within 100 feet of his office door constantly hears his loud, booming voice on the phone or in conversation with visitors. Aides move around the office swiftly, aware that at any second Trump might call out "Rhona" or "Robin" and ask them to get someone on the phone or "come inside."

Trump prefers the lack of formality, for it plays into the kind of business life he is leading in 2004: It seems as if everyone wants a piece of him. And unlike most business leaders, he wants to hear what these people have to say. To be sure, his long-time aide Norma Foerderer filters out some of the more extreme proposals, but Trump insists that he hear quite a number of proposed projects directly. That eagerness to listen to ideas requires the kind of spontaneity that he loves, for he is impatient with events and meetings and people that go on for too long.

He often arranges meetings on his own, writing down details in pencil in an appointment notebook. He sometimes makes his own calls as well. Though aides and visitors stream into his office and the phone rings continually, he never seems rattled by the seemingly frenetic pace of life in his midst. Indeed, he seems to thrive on it.

Whatever he is doing, he finds time to freshen up. Personal cleanliness is of extreme importance to him. Occasionally, he takes a time out to wash his hands in a restroom inside his office. He asks a visitor if he, too, would like to "wash up." Trump's penchant for avoiding handshakes has become part of his personal lore. Knowing of that lore, visitors often wait for Trump to see if he will extend his hand. Usually, he does. In the world he inhabits, where reaching out to people is part and parcel of his daily behavior, Trump is unable to steer clear completely of shaking hands. He is not obsessed with personal hygiene, as some have put it, but from time to time, he is eager to get the grit and grime of life out of his system. Other CEOs, getting into their limousines, unwind with a soft drink (or a hard one), but as soon as Trump takes his seat in his limo, he searches for a package containing those small wet cloths to wash his hands. Along with his predilection for cleanliness, he takes time to check his personal appearance in a mirror, checking especially his hair and his face. He is one of the most photographed men in the world, and he wants to make sure he looks good the next time a camera appears— which might well be in the next five minutes.

Donald Trump might be the ultimate multitasker, skipping back and forth between a seemingly endless number of projects that range from routine construction meetings to the shooting of *The Apprentice*. He has also published three books in 2004: *Trump: How to Get Rich: Big Deals from the Star of the Apprentice* (March), *The Way to the Top: The Best Business Advice I Ever Received* (May), and *Trump: Think Like a Billionaire* (October). He abandoned the practice of using ghost writers, instead relying on Meredith McIver, who, as a staff writer for the Trump Organization, sits behind a desk just outside his office, exploiting her proximity to the author: "I hear his voice all day, and it helps me in getting the words right."

Apart from the buildings, the television program, and the books, Trump stars in television commercials, deals with the restructuring of financial arrangements for his Atlantic City casino hotels, handles his own public-relations shop, and keeps himself available to respond to what comes cross the transom.

NO LYING ON THE BEACH

Of course, when the boss makes a point of staying close to the office, subordinates get the hint that they must be on hand as well. Sometimes, Trump gets that point across subtly, sometimes not. When his son, Donald Trump Jr., planned a two-week trip to Africa in the summer of 2004, his father told him that he did not like his going away for that long "because you can come back and your business is no longer there." Trump's fear was that his son would be out of touch for too long. "You've got to find some other thing that you like to do," he urged his son. Golf was the father's own passion, if only because "you play for three hours and you come back to the office."

For much the same reason, senior executives who fly to exotic places for a vacation get no praise from Trump for getting good suntans. "He never takes two weeks off," says an exasperated but respectful Mark A. Brown, the president and chief executive officer of the five Trump hotel and casino resorts. "That's why I don't." Brown has had the experience of being in the Bahamas with his sons and getting a Trump "checking up" phone call, simply asking, "What's going on?"

Brown's guilt barometer rises off the charts. "He makes you feel so bad. So I can't just lie on the beach. I'm always afraid I'm going to miss something."

Indeed, Trump keeps employees on their toes. He warns them that he does not want to hear about some problem after it is too late to solve it. Hence, he encourages employees to drop in on him at the office or seek him out on the phone.

Trump uses the phone not just to keep tabs on employees, but to keep in touch with an army of acquaintances. Indeed, the phone is perhaps his most important business tool, more than the jet plane or the helicopter. Because he is so reluctant to leave his office, he needs an instant connection to the outside world. He does not take every call, though at times it seems that way. Ironically, getting him on the phone is often easier than reaching one of his subordinates.

His aides know instinctively when to interrupt him to say that some VIP or some journalist is on the line. They wait outside his door until he is off the phone, or they enter the office and hover in the background, waiting for him to acknowledge their presence. When he does, they quietly inform him who is on the phone. Grabbing for the phone as if it were trying to get away from him, he embraces the device familiarly. He rarely asks a guest to leave while he conducts business on the phone.

Embarrassed guests sit quietly, hoping not to appear like an eager eavesdropper. "Hold my calls" is not part of his vocabulary.

Even when Donald Trump wants to wander off to visit one of his properties, they are situated so close to Trump Tower that he can conveniently slip away and be back in the office after an hour or two. Within walking distance of the Trump Organization's headquarters at Trump Tower are such properties as Trump Parc, Trump Palace (the tallest building on the East Side, so Trump contends), Trump Plaza, 610 Park Avenue, the Trump World Tower, and Trump Park Avenue. Just by visiting a property, he earns as much as a half-million dollars, he likes to joke, because that is the amount of revenue he will generate by accelerating work schedules and insisting on needed improvements.

One August afternoon in 2004, in one of those unusual departures from the routine, he departed his office at Trump Tower and walked over a few blocks to inspect the construction of Trump Park Avenue at Park Avenue and 59th Street. Having purchased the Delmonico Hotel on that site in 2002, he is now turning the place into a state-of-the-art luxury 35-story condominium apartment building. What for anyone else would have been an uneventful stroll is an adventure for Donald Trump. Nearly everyone he passes recognizes him or realizes he is "somebody." Those who cannot identify him by name simply stare. They know that he is somebody famous. Those who identify him usually shout, "Hi, Donald" or, "Give it to them, Mr. Trump." One woman whom he obviously knew said simply, "See you at Mar-a-Lago." She was referring to Trump's private, ultraluxurious club in Palm Beach, Florida, that once was owned by Marjorie Merriweather Post and E. F. Hutton.

A bodyguard walks discretely nearby at all times.

YOUR CURBS DON'T MATCH

Trump reached the site. The project manager stood outside the front door, waiting to greet the boss. As he approached his man on the spot, Trump noticed a fault in the construction of the sidewalk surrounding the front door. "Your curbs aren't matching here," Trump pointed out to the manager. "Why don't we have matching curbs?" His disposition changed instantly from warm and friendly to his walking companion, to sullen and angry to the project manager.

"I can't believe you approved this," he shouted like a parent scolding a child. "You think I'm going to pay for this fuckin' job? This is supposed to be one solid piece of granite. Who gave out the job? I didn't give this out. If I would have given it out, it would have been a better job. This is the worst job I've ever seen. Go find out the name of the contractor."

The project manager took the verbal assault quietly, as if he knew that it was better to button up than make excuses. By the dismal look on his face, he clearly was frustrated and embarrassed at being on the receiving end of Donald Trump's venom. None of the contestants on *The Apprentice* ever received such a dressing down or witnessed Donald Trump so steamed up. Was the real-life Donald Trump on the verge of actually firing this man on the spot? Might this be an actual instance of "You're fired"?

Not really. This was not a television show. Trump did not want this man's head. He simply wanted him to get someone else to redo the curb.

Walking into the lobby, Trump found another item that displeased him: white flowers on the reception counter. To the attractive, Russian-born woman behind the counter, Trump said, "They make the place look like a funeral parlor." Agreeing, the woman noted that previous visitors had registered similar complaints. Trump issued orders on the spot: "Remove the flowers, fire the florist, and get the name of the florist who does the flowers at Trump Tower." Though she is not exactly the key decision-maker in the builder, the receptionist promises to get the job done at once.

Walking into the elevator, Trump confided to someone tagging along on the visit that his attack on the project manager was "mostly an act, but I *did* feel that way. It was a terrible job." Then, as if removing himself from the scene and offering some instant analysis, he suggested,"That's the way I get things done."

He arrived at a floor containing a model apartment and, once again, immediately spotted flowers that he didn't like arranged on a table. A woman who worked in sales arrived with a chirpy greeting, only to listen as Trump abruptly insisted that she remove the offending flowers. Unlike the woman at the counter in the lobby, she got defensive, suggesting that no one had ever complained before.

"They are fake, right?" Trump asked her, wondering why all the flowers in the building so far were not real.

Well, sure they are, she replied, beginning to understand that it's not worth arguing with the boss.

"I don't want fake flowers. It looks like shit, whether it is fake or real."

The woman nodded her head, as if to say, "Point taken."

Trump moved on to a kitchen done in marble, noting how beautiful it was and adding how much tougher it is to build a kitchen than a street curb.

He was clearly enjoying himself. "Every time I come over to a site, I make a lot of money," he boasted. "My father (a real-estate developer in Brooklyn and Queens when Donald was a child) used to tell me that you can't make money sitting behind a desk."

The faulty street curb stuck in his mind like a nagging headache. The project manager returned with the name of the contractor. Trump unleashed a new tirade:

"I want the curbs ripped out and new ones put in. Rip out that shit in front of the building. Put concrete down. I don't give a shit if you ever put that phony crap down. You know, the panels. I want that stuff tomorrow. Don't worry about the city. I want it ripped out, and I want concrete to be put in front. There's nothing worse than what you've done here, to leave that shit."

The project manager replied meekly, "Okay."

Trump did not let go. "I want the curb taken out. This is the worst fuckin' job I've ever seen. I can't believe you did this. I can't believe it. Unbelievable."

He walked away in a huff.

Settling down a bit, Trump noticed that the ground-floor storefront exteriors were being done in aluminum. Why is that, he asked? Trump believed that bronze or brass was a better finish; he did not want the aluminum. The project manager explained that Trump's senior executives had not made a final decision yet.

Trump blew up again. "I can't believe it." He paused for a moment and then said, "You have a decision. It's brass. Order it right after I leave."

As he walked out of the building, Trump passed the counter with the funereal flowers. "You negotiate a good price," he urged the receptionist, as if she did the deals for the buildings. "Let me see what kind of a negotiator you are."

Trump had been at the site only 45 minutes, but he shook things up.

Walking back to Trump Tower, he admitted that he yelled at the project manager simply to get him to do the job properly. He has to stay on top of his people, he said. He might well have been acting, but his anger at the project manager seemed genuine. He has learned to exaggerate for effect—with very positive results.

(Returning to the site without Trump at a later date, I could tell that the curb had been fixed and the brass assembled on the storefront exterior.)

Determined to stay focused, finding value in sticking to the office as much as possible, delighted to be in such demand, Donald Trump has a hard time taking a real time out, easily qualifying him as a workaholic. "He's a machine," says his son Donald Jr., who works just down the corridor from his father as part of the senior team that runs the Trump Organization. "He's always working. Even in his free time, he's working. There's little that he's very passionate about that doesn't involve work or some off-shoot thereof. It's his hobby, and it's also his job." Trump has all the classical personal traits of the workaholic: He concedes that he does not believe in vacations, and he finds that he needs only four hours of sleep a night. He boasts that this gives him a competitive advantage over other businesspeople who sleep ten hours a night.

Even when he's playing golf, he's thinking about work. His son recalls the time Trump was on the 12th hole of one of his courses and suddenly turned to the course manager, saying, "Move that tree." His courses are in the best possible shape, he notes proudly. "You know why?" he asks rhetorically. "It's because I play them."

Trump never admits to being a workaholic; he prefers to use the phrases "total focus" or "controlled neurosis" to describe his attitude toward work. Both phrases imply someone who is obsessive, driven, single-minded, and nearly maniacal about the work at hand. The phrases are shorthand for the way Trump works to make sure things go right.

IT'S HIS MONEY

As a workaholic and a perfectionist, he enjoys taking on numerous tasks that, in other large organizations, would be delegated to subordinates. Believing that he is the best negotiator, he does the negotiating, handling the hundred-million-dollar deals and the thousand-dollar items with equal devotion. Because he is certain that he knows the media better than all others, he runs his own public-relations shop. As a general rule of thumb, managing a large organization should never degenerate into micromanaging. Trump disagrees. He loves to get hands-on. And he has a good reason. "It's his money," says Matthew F. Calamari, the executive vice president for operations for the Trump Organization, the one-time semi-pro football player who Trump hired in 1981 as his chief of security. "And," Calamari adds, "Mr. Trump watches it carefully."

When he does leave the office, he dislikes traveling too far from New York. It is no coincidence that most of Trump's operations are in Manhattan and Atlantic City, New Jersey, 127 miles to the south. (Only in the past few years has he taken on projects in Los Angeles, Chicago, and Las Vegas.) Earlier in his career, upon learning that a planned flight to Australia on business would take 27 hours, he cancelled the trip. Today's typical business leader hops on a plane routinely and flies halfway across the world. Not Donald Trump. He likes the comfort and security of being at home and near the office. When it comes to traveling, he seems most at home in his helicopter. The trips are short, often 30 to 45 minutes; he uses the chopper to fly back and forth between New York and Washington, D.C., saving time by not having to travel to and from major airports (where he could use his own 727, if he so chose).

But of all the places where he works, it is Donald Trump's office on the 26th floor of the Trump Tower where he seems most comfortable. It is a lean office over which he presides, with no more than a dozen or so senior executives making day-to-day decisions. Trump is the center of the operation, with a personal power and influence over the daily rhythms of the place that typifies few other CEOs. He wants to keep track of the ebb and flow of the people in the executive offices, one more reason why he keeps his door wide open. He cannot tolerate being shut off from his support staff, so he communicates to his assistants by shouting their names instead of pressing three-button codes on some telephone.

He has an inherent dislike of technology—the office kind. He does not use a computer and insists that e-mail is for wimps. If he has something important to say to someone, he prefers to do it in person. In general, he thinks the new, modern office technology does not add that much and is quite expensive.

In the summer of 2004—between the first and second seasons of *The Apprentice*—the notion of a quiet day at his office does not exist. Phone calls come in record numbers; so does the mail. Trump has conveyed to millions of people on television the past year that he is a business leader who knows how to get things done, how to make money, how to handle people, and how to turn an idea into something profitable. He has also become the most recognized business leader in America. Consequently, more than a thousand calls asking for all sorts of things from him come into the office each week. That is far more than most CEOs get in a month.

THE GATEKEEPER

The people who supply the help in his executive offices often feel that they need an army to deal with the requests. But Trump does not want an army traipsing through the place on a regular basis. He wants only a handful of aides to organize the incoming requests and the outgoing responses, and for more than two decades, he has given chief responsibility for all that organizing to a woman named Norma Foerderer, who went to work for Trump in April 1981. Her office is located just to the right of Trump's front door. She puts in the same long hours as her boss, looking at the 300 letters that arrive daily, deciding how to react to the numerous ideas that arrive every day, and dealing with all sorts of media-related requests that have to be put to Donald Trump. It is for her a full-time job and a half. When a visiting writer suggests that their interview might take an hour, she says politely but firmly, "Oh, I won't have an hour."

And indeed she does not. Thirty minutes later, she and the writer part company and she goes back to the task at hand, serving as chief gate-keeper to Donald Trump. She is a nice blend of old school and new school: Next to her desk is both an electric typewriter and a computer. On this day, she is juggling requests from reporters in countries where *The Apprentice* and Trump's latest book, *How to Get Rich*, are about to appear. She also fields requests for him to travel to those countries, but Norma Foerderer issues a reminder: "He doesn't like to travel."

Foerderer is one of the few veterans whose service with Trump dates back to the early 1980s, when his career was gaining momentum. She had worked for the U.S. Foreign Service in the 1970s, serving in East and North Africa; then she worked for the private sector in both the former USSR and Monaco. She was ready for a job change, and as part of her job search, a young woman named Ivana Trump, Donald's first wife, interviewed her. The next thing Norma knew, Donald Trump asked to interview her on a Saturday morning. Having been abroad, she knew little about the man. Showing up for the interview, she heard him say, "I like this. You're on time." He hired her, and she joined Trump and his tiny staff in a sales office across the street from what became Trump Tower.

More than two decades later, she takes time out from sifting through fan mail, autograph requests, and business proposals to note how the pace of work has picked up in the office lately. For one thing, she notes, "Everyone in the world wants a job with Mr. Trump." It is little wonder. Millions of people watched *The Apprentice* week after week earlier in the year as one contestant after another sought the grand prize: a one-year $250,000-a-year job apprenticing to Donald Trump. It clearly occurred to countless others that perhaps there was additional room in the Trump Organization for someone as street-wise, enthusiastic, and solid as *Apprentice* winner Bill Rancic.

Norma Foerderer looks through proposals to buy property, to endorse someone's invention, to take a look at an architectural design. Then there are the hardship cases. Trump finds one of them so compelling that he immediately writes a check for $5,000, but Foerderer suggests that it's impossible for him to deal with every hardship letter that comes along: "It's a haphazard way of doing it," she says apologetically. "We're not a big operation."

Trump never tells Norma Foerderer what to send in to him and what to hold back, but she notes that "what is on his desk now is the result of my eliminating more than he sees. I throw out tons because he could never go through all of it." Has she ever kept something from him that she realized later she should have shown him? "Not to my knowledge. I am familiar with his priorities, and if there is a question, I will check it out with him. Also, there is a good deal of material that I pass on to Mr. Trump for informational purposes."

Norma Foerderer, the gatekeeper, frees up Trump so that he can spend a good deal of time supervising the day-to-day real-estate operations that are the bread and butter of the organization. Though he still owns three casinos in Atlantic City, they seem more like a nagging toothache to him than a source of joy. At times, with no apparent prelude, he bursts forth with a vow that he is going to make the greatest deal ever in connection with his casinos. But then his words drift off just as abruptly, and he is back to talking about one of his building projects.

Judging by the company he keeps at the office and the subjects of his conversations, it is his real-estate dealings that are the center of his attention. He believes that he was—at least, in part—responsible for his real-estate business nearly slipping away from him in the early 1990s; now he is intent on not letting that happen a second time. He promises himself that he will monitor the tiniest detail, negotiate the smallest contract, and meet with the most junior member of a building team to make sure that things are running smoothly. In another business, Trump's micromanaging might seem intrusive. But his senior executives do not seem bothered by his personal intervention. They acknowledge that he is better at negotiating than they are. So, they seem to be saying, if he wants to handle matters instead of delegate them, that is fine with them.

He is hands on, but he also knows his limitations. One of them is reading long, convoluted contracts. For such technical tasks, he has his legal staff. "I know it sounds a little slipshod if you don't read contracts, but I have trained killers who read them better than I do." All too aware that he is better off spending his time on other matters, he issues guidelines to his attorneys on what should or should not be in a certain contract and then leaves them to the reading.

Reading contracts is one notable exception to the Donald Trump rule of being involved in anything and everything around the office. "He can't sit still," comments Dan Klores, who organized the public relations aspects of certain Trump projects early in his career. "He has to be in the fray, in the mix." And so he does everything he can to stay involved, to stay *au courant*. One day, Pam Liebman, the chief executive officer of the Corcoran group, a real-estate firm in Manhattan that works closely with Trump, visited his office. She noticed that on his desk was a stack of checks that he was signing as he talked to her. Noticing her staring at his check-writing, he explained that he signed most checks because that was the way he kept on top of what was going on. (In fact, as his son, Donald Trump Jr., explained, he signs off on any check larger than $100,000; but for certain projects, he insists on seeing and signing all checks, including phone bills.)

> *So much of his time appears to be spent on such haggling that he sometimes says in mild frustration, "My whole life is just one big negotiation."*

Nowhere does he micromanage more than in negotiating building contracts, large and small. One moment, he is talking to a potential partner about doing a deal that adds up to hundreds of millions of dollars. Later that same day, he is on the phone with a supplier, haggling over the price for furnishings for a locker room in one of his golf clubs, hoping to lower that price by thousands of dollars. The size of the deal does not seem to matter to him. He simply wants to be involved in everything.

So much of his time appears to be spent on such haggling that he sometimes says in mild frustration, "My whole life is just one big negotiation."

Even on a golf course, where he is seemingly in vacation mode, he cannot resist making a deal, if he thinks it has merit. One day, he was playing 18 holes when fellow player Lou Cappelli proposed partnering with Trump in a luxury condominium tower that would be known as Trump Tower at City Center in White Plains, New York. By the time they reached the 18th hole, they had an agreement in principle. Lunching at a restaurant afterward, they wrote down details of their new partnership on a napkin. Cappelli was ecstatic. "His name will add tens of millions of dollars literally." The 35-story tower, due to be opened in the summer of 2005, has 212 luxury condominium residences. A golf course, a napkin, a Trump-Cappelli partnership—indeed, a large part of Donald Trump's life is about negotiating.

Convinced that deals can easily and unpredictably go sour, Trump likes to pursue a lot of projects at once. "Nothing is ever enough for him," says Mark Brown. "He's never not looking to hit the jackpot so he can go lay on a beach somewhere. For him, it's the thrill of the deal. It's winning."

But winning with what purpose in mind? Does he simply want to make more money? Does he want to erect one luxury tower after another? Or does he negotiate to feel the thrill of negotiating? Apparently, it's the latter. "I do it to do it," he writes in the opening words of his first book, *Trump: The Art of the Deal*. "Deals are my art form. Other people paint beautifully on canvas or write wonderful poetry. I like making deals, preferably big deals. That's how I get my kicks." What is it about negotiating that gives him such a kick? "It's just a thrill for me. I love it when someone comes in with a $10 million price and they won't lower it, and I get them for $8.2 million. And they didn't even know they were going down. You don't feel like a sucker."

> "I like making deals, preferably big deals. That's how I get my kicks."

He negotiates, therefore, because he wants to avoid feeling like a sucker. He never wants to overpay for something. So he makes sure at all times that he knows what things are worth. One day in the summer of 2004, fellow executives told him that a certain contractor wanted $1.2 million for a job. Trump called the man to tell him there was no way he was making such a deal.

Within a few minutes, the man had agreed to chip off $700,000 from the price.

"That's a pretty big discount," Trump said later. "Suppose I didn't call this guy because I was too lazy. He now picks up $700,000 that is pure profit to him. I'd feel like a jerk; I need to negotiate for my own self-esteem." He knows that others might accuse him of meddling, but he insists that when the outcome is that good, not to meddle would be disastrous. He knows that his executives are good, "but I got $700,000 off by being hands on, so at a certain point, you say I better be hands on."

He clearly feels a strong need to show that he is a superb negotiator. That feeling might have to do at least in part with the criticism that he is little more than a showman or a promoter. To counteract that impression, he constantly makes the point that he is, first and foremost, a great builder. He does not want to be known *only* as a great promoter. Certainly, the way to become known as a great builder is to strengthen his reputation as a deft negotiator. So he gets personally involved—in negotiations, in visits to his properties to fix flaws, and in every aspect of the building process.

It is, he suggests, the unique nature of the building trade that requires his constant intervention. In the building business, he notes, a good deal of success has to do with building design, so "if you're not hands on, architects can put you out of business very quickly and easily. You have to build on or under budget." Donald Trump Jr., explains the parameters: "There are times when he is hands on and then pulls back. He doesn't over-micromanage. He'll pull back and let people do their stuff and make their own decisions. You just better be right, or you'll hear about it for the rest of your tenure at the organization."

Donald Trump has obvious advantages in doing the negotiating personally. He possesses the necessary skill set, and he has that daunting fame. He has the household name. Trump knows that no one wants to disappoint a celebrity. And so Trump can be soft and gentle in one instant, and tough and unbending a nanosecond later. But none of those tactics is nearly as effective as the simple act of picking up the phone to a supplier and uttering those intimidating words, "This is Donald Trump." Few want to say no to an icon. Most want to be able to say later that they did business with him. On top of those advantages, Trump knows how to play his adversaries to perfection. "He has a combination of gifts that's very rare," says Dan Klores. "He sizes up people as well as I've ever seen anyone do within three to five seconds. And he has an ability to make people feel important." But no less important, adds Klores, "He has steel balls."

Other business executives know how to negotiate. Some even have steel balls. None, however, have Donald Trump's fame or his willingness to get down and dirty in the negotiating arena. If other business leaders possessed Trump's fame, they would have one more reason to think such negotiating on small-scale items was a waste of their time. What is the value of being famous if one has to work so hard? But negotiating the nitty-gritty items of a construction project is not a waste of time to Donald Trump. "He loves it," observes Donald Trump Jr. "He doesn't consider it a waste of time. He sees it as a five-minute conversation that can save a million dollars."

To those on the other side of the negotiating table, the experience of squaring off against Donald Trump can be frustrating and intimidating. "We call it 'Trump-it-is,'" observes Greg Cuneo, the president and COO of HRH Construction and a close Trump associate. A negotiating session with Trump at one end of the phone becomes a war of attrition that the real-estate titan wages—and often wins.

Often, a veteran contractor swears to himself just before a negotiating session with Trump that he will not take anything less than a certain figure from Trump for a job the contractor was bidding on; in one case, it was $5 million. Then the negotiation begins and the veteran contractor notes: "I'll stand my ground, but we end up at $4.5 million." It's "Trump-it-is" at work.

He is perfectly willing to be the tough guy on the phone. "There's certainly an intimidation factor," says his son. "There's something beyond his skills. He's assertive, aggressive, and very in your face at the same time. He can be very scatter-brained when he's talking to someone, but it's all for a purpose. He can get people confused. But he ultimately gets what he wants."

Trump is clever, all right. When talking to suppliers, he assembles a team of senior executives for the particular building project, and they sit around his desk, ready to give background information and advice on a second's notice. They have seen the various bids that Trump will negotiate on. They have their own preferences of who should get the contract. But they are careful not to reveal too much of their feelings. They don't want to intrude on Trump's negotiations that, if conducted properly, will result in getting the right person for the job and saving the project thousands of dollars—perhaps even hundreds of thousands of dollars. Some of them already did the hard work before entering the room. They have called the bidders and issued the clear warning that they'd better be prepared to lower their prices. "If Donald Trump doesn't like your price and he says he will call you back, you better believe that he won't call you back. If you want the job, you better be ready to lower your price on the spot."

Trump talks for a few minutes with the assembled delegation. They talk about who has done a good job for them in the past, who might be negotiated down sharply in price, who the assembly wants, and who Trump wants. From watching him at work in these "buy-out" sessions, it is clear that he wants the best person at the best price.

Then Donald Trump dials the number of the first supplier.

A secretary answers. "Who's calling, please?"

"This is Donald Trump. Can I speak to John?" (John is a composite character.)

It seems clear that Trump has phoned the office before because the secretary keeps her cool. "Hello, Mr. Trump. Let me get him for you."

John comes on the line; there is the usual brief banter back and forth, and then Trump gets down to business.

He sneaks in a question: Are you really able to make a decision? Or should I talk to someone else? He does not want to waste his time talking to an underling.

Usually, the person says yes, he has the power to decide. No one wants to admit to Donald Trump that he is out of the decision-making loop. If the person were to say no, he cannot finalize things, Trump quickly checks to find out who can make decisions and how to reach that person.

In this case, John says quickly that he can make the decisions.

Hearing that, Trump takes the offensive immediately. He combines toughness with a dollop of gentility.

"Look, John, your prices are way too high. If you really want this job, you're just going to have to come down a lot."

John says nothing. The silence on his end of the line carries on for what seems like ten minutes. In fact, it's only a matter of seconds. John knows that he has little choice. He can either succumb to Trump-it-is or try to find work elsewhere. But he wants to be able to say that he has worked for Donald Trump. That alone can get him other jobs—with Trump and with others.

Trump will get him to lower his price. John took that into account when he placed the original bid. Still, it is painful to be on the receiving end of such artful no-holds-barred negotiating.

Throughout the conversation, both sides know the outcome of the give-and-take even before they hang up. The advantage seems to be all with Trump. He has a winner's air even before hanging up the phone. He does not lose his temper; he never yells at anyone while negotiating. He does not need to. Matthew Calamari plays a game with himself during the buy-out sessions. He writes down a number that he thinks will be the most amount of money Trump will save on a certain bid. "He always beats that number." The day before, Calamari had sat in on a "buy-out" session in which suppliers bid for a window rig that would be used to clean Trump Tower. The lowest bid came in at $350,000, but Trump negotiated the price down to $265,000. "The suppliers know he is the top builder in New York," noted Calamari, "and if they do the right thing, he'll ask them to bid on the next job, too."

The outlines of the contract fall in line quickly. Trump wants this supplier for the job at hand, but at a much lower price. He will get his way if only because John wants the prestige of being able to tell his business acquaintances that he works with (not for) Donald Trump.

Trump does not mind triumphant suppliers passing word that they do work for him. He gets bothered if the supplier seeks to take advantage of the connection, as one plumber did after working on two Trump projects. The man went around boasting that he was "Donald Trump's plumber," letting other plumbers know that it was not worth their time to bid on new Trump contracts. When Trump learned what the man had said and how cocky he had been, he vowed that "Trump's plumber" would never work for him again.

When the negotiation ends, Trump is exhilarated. He knows that he has saved a goodly sum and has gotten the supplier he wants. He cannot imagine that he could spend his time more usefully.

Greg Cuneo sits in on countless of these Trump-led "buy-out" sessions and he grows more uncomfortable with each event. "I don't do the buys for my own company," he acknowledges. "I feel guilty seeing him doing it." One Trump "buy-out" session, he recalls, lasted 90 minutes, and it was entirely devoted to buying lockers for a golf course. "That was bizarre," he suggests. "In my company, where we have annual revenues of $500 million, I wouldn't have the time or the brainpower to spend 30 seconds on such a thing." Cuneo says that Trump handles his own "buy-out" activities as a way of ensuring the finest buildings. "If you spend time with the locker guy and your name is Donald Trump, you're going to get a quality job."

Aides agree that Trump does well at the "buy-out" sessions. He does not use a computer. He does not pore over spreadsheets but, says Donald Trump Jr., "He remembers everything. He won't forget that he bought a $50,000 contract from the guy on the phone 15 years ago, and there were $5,000 in extras that the guy screwed my father with. He doesn't forget, especially if there's a negative associated with the recollection."

The "buy-out" sessions are not the only area in which Donald Trump micromanages. He reserves a right to intervene at any moment under any circumstances—and sometimes it seems that the more spontaneous he can be at micro-managing, the more he likes it. Ashley Cooper, the chairman of Trump National Golf Club, Bedminster, New Jersey, will never forget the time in 2004 when his employees were finishing up a paint job on the exterior of the club's new offices. As he did daily, Cooper phoned Trump and noted that today he was having trouble with the color of certain paint. It was too pale.

"All right, I'll be out."

Cooper thought nothing of Trump's seemingly off-handed remark. It was a Tuesday, and Cooper assumed Trump would show up as he usually did on a Saturday.

An hour and a half later, a helicopter landed on the front yard of the office building and Trump emerged.

"Why are you here?" a startled Cooper asks, visibly shocked to see the man.

"You said you were concerned about the paint. I had two free hours."

The two men made a few tweaks and the paint job continued.

"That's Donald Trump," Cooper said later. "He notices everything."

He seems to notice almost everything indeed. For one thing, his eye is always casting about looking for flaws in a building design. It is hard to hide things from him. Alex Yemenidjian, chairman and CEO of MGM Studios, and president of the MGM Grand, found that out when Trump showed up at the MGM Grand in Las Vegas in the mid-1990s to attend a championship boxing match. Trump asked for a hotel suite, but all the suites were occupied by high rollers.

"What should we do?" a hotel executive asked Yemenidjian.

"Take two rooms, knock down a wall in between, and make a suite out of them."

Alex had never done that, but for Donald Trump, he was willing.

A week after the fight, Trump called Alex to say, "I am in the construction business. I know what you did."

Alex was taken back. "What are you talking about?

"I could see the carpet patch," Trump said gleefully, "Where you moved the wall. And I'm never going to forget that."

Moving ahead to April 2004, again, Donald Trump's eye is casting about for flaws. From his office in Trump Tower, he is staring at the eastern wall of a building that Richard S. Lefrak, president of the Lefrak

Organization, is redeveloping at 40 West 57th Street. Trump spots a flaw in the panels that are being used to reskin the building.

He picked up the phone.

"Richard, they're putting these panels up and they look great, but 15 out of the 100 panels don't match. No one can see it from the street, but I can see it."

Trump invited Lefrak to come over to see the flaw for himself, which he did. The flaw got corrected.

Time after time, Trump's business friends recall examples of his attention to detail. For John Myers, president and CEO of GE Asset Management, it was the moment in 2002 when he spotted Trump in a discount store in New York City. Myers and his wife were shopping for a chandelier for their apartment; Trump was looking for one for the ballroom of his golf course. "He came personally to do that," said Myers, shaking his head in disbelief.

For David Friedman, an attorney who has worked closely with Trump, it was the time he was flying on Trump's plane. Along for the ride was the designer of a new golf course Trump was building. On a conference table was the building design. "Donald takes out a black Magic Marker and goes through it tree by tree, sand trap by sand trap, and hole by hole. 'I don't like this tree here,' he said, crossing it out with the Magic Marker."

The kind of person Donald Trump was in 2004, and the way he worked had a good deal to do with those people and environs that influenced him years earlier. We therefore turn to his childhood and formative years in the next chapter for a look at the main influences on his career.

PART

II

Seizing an Island

CHAPTER

3

MARCHING UP FIFTH AVENUE

Children often want to be like their parents, but they are eager to establish independent identities as well. Donald Trump was no different. But he carried an extra "burden," the kind borne by children of very wealthy parents. The burden was how to develop a successful career that was identifiably one's own, with parents who possessed the wealth to take care of one's every need? The burden is that much greater when a son admires and respects his father as deeply as Donald Trump did.

In his youth, young Donald vacillated between wanting to follow in his father's footsteps as a real-estate developer and searching for ways to stand apart from his parents and his peers. The turning point came when his parents sent him to military school. His parents rightly thought he required discipline. It was less important to them at the time that young Donald gain self-confidence, but he acquired that as well. At military school, Donald was pleased to find that he could compete successfully among his young peers both in academic work and in sports; that self-confidence became his most enduring and distinguishable character trait.

From his father, Fred Trump, Donald learned many things, none more important than making sure to select as his career something he loved. From Fred, the young man also acquired a deep familiarity with the real-estate business. "My father had a great sense of the nuts and bolts," Donald Trump said years later.

From his mother, Mary Trump, the youngster acquired a love of glamour: "My mother had a great sense of pageantry." Donald's older sister Maryanne agreed, recalling how, even when ill, Mary Trump rallied for family parties and other events. "When the lights went up," Maryanne noted, "she was the star."

That is Donald Trump wrapped up in a neat package: the flair for the dramatic a gift from Mom, an intimate knowledge of the real-estate business from Dad.

Donald's father had this great self-confidence, a strong conviction. He communicated it to the children, who were taught that they had to believe in themselves; that they should remain optimistic no matter what obstacles lay in their paths; and that ultimately they would succeed. Some would say Donald was brash, Maryanne suggested. "He had guts, confidence, he bulled ahead. Most people don't have his guts. He believes in himself. He takes chances that others might not."

New York and the real-estate business in Manhattan formed the critical backdrops for Donald Trump. He was born in New York City on June 14, 1946. Both his father and his grandfather Friedrich were businesspeople. Born in 1869, the German-born Friedrich came to America in 1885. Friedrich was a barber who became wealthy by offering lodging, food, and female companionship to gold miners in the Klondike in the late 1890s and early 1900s. In German, the family name was Trumpf. "Nobody knows where it came from," recalled Trump. It's very unusual, but it's just a good name to have." Friedrich's son, Fred, born on October 11, 1905, in New York, built affordable urban housing and grew very wealthy. Exploiting the huge demand for low-cost multiunit housing during the 1940s and 1950s, Fred used government subsidies to build such housing. His profits helped launch Donald in the real-estate business.

OUR HERO

Maryanne remembered their father as their hero, "He was everything a husband should be; a very hard-working guy who started at the bottom and ended up at the top through sheer dint of work." Fred expected his daughters to become wives and mothers. Maryanne lived that life for a long time before going to law school. Her brothers were expected to enter the family real-estate business. "Our father set high standards for us," Maryanne recalled, "standards of hard work, excellence."

Ultimately, Fred was one of the largest landlords of New York's outer boroughs, and when he died in 1999, he was worth $200 million.

In 1935, at age 30, Fred met his future wife and Donald Trump's mother, Mary MacLeod at a party. Immediately afterward, Fred told his mother that he had just met the girl he wanted to marry. They had five children: Maryanne, Fred Jr., Elizabeth, Donald, and Robert, in that order. The family lived in Jamaica Estates on Long Island at the time of Donald's birth.

Maryanne, 65 in 2004, became a judge on the U.S. Court of Appeals for the Third Circuit in 1999. Elizabeth, 61, is married and lives in Palm Beach, Florida. Donald's brother Robert, 56, and Donald ran their father's business after Fred Trump died in 1999, although they later sold it; Robert is still involved in real estate.

Fred Jr. joined his father's real-estate business and then became a TWA pilot. An alcoholic, he died at age 43 in 1981. Trump called his death "the toughest situation I've had." Because of his brother's alcoholism, Trump himself never drinks. Trump said, "I saw people really taking advantage of Fred, and the lesson I learned was always to keep up my guard 100 percent, whereas he didn't."

Not keeping his guard up, observed Trump sadly, was a fatal mistake for Fred Jr. As a result, Donald Trump feels it is better to be untrusting and skeptical about people, better to assume that they are out for themselves.

Fred Jr. taught Donald Trump a lot. Trying real estate, Fred Jr. did not enjoy the business, especially dealing with suppliers and contractors; his father intimidated him. Donald drew conclusions: The way to gain his father's respect was, first, to be tough in business and, second, to stand up to him when called for. Just how tough was his father? "He was," Trump said, "a strong, strict father, a no-nonsense kind of guy, but he didn't hit me. It wasn't what he'd ever say to us, either. He ruled by demeanor, not the sword. And he *never* (emphasis added) scared or intimidated me." Still, said Donald, he "ruled all of us with a steel will."

In contrast with what came later, one of the strong undercurrents of Donald Trump's youth was a lack of flash and glitter. His father's stamping grounds were Brooklyn and Queens, the proverbial other side of the tracks to snobby Manhattan. Eager to succeed, but harboring no grandiose ambitions, the self-made Fred Trump Sr. had no interest in tooting his own horn. Like the other real-estate developers who made sizeable fortunes, he had no desire to publicize his worth or how he achieved his fortune. Real-estate executive Tom Barrack thought of Fred Trump Sr. as "humble, modest, but not flamboyant." To Allen Weisselberg, executive vice president and chief financial officer of the Trump Organization in 2004, and someone who worked closely both with Fred Trump Sr. and Donald, Fred Trump Sr. was neither a great builder nor a man who possessed his son's flamboyance. "He built typical brick buildings which didn't have the flash of bronze and marble. He built more for the outer boroughs, and he didn't require the kind of marketing that we (at the Trump Organization) did." Still, he had great business acumen; he built a huge empire, and he dispensed enough knowledge to his son to set in motion a second, much larger Trump empire.

> *I understood the construction business from a young age because I grew up at my father's knee... you learn by osmosis.*

Long after Donald had built his own empire, long after he had established his own identity, he credited his father with being his most important influence. To hear Donald tell it, he began learning the real-estate business at the age of three. "I understood the construction business from a young age because I grew up at my father's knee...you learn by osmosis. I grew up listening to my father negotiating with contractors on a telephone from the time I was 3 years old sitting down playing with blocks. When I was 10 years old I knew how to build a building, whereas people who are 50 years old can't figure it out."

Could a child that age absorb such technical information? Donald Trump wants us to believe that it was possible.

FOUR-STEP FORMULA

Not only did Fred Sr. teach his son to be tough, but, as Donald pointed out, he also taught him how to motivate others. Most important, the father taught the son to be efficient. Fred drummed into his son a four-step formula that Donald never forgot, "Get in, get it done, get it done right, and get out."

As he assisted his father during school vacations, Donald learned to recognize and appreciate a good business deal, always remembering the time that, when his father discovered that a competitor had gone bankrupt before finishing a building, he bought out that competitor—and completed the building. Father and son applied this lesson when, during his college years, Donald Trump and Fred purchased an apartment complex in Cincinnati, Ohio, called Swifton Village, for less than $6 million; it was a 1,200-unit development that had gone bankrupt. They cleverly obtained financing above the purchase price so they could do the necessary remodeling. Eighteen months later, the Trumps sold it for twice the price. It was the four-step formula put to an early test by Donald—and it worked beautifully.

Hanging around his father, eager to absorb key lessons from that experience, young Donald Trump acquired a fingertip feel for the best way to negotiate with contractors (Rule Number One: Know precisely how much contractors needed to spend). He also learned the value of being reliable, paying people on time, avoiding building delays, and providing long-term labor to contractors.

Fred made no secret of his hope that Donald would go into the real-estate business. His mother had no specific dreams for her son. "She just wanted me to be happy," recalled Donald. "She didn't care (what I went into), as long as I was happy." To his father's joy, Donald liked real estate from a very early age "because it's hard, it's tangible. You can feel it."

Always Fred Trump served as a role model for his son; Donald especially admired the way his father micromanaged his business. That allowed him to stay on top of things. He also liked the way his father wrote notes to himself during coffee breaks. That was zeal. That was ambition.

Donald Trump learned to value money from his father. As an adult, Donald encountered constant criticism that he was more frills than substance, that he knew how to promote but was not a first-class builder, that he was motivated purely by greed. Accordingly, it was of great importance to Donald to show that Fred and Mary Trump had all the right values regarding money. Although he was wealthy enough that his children did not have to work, Fred insisted that they find gainful employment. The daughters worked either in banks or in local department stores. The sons joined their father in the real-estate business.

Fred was determined that his children appreciate the value of a dollar. When young Donald came home one day with news that a friend had just been presented with a $45 baseball glove and asked his father for a similar gift, Fred said no, fearing that his son would not understand the value of items if he were simply given them.

In his adult years, Donald Trump gave new meaning to the term *self-assured*. He said what was on his mind. He was blunt. He did not mince words. He used colorful language to underline his bluntness. He was not

He was not much different as a child— "very assertive, aggressive," in his own words. "I never respected authority. I was a little wise guy, a little brat." He admitted that he was a "rebellious kid in school...a ball-breaker."

much different as a child—"very assertive, aggressive," in his own words. "I never respected authority. I was a little wise guy, a little brat." He admitted that he was a "rebellious kid in school...a ball-breaker." He once punched a music teacher for not being up to snuff. The teacher received a black eye. Donald was nearly thrown out of school. It was, Donald Trump acknowledged later, an early sign of his outspoken and forceful nature. Young Donald was a self-admitted hellion, not very studious, a kid who threw balloons and spitballs at parties, and chalk and erasers in class. Maryanne recalled her brother as full of mischief, "We used to call him, when he was a little kid, when he had that brat-like quality, the great I-am."

At a certain point, Fred Trump became persuaded that his hellion son needed the kind of discipline and training that only a military academy offered. So he sent Donald to New York Military Academy (NYMA), on the edge of Cornwall-on-Hudson, next to West Post, 55 miles north of New York City.

THE DISCIPLINARIAN

At home and in school on Long Island, Donald had learned to break the rules largely with impunity. At NYMA, where he began seventh grade in 1959, breaking the rules was not an option. He could not get away with the shenanigans he had pulled on his teachers back in Long Island. The man who embodies this take-no-prisoners spirit was a former drill sergeant in the U.S. Marines named Theodore Dobias. Major Dobias, who served as a tactical training officer and an athletic coach at NYMA, immediately singled out Donald as a problematic new student who needed extra attention. Donald was somewhat nervous about Dobias at first. "You said the wrong thing, and you'd end up in a very negative position. This guy would come at you and knock hell out of you until you got it right."

Eventually, Donald realized that he had to learn to stand up to the major. But Dobias did not make it easy, landing blows against students to whip them in line. Some tried to ward off the blows. Others passively stood by. To the young Donald, neither approach seemed particularly wise. He sought a third way, simply letting Dobias know that he was not intimidated by him. The tactic worked. The young student vowed that he would never show weakness to anyone.

All that discipline at NYMA led Donald to channel his instinctive competitiveness and aggressiveness into more positive pursuits than hurling erasers and hitting music teachers. Other NYMA students fell by the wayside, failing to make a smooth transition from their soft, cushy homes to the stern disciplinarians at the academy. But Donald, none the worse for wear from the major's drill sergeant antics, flourished in the new environment.

He learned to march—the hard way. Failing to march correctly earned him 20 push-ups. Failing to do his manual of arms properly required running around the perimeter of the field double-time while holding his rifle. He learned to salute. He received the highest grades in geometry, and he did well in sports, especially baseball.

Had professional baseball been more lucrative in those days, Trump might have considered pursuing it. He was that good. Major League scouts looked him over. Years later, his close friend TV personality Regis Philbin noted that "he was perfectly built for first base," a position Trump played as an adult in celebrity games at Yankee Stadium.

THE VALUE OF WINNING

At NYMA, he learned the value of winning. Major Dobias drilled into Donald and the others that winning was not everything—it was the only thing. Learning how to win became crucial. The secret was preparation. When it came to football, baseball, and basketball, the youngsters had to prepare by learning all they could about the other teams. When it came to studies, they had to do their homework. Winning mattered, Major Dobias taught the boys. Donald did his best to make sure he won at whatever he did. He was a good listener. And he made sure to correct those things his teachers told him needed correcting.

Though he met girls only at mixers, already as a teenager, he acquired a reputation for knowing how to attract women. His classmates voted him "Ladies' Man."

The life at Cornwall-on-Hudson turned Donald Trump, both an honors student and a star athlete, into a new, more accomplished young man. Promoted to cadet captain during his senior year, he had charge of the honor guard. He was newly motivated: He had to be number one in whatever he did, whether having the best appearance or getting the highest grades. As a reward for his excellence, Cadet Captain Trump, then 17 years old, led the New York Military Academy up Fifth Avenue in the 1963 Columbus Day parade. Years later, the irony of that day was not lost on him. When he thought back to that parade, he realized that, as a youngster, he had passed right by the future site of one of his proudest accomplishments, the Trump Tower, on the corner of 57th Street and Fifth Avenue, the crown jewel in his real-estate empire.

Graduating from New York Military Academy in 1964, Donald Trump had to choose between trying to become a Hollywood movie producer and getting a college education. "It was a glamour thing," he said later. He loved the whole Hollywood scene—the glamour, the glitter—and he admired moguls such as Sam Goldwyn, Darryl Zanuck, Louis B. Mayer, Flo Ziegfeld, and Harry Cohn as great showmen. To him, Mayer and Ziegfeld led the ultimate lives; Zanuck and Cohn were, in his view, especially creative. Oh, how Donald Trump would have loved running MGM in the 1930s and 1940s—his ultimate business fantasy: "There was incredible style in those days that's gone now."

He considered enrolling at the film school at the University of Southern California. "I wanted to make movies," Trump said. He never thought of acting, only producing. But then a friend, experiencing great difficulty in finding a suitable apartment posed questions to the young man about real estate and, listening to his astute answers, told him, "Donald, you know more about this than anybody I've ever spoken to. Why aren't you going into real estate?" All Donald could say was, "I just want to make movies."

Whatever profession he chose, Donald did not want to blend into the scenery. He wanted to be taken seriously. He had seen firsthand what it was like to be shunted aside, and he wanted none of that. In November 1964, his father took him to the opening ceremony of the Verazanno Narrows Bridge linking the New York boroughs of Staten Island and Brooklyn. For years, Donald Trump could not get out of his mind the memory of the bridge's chief engineer, Othmar Ammann, standing off to the side of the politicians, ignored by one speaker after another; yet this Swiss engineer had actually built and designed the bridge. "I was young," said Donald, "but it left an impression because I didn't want to be treated that way."

He abandoned his thoughts of Hollywood and spent the next two years at Fordham in the Bronx, near enough to his Long Island home for him to commute daily. He seemed more polished and refined, more sophisticated than the other college students. With his sports car and fine clothes, he appeared wealthier as well. In some other ways, his lifestyle was decidedly conservative: He neither smoked nor consumed alcohol.

After two years at Fordham, Trump spent his final two years of college at the Wharton School of Business at the University of Pennsylvania in Philadelphia. Wharton was considered one of the finest business schools in the country. Thinking about a career, he found that he admired entrepreneurs and clearly liked real estate. Wharton had turned out some leading entrepreneurs and had one of the few real-estate departments around, so the place was a natural for Trump.

Wharton's real-estate department was small, with one professor and six students—ideal for learning. Most of the department's students came from families who had worked in real estate. The curriculum called for visits to neighborhoods to check out demographics. Young Trump loved the curriculum and delighted in finding that he could keep up with other students. But he did more than just keep up; whenever he chatted casually with the department head after hours, he sounded like some real-estate insider. One Wharton classmate recalled that, with Trump, it was as if he had been playing with real money, and all the other real-estate finance students were playing with Monopoly money.

BRICK AND MORTAR

Even after graduating in 1968, Donald Trump had reservations about the value of a college education. He did not think his father had suffered from not attending college. Nor was he convinced that fellow classmates were exceptionally brighter than he was. Yet a Wharton degree seemed to impress others. So, even with his doubts, he thought he had made the right decision to get a college education. Wharton, he believed, had taught him how to succeed, how to deal with people, how to avoid others playing him for a sucker, how to be tough. These were valuable lessons for whatever he pursued next.

By graduation, he had decided on a career in real estate. "There's something about Mother Earth that's awfully good," he said in a 1990 interview, "and Mother Earth is still real estate." Publishing, movies, and broadcasting were all tougher, in his view, and the stock market was "a crap shoot": "Real estate is something solid. It's brick, mortar."

Above all, he wanted to make it on his own. He wanted to engage in real-estate development in a way that his father had not. He admired his father greatly, but he needed to carve out an individual identity. "He wanted to crawl out of the very large shadow of his father," said George H. Ross, executive vice president and senior counsel at the Trump Organization. "He was very well known, very reputable, and very successful. Donald was uncomfortable with that. He said to himself, 'I'm his son; I can do things, too. It's not just because of my father.'"

He wanted to prove that he was something special. The way to do that, young Trump decided, was to make a name for himself in Manhattan. That would allow him to put some distance between himself and Fred Trump's real-estate initiatives in the outer boroughs. To young Trump, Manhattan represented the *big leagues* in a way that the outer boroughs did not, and he wanted to be a major league player: "I wanted to be in the big real estate and the glamour real estate." Donald Trump knew that no one became famous by sticking to Brooklyn and Queens, not even the very successful Fred Trump. Even for Fred, Manhattan seemed like a world apart from Brooklyn and Queens: Fred's greatest joy, Donald said later, was to have a meal at 21, one of New York's finest restaurants. (Upon his death, a table was named after Fred.)

Donald felt he had good reason to jettison the outer boroughs. During his summers at Wharton, he worked for his father in Brooklyn and Queens, where he found developers to be "petty." "They weren't worthy of the big picture or the big story. They didn't think big. They didn't have great style. They were great competitors, but at a very local level. They were great negotiators, great chiselers, because in Brooklyn and Queens, you had to negotiate every penny." They did not buy a whole mop; instead, they bought the handle and the end (or whisk) separately—to save money. They purchased paint directly from the supplier, again as a money-saver. These were the greatest negotiators in real estate, Trump said later, but he did not want to be a part of them.

Young Donald had tried to convince his father to spread his real-estate wings into Manhattan, but Brooklyn and Queens were familiar territory for Fred; Manhattan was not. The risks seemed too great in Manhattan. A property in Manhattan that cost thousands of dollars per square foot cost Fred only 30¢ in Brooklyn. So Manhattan made no economic sense to him.

Donald hoped to succeed in Manhattan even though the real-estate community was in the hands of a few players. One of them was Harry Helmsley. Eventually, the young Trump and the much older Helmsley got along well. Leona, Harry's wife, used to call Donald "the young Harry Helmsley." With Helmsley and a few others at the top of New York real estate, Fred Trump cautioned his son to stick to Queens and Brooklyn: "Don't go to Manhattan, it's too tough, it's too tough." But Donald could not be deterred. He equated making it big in Manhattan with being taken seriously. "Maybe it had to do with competing with my father, who I adored, but we were still competitive."

Allen Weisselberg, who began working for Fred Trump in 1973 as a staff accountant in Brooklyn, always thought Donald set higher expectations for himself: "He respected what his father did and thought he was a brilliant man, but he had higher ideals, a bigger picture in mind."

Donald Trump had to wait a while to implement those higher ideals. In the late 1960s, the Manhattan real-estate market was very pricey, not allowing Donald Trump to pursue an acquisition strategy that worked so well for him in later years: gobbling up underpriced properties. And so he worked for his father, convincing himself that it was only temporary; meanwhile, impatiently, he waited for an opportunity to get into the real-estate business in Manhattan.

Finally, in 1971, he rented an apartment on 75th Street and Third Avenue, and though it was small, dark, dingy, and had no view, it represented his first big step into a much larger world than he had been used to: It was, he thought much later, even more exciting to live in that first apartment than to move into the top three floors of the Trump Tower 15 years later. He got to know the city, and he began to search for good properties. He was still commuting back to work in Brooklyn, but he had established a foothold, and he liked the feeling.

Whatever business and real-estate talents he possessed, Donald Trump was smart enough to understand that a young man, even one with a Wharton degree, was not going to get very far in Manhattan without the right connections. If he was going to break into the business world in Manhattan, he had to break into "society." Trump was realistic enough to know that he had to start somewhere, so he sought to join one of the most exclusive clubs in New York City, Le Club, a members-only restaurant and nightclub on East 54th Street, founded in 1960 by society columnist Igor Cassini. But constant phoning to Le Club got him nowhere. In exasperation, he asked for the name of the president of the club. The man at the other end of the phone supplied it.

Trump called the president, asked to become a member, and kept talking until he was told that he sounded like a nice young man and that the club was looking for nice young men. The president invited him for a drink at 21. A teetotaler, the young man sat by while the club president got sloshed, but on a second visit to 21, the president said he planned to propose Trump for membership—on one condition. Finding Trump young and handsome, he insisted that he agree in advance not to steal any of the members' wives. Astonished to hear the condition, young Trump agreed. Membership came quickly thereafter.

Even with that triumph, Donald Trump was a nobody to most of the Manhattan business community—but he was a nobody inside a very swanky, exclusive club. He tried to make inroads anywhere he could: Young and inexperienced, he fell in with a notorious celebrity attorney named Roy Cohen who helped him get connected. Cohen had first gained national attention as the assistant to Sen. Joseph McCarthy as the Wisconsin senator chased alleged subversives within the federal government. Cohen had been indicted a number of times on charges of bribery, conspiracy, and bank fraud, and had been exonerated each time. One writer suggested that what seemed to appeal to Donald Trump was Cohen's willingness to do almost anything to win.

PASS THE GRAVY

Cindy Adams, the *New York Post* gossip columnist, met young Donald Trump at a New York dinner party around that time. In attendance were some pretty high-fliers. "And being piloted around was this young, tall drink of water with blond hair named Donny Trump. No one knew who he was. Nobody cared. But his pilot was Roy Cohen, who everybody knew. Roy introduced me to him and said, 'See this kid? This kid is going to own New York one day.'" To which Cindy Adams replied with great cynicism, "Yeah, lots of luck, pass the gravy."

The young drink of water with blond hair might have seemed like he was on the fast track to some, but his early forays into real-estate development were difficult. He was going up against all sorts of odds heavily stacked against him. In the early 1970s, New York City was going through an economic downturn. Donald Trump had no proven track record. He had not built one building in Manhattan. To negotiate deals, to acquire properties, he had to convince others purely on the basis of his energy and enthusiasm, not on his abilities, which as yet were not evident. "A lot of people thought he was a big mouth in the beginning," said Richard Kahan, president of the New York-based Urban Assembly in

2004. "He was always brash, a kid in a white suit, bad-mouthing people. So people asked who this 28-year-old kid was. He wasn't taken seriously until he started doing serious things." The politicians, whose support Trump needed for all sorts of issues, did not know him; he was known, and only fleetingly, to a few members of New York's high society.

Eager to become widely known, young Trump scrambled to dive into Manhattan real estate. He had admired Hollywood moguls and had great respect for Manhattan, with its seemingly unlimited potential for him. He hoped to find his niche and to build on it. But he had much going against him. Most important, he was largely unknown. He planned to change that.

CHAPTER 4

CHANGING A SKYLINE

Long before the marketing of Donald Trump began in earnest, long before he understood how valuable a business strategy it was to promote his name as a brand, he set out to impose his presence and his personal stamp on Manhattan. He was only 30 years old, with no track record in building—only a burning ambition coupled with a boyish enthusiasm. Back then, as in later years, he was brimming with self-confidence. He had boasted to a college friend that he planned to change the skyline of New York, but such youthful dreams were part and parcel of every young real-estate developer's fantasies. No particular reason existed at that time to indicate that this tall, solidly built, golden-haired young man might have such a significant impact on the city.

From the onset of his career, young Trump did not make it easy on himself, setting the bar very high. Instead of carrying on his father's tradition of putting up buildings that offered wonderful opportunities for many people and won the plaudits of the real-estate community, young Donald sought a larger stage. "I believe in doing things big. ... If you're going to do it, go for it. Make it the biggest, make it the best."

The same young man who had dreamed of producing movies on the big screen imagined doing more with his life than simply making a good living. Many did that and got no recognition for it. Though he insisted that it was never part of his game plan to pursue recognition, he certainly seemed eager for it.

> *"I believe in doing things big. ...*
> *If you're going to do it, go for it. Make it the biggest, make it the best."*

He was simply not satisfied with being an ordinary real-estate developer. He thought big thoughts. He wanted to build large buildings. He wanted to make grand statements. In contrast with many other real-estate developers, he understood from this early stage in his career that it took no more time, no more effort to organize a large project than it did a much smaller one. It was that insight that gave him the incentive to think big—and to take on large projects from the outset of his career.

Perhaps most important, his still-burgeoning sense of marketing told him that only by acting boldly could he attract the financial resources required, and only by building the biggest and the best could he grab the attention of the media: "I was out to build something monumental, something worth a big effort." That meant, in his view, putting up buildings that had a unique style and a unique feel, that were grand and of high quality.

These became the enduring traits of every building project he undertook.

Thinking big thoughts would prove costly, but here the young Trump had the good fortune of coming from a well-to-do family. Thus, he did not exactly start from zero when it came to financing. His father helped get him started by providing him with $350,000. The son used that sum to pay for expenses on his earliest building projects.

To the more veteran, experienced real-estate crowd, that "make it the biggest" line of Donald Trump's sounded like so much hot air. Searching for underpriced properties, he tried to sell himself on the basis of his energy and enthusiasm, but these were qualities every young real-estate developer claimed to possess. His great frustration came from being virtually unknown. Because of that, almost no one at the outset of his career in Manhattan took him seriously. Hard as it is to imagine today, in the early 1970s, journalists had no idea who Donald Trump was. His phone did not ring off the hook with requests for interviews, and no matter how much he hoped to gain attention in New York City, he attracted no publicity.

He was certainly not averse to attracting media attention. But he knew that to attract journalists, he had to do something special. In the mid-1970s, he proposed that a convention center be built on West 34th Street. Gerald Schoenfeld, chairman of the Shubert Organization,

America's oldest professional theater company, recalled being invited to a meeting at Gracie Mansion to hear a young man named Donald Trump make a presentation about building a convention center on the site where the Javits Center was eventually built. Attending were various corporate executives, along with Donald's father Fred. Trump's presentation was impressive, and he seemed to Schoenfeld to be a young man on the rise.

JUST DONALD AND ME

Some time later, Donald Trump called Schoenfeld to invite him to attend a press conference that Trump was giving at the potential site. When Schoenfeld arrived for the press conference, the place was covered in heavy snow. "It turned out that the only people who showed up at the press conference were Donald and me. Nobody came." For years later, when they met, Trump expressed appreciation to Schoenfeld for making the effort on that snow-filled December day. The incident revealed a good deal about the Donald Trump of the 1970s: He was indeed hardly known, certainly not well enough to attract a crowd of journalists. Years later, journalists would not let a tiny matter such as a snowstorm deter them from a Trump-organized news conference.

But back in the 1970s Trump understood that to attract the media, he needed a track record; he could not get by on bombast. Howard M. Lorber, president and chief operating officer of Vector Group, and a close friend of Donald Trump's, understood how important it was for Trump to be more than just a great marketer: "Before he was able to promote, he had to have something to promote. There has to be substance first. It wouldn't last a long time if he had been a flim-flam person and there was no substance."

Naturally, the very first project Donald Trump undertook in Manhattan had grandness to it: rebuilding the Commodore Hotel, and thus reviving one of the city's great landmarks. At the time, the entire area around Grand Central Station on 42nd Street was deteriorating; Trump hoped that by putting a high-quality, elegant building adjacent to the railroad station, he would contribute to the more broadly based revival of what most considered the heart of New York. Trump's goal, Howard Lorber remembered, was to take "an old piece of garbage and turn it into a diamond."

Ever the blunt and candid figure, Trump embarked on the Commodore Hotel project not out of some sense of altruism, not to give a part of New York City a face-lift, but simply to purchase a property on the cheap. In his search for cheap properties, he learned that the bankrupt Penn Central railroad, which owed $6 million in back taxes, was interested in dumping the money-losing Hotel Commodore. Trump leaped into the fray.

The hotel, along with the rest of the neighborhood, had a run-down look that had driven customers away. It was an open secret that part of the hotel was used as a brothel. Other parts had been closed up. Touring the hotel for the first time, Donald Trump looked sorrowfully at its filth and the nearby homeless. Glancing at the bad ventilation and tiny rooms, he thought the place looked more like a welfare institution than a major tourist attraction.

Yet when Trump gazed outside, he noticed thousands of middle- and upper-middle class commuters emerging from Grand Central Station and the underground subway stations, passing by the Commodore on their way to work. These, he thought, could become regular customers if the hotel became appealing. Now that he saw an opportunity, he wanted to purchase the building.

DONALD, YOU'RE CRAZY

Most of those from whom he sought advice, including his father, thought he was out of his mind to get involved in such a project. It was, they argued, simply unwise to purchase a New York hotel at a time when the city was so economically depressed. However cheap the property, the risks outweighed any potential upside. Trump got in touch with the same George H. Ross who later became a senior executive at the Trump Organization; he was then a senior partner in a major law firm; Trump asked him to sign on as his attorney for the Commodore project. Though Trump was brimming over with enthusiasm, Ross "thought he was crazy."

What Trump proposed was to make a deal with a bankrupt railroad to buy the land under the building, to ask the city to forego taxes and take only a share of the profits, to induce a major hotel operator to buy in and operate the refurbished hotel, and, finally, to convince a bank to loan him more than $60 million. It was indeed, insane, Ross thought. The mere fact that the city was one step away from bankruptcy and that buildings near the Commodore were going through foreclosures made Trump's deal unsound. "The atmosphere for constructing a new hotel in this area just wasn't there," said Ross nearly 30 years later. "To me, this seemed an impossible project."

But Ross came around. "Donald Trump sold me."

Trump was young, brash, and, Ross recalled warmly, "full of enthusiasm. His enthusiasm and perseverance made the project a reality." To make the project economically feasible, Trump felt he had to secure tax abatement from the city. Seeking such a favor from the city was unheard of, but Trump went ahead anyway. He asked for a tax abatement scheme from the city of New York amounting to tens of millions of dollars—without having first obtained financing for the project. It would be a coup if he were to succeed. Getting those tax breaks, Trump was convinced, would bring the banks around, even though the banks had been highly resistant to lending money in good neighborhoods, let alone the financially strapped 42nd Street area.

He made sure to invest as little of his money as possible, relying instead on big-name financial partners to foot the bills. Such partners solidified his own standing with the banks once he sought them out for the hotel's financing.

He was hoping to create a 1.5-million-square-foot hotel with 1,400 rooms that would be the most spectacular hotel project since the building of the New York Hilton a quarter-century before. The only logical approach was to sign on a big-name hotel chain as a partner because he knew nothing about running a hotel; indeed, he had hardly ever slept in one. He cast his eye on Hyatt mostly because he liked the image its hotels possessed: light, clean, and a bit glossy.

He was, as it turned out, knocking on an open door: Because Hyatt was eager to create a flagship project in New York City, Trump managed to secure a deal with Hyatt boss Jay Pritzker to become equal partners: Trump was to build the hotel, and Pritzker's Hyatt was to manage it. They announced their new partnership at a joint news conference on May 4, 1975. "The idea that Donald Trump was going in with a substantial partner made him feel very comfortable," recalled Saul F. Leonard, a project accountant.

Trump then went to the banks; but they were not impressed by the potential partnership. He feared that the banks' resistance had much more to do with his being untested and inexperienced. Only if he got the tax abatement from the city did he believe he had a chance to win over the banks. But he faced all sorts of obstacles. Politicians and hotel groups groused that granting Trump a 40-year tax abatement gave him an unfair advantage. The hotel owners were expected to pay taxes. Donald Trump was not.

Nothing helped Trump's case more than media reports that Penn Central was nearing a decision to board up and close the hotel. No one wanted that. No one wanted the eastern part of 42nd Street to turn into the same kind of eyesore as the western part. Better than anyone else, Trump understood the pride that New Yorkers felt about this section of the city. Richard Kahan, then president of the New York City Urban Development Corporation (UDC), Trump's public sector partner in the Commodore project, suggested that Trump "saw that lenders—and this had never been recognized—would throw away the usual rules so that things that didn't seem to make a ton of sense on paper suddenly made sense if the government was pushing the project as in the public interest." Trump grasped uniquely that if the government wanted the project to happen, the banks would go the extra 10 percent. "He was," suggested Kahan, "the only one who saw this connection between the private and public sectors."

Four days after the news conference announcing the Trump-Hyatt partnership, on May 8, the Board of Estimate voted to give Trump a 40-year tax abatement program, thus saving him millions of dollars. He was granted an option to purchase the land from the railroad for $12 million. The UDC took the title to the site and the building; Trump leased the site from the UDC for 99 years.

TRUMP TO THE RESCUE

The project, in George Ross's phrase, "made his reputation." Trump became known as someone who, despite his youthful age and inexperience, somehow had excellent connections to banks and to government agencies. He did not have those connections before the project, and they proved enormously valuable then and in later years. He also became known as someone who had the nerve, or perhaps the youthful innocence, to buck convention.

The media followed all this fleetingly. It was still too early for Trump to gain much traction with journalists. Media coverage of business figures in the 1970s was modest compared to the intensive coverage that developed in the three subsequent decades.

Yet although he was still unknown to the wider business community, Trump managed to draw crowds at press conferences.

How did he do that?

By masterfully playing the rescuer card, he convinced politicians and financiers—and, eventually, journalists—that because he was the only developer willing to take a chance on a losing hotel in a decaying neighborhood in a financially depressed city, he deserved a good deal of credit. He was doing all this, he argued to city officials and bankers, not simply to make a profit, but to help the city get back on its feet.

By creating thousands of new jobs in construction and service, and by showing that progress could be made with respect to at least one major landmark in the area, he was helping to save a neighborhood. Evidence began to accumulate to support his point: Shortly after he went ahead with the Commodore project, others projects that had been stalled, such as the Helmsley Hotel down the block from the Commodore, and the nearby Philip Morris headquarters, went forward. Certainly, Trump looked like a savior in rebuilding the Commodore.

This was a key turning point in his broader quest for recognition. Had the journalists attending those news conferences been sufficiently turned off by Trump's colossal ego or by his effort to pose as a rescuer of the heart of Manhattan, he would have found it almost impossible to sustain media interest in him and in his projects. But he had one thing going for him, and that was that his ability to execute: Quite simply, he did what he said he would do. Few imagined that he would succeed in getting the project launched. But he got the job done. Consequently, in turning the old Commodore into the new Grand Hyatt, he *did* come across as a savior at a time when precious few others were doing anything positive for a city that was falling apart. The result was that the journalists bought into the "Donald Trump as savior" narrative.

Ironically, rescuing the heart of Manhattan was not his prime motivation. "He wanted to establish himself as a major Manhattan developer," insisted Richard Kahan. "He saw an opportunity and managed to shape it where no one else saw it because the others were looking at it conventionally." Trump knew that he had to establish himself carefully, methodically. For one thing, he was not yet ready to put his name on buildings. It was too early for that. Besides, had he made such a suggestion to the Pritzkers, far more famous than young Mr. Trump, they surely would have balked.

Donald Trump decided that the only way the Commodore project would work architecturally was to design a building that looked brand new: The dark, dingy hotel had failure written all over its exterior. He wanted a sleek, contemporary feel that had sparkle and excitement. To achieve that look, he deployed high-quality workmanship combined with a good deal of flash and glitter. Above all, he wanted people to take notice of his effort. To that end, although he could have saved millions of dollars by simply refurbishing the existing hotel, he erected an entirely new building.

Rejecting the limestone-and-brick facades of the nearby buildings, he did not want the Hyatt simply to blend into the adjacent structures. He wanted it to stand out, to be shiny and to glisten, diminishing the dark gloom that pervaded the neighborhood. And so he put up a wall of highly reflective glass on the hotel's exterior, producing a mirror effect that enabled passersby to see the reflection of the Grand Central Terminal, the Chrysler Building, and other New York edifices, in the Grand Hyatt. To get visitors to take notice after they stepped inside, he conceived of a magnificent lobby with brown Paradisio marble along with brass railings and columns.

From working with his father, Donald Trump knew that big statements such as he had planned for the new Grand Hyatt meant nothing if they were not done efficiently. His father had given him that wonderful formula ("Get in, get it done, get it done right, and get out,"), and the son made sure to apply that formula in rebuilding the Commodore. Promising to bring the project in on time and within budget proved a great selling point to the banks.

It was almost unthinkable for someone as young as Trump (a tad under 30 years old) to mount a project of this scope, an outrageous act of chutzpah to the cynical. The only way to counteract such cynicism, he knew, was to execute. Words went only so far. Ultimately, he had to show that he knew how to get the job done. "You can't con people, at least not for long," he wrote. "You can create excitement, you can do wonderful promotion and get all kinds of press, and you can throw in a little hyperbole. But if you don't deliver the goods, people will eventually catch on."

He hired the best architects and the best engineers and told them, "Don't tell me it can't be done; tell me how it can be done." Instead of being impediments, his youth and inexperience seemed to work in his favor: As Edward Gordon, a New York–based real-estate broker, noted, it was a classic example of a person being too young and not being smart enough to know that something cannot be done. In the end, he brought the project in under budget and ahead of schedule. "I did a great job," he declared, sounding very pleased indeed.

The Grand Hyatt opened in September 1980 with 1,400 rooms and 1,500 employees, and a presidential suite that cost $2,000 a night. Trump asked his wife, Ivana, whom he had married in 1977, to oversee the interior decorating. An instant success, generating $30 million of profit a year, the new hotel jump-started Trump's career. He now had his first solid body of work. Plus, he had the ambition and the talent to keep going. "He was incredibly hard working," remembered Richard Kahan. "And he took risks that others wouldn't take. He was not afraid to lose it all. When you have that aggressiveness, when you work hard, when you're smart, and when you know the business from the ground up, you have a very good chance of succeeding. There aren't many people with all those characteristics."

Twenty-four years later, observers of the New York real-estate scene admitted, some cheerfully, some grudgingly, that Donald Trump had made a huge success of the Commodore/Hyatt endeavor. "He turned it into a successful hotel," said Steven Spinola in 2004, the president of the Real Estate Board of New York. But more important, "it was the beginning of the revival of the Grand Central area. He deserves tremendous credit for the foresight and guts to do that." New York's attorney general, Eliot Spitzer, noted in 2004 that he always pointed to the Grand Hyatt Hotel as an example that "we now take for granted. Few people remember at the time what Donald Trump did. The project was viewed as a highly risky venture in a city that couldn't support a good hotel, yet it sparked something significant for New York."

A less heartwarming endorsement came from Roberta Brandes Gratz, the urban critic, author, and lecturer on urban-development issues who later allied with Trump on his Riverside project. She offered grudging praise for Trump and the Commodore. "He made a good deal, and then he made a big deal out of the deal." The rejuvenation of the Grand Central Station district would have come with or without him, she insisted, "but he did the first project. He did it early. He got the credit, and then it got magnified in a way that he then capitalized magnificently." (In 1998, Trump sold his half of the Grand Hyatt to the Hyatt chain for $200 million.)

If the Commodore project had been Trump's baptism under fire, his next project put him on the map as a major developer.

In 1978, 15 years after Cadet Captain Donald Trump marched up Fifth Avenue leading the New York Military Academy contingent, he began planning a residential tower at 57th Street and Fifth Avenue that was meant to shake the very foundations of New York real-estate. Until then, the buildings along Manhattan's most famous shopping boulevard lacked an exciting modern design. Trump wanted to change that. Acquiring the site of the former Bonwit Teller building for $25 million, he also negotiated for the air rights so that he could build a 68-floor residential tower on one of the great locations in Manhattan. The budget was put at $200 million.

He encountered critics, among them Roberta Brandes Gratz: "He wants to tear (the Bonwit Teller building) down and build a $100 million, 60-story tower that will overshadow an avenue rich in moderate-size buildings and pedestrian pleasure. Suddenly, the image of a new Fifth Avenue has emerged—a specter of similar behemoths of slick design rising from the ashes of the city's most famous department stores, from Bergdorf's down to B. Altman." (Years later, when Trump was asked what he thought of Gratz, he replied with a resigned look, "She's a ball-buster.")

Other criticism emerged as well. A high-priced luxury residential tower would simply not work, critics were convinced, because the apartments were too expensive. Besides, the concept seemed all wrong: the marble, the glass, the huge waterfall.

WHY USE GLASS?

Even Trump's father attacked one aspect of the project. Donald had decided to use glass instead of brick for the exterior because he thought it was "cute as hell." He knew that he could build four floors a week using brick, while glass took longer; but he did not care. One day, Fred Trump was standing outside Harry Winston's jewelry store looking up at Trump Tower in amazement. "Why the hell are you using glass?," he asked his son. "It takes too long to put up. Use brick. Nobody looks at the outside of the building. All they care about is their closet size." In the end, Donald kept the glass exterior.

When the building opened in April 1983, it became one of the city's most recognizable, heavily visited, and unique attractions. By 2004, more than 2.5 million visitors were walking through the premises each year. It contained some of the city's most exclusive residential, retail, and office properties—but it was the six-story pink marble atrium with its 80-foot waterfall that became its instant signature. The pink marble certainly caught everyone's attention. Trump boasted that he had bought the "whole damn mountain" after Ivana had suggested that the color pink made people look better. Along with Ivana and their two children, Trump moved into the top three stories, where he installed rare marble in the bathrooms, gold fixtures, a fountain in the center of the living room, and white carpet. Other famous residents included Johnny Carson, Paul Anka, Liberace, Steven Spielberg, Sophia Loren, and Andrew Lloyd Webber.

Trump had just finished the building when a young television reporter called him one day to say that he wanted to do a little feature on the brand-new building that Trump had built that was "saving Fifth Avenue and saving New York City." The reporter was Regis Philbin.

Naming the new Fifth Avenue skyscraper became a matter of debate among Trump and his closest business associates.

His first instinct was to call it the Tiffany Tower because nearby Tiffany's was the premium name in high-quality jewelry and had broad brand recognition. But then he had a brainstorm. Why not call it the Trump Tower? He had never named a building after himself. It was the kind of bold step that he loved to take. Yet it was high risk. If the building failed, his name would forever be associated with that failure.

But he was optimistic, and he loved the idea. "The name Trump was a good name. I have a lot of friends who are named Smith, Jones, Rosenberg, names that won't work necessarily. Trump is a great name. It's the winning card."

Before finalizing his decision, Trump turned to others for advice. Among those who challenged him was attorney George Ross. "The name Tiffany is well recognized. Trump is not." That was true enough. Although he had pushed for a convention center in Manhattan and rebuilt the Commodore, outside of some in the real-estate community and a few journalists, Donald Trump was largely unknown.

Trump was determined. Not only did he name the building Trump Tower, but he put the name in 2-foot-high gold lettering on the outside above the front door. That gold lettering was a first for Fifth Avenue.

The success of Trump Tower encouraged Trump to think about moving forward. He shrewdly decided to focus on the very narrow but highly lucrative luxury condominium market. "He wasn't Wal-Mart," commented fellow real-estate developer Richard Lefrak. "He was Bergdorf."

The Bergdorf builder further decided to concentrate his building efforts on a

> "He wasn't Wal-Mart," commented fellow real-estate developer Richard Lefrak. "He was Bergdorf."

20-block area near Central Park. It was a great strategy for someone who wanted to stay close to the office.

Seventeen years later, Trump declared that, when he was building Trump Tower, he had hoped it would become the greatest building in the world because then people would come and they would spend money. That became the Trump formula: creating a marvelous product and then wrapping that product in his persona, mixing in some hyperbole.

One of Donald Trump's more image-burnishing projects in the mid-1980s had nothing to do with skyscrapers or large tracts of land. It had to do with an ice-skating rink. At first blush, the project seemed counterintuitive for Trump: Where was the big statement? What was grandiose about an ice-skating risk?

But, in retrospect, the ice-skating rink project was highly illustrative of a central part of Trump's business approach: to think out of the box, to go against the grain, and to look like a savior.

By 1986, Trump had watched with growing bemusement as the City of New York had spent seven years trying to rebuild the Wollman ice-skating rink in Central Park. He had rebuilt a major hotel and constructed a 68-floor residential tower, and the politicians could not even rebuild a skating rink. Thus far, the city had spent $20 million on the project, to its great embarrassment. Realizing that he could once again look like a knight in shining armor, Trump plopped down $3 million, and within four months the rink was open—on November 14, 1986, just in time for the winter skating season. He came in $750,000 under budget.

Most important, the project put him in front of the media on a continuing basis, for doing something positive—even heroic, some thought.

"We ran a news conference every two minutes," said Howard J. Rubenstein, president of Rubenstein Associates, Inc., the prestigious New York–based public relations firm that handled Trump's media relations at that time. "Donald was brilliant. He said, 'I can do it faster and cheaper than the government can.' And he did it. When he proved to be successful and got it done, when he cut the time dramatically, everyone applauded him. And every single step of the way, we held a news conference. And they gave him the front pages and back pages. The New York Times would write one or two stories, but television kept coming back for more and more."

Dan Klores was helping with the Trump public-relations campaign surrounding the Wollman rink and recalled how easy it was to attract a crowd of journalists for a news conference even when the news was, to say the least, thin. "Each of the seven or eight news conferences I arranged were about the same thing: Trump announces, Trump is going to show his plans, Trump is breaking ground, Trump is ripping up the ground, Trump is laying out the ice, Trump announces the ice is ready. But the journalists came." They came because Trump was a New York City hero. "Every time they dumped a load of cement, we called a press conference," recalled Trump's veteran right hand, Norma Foerderer, "and the press would come because Donald Trump was their champion. To think that a cement fixer would get the press out—but they came."

The success of the Commodore project, Trump Tower, and the Wollman Rink transformed Donald Trump's image. No longer was he the inexperienced, untested developer. He was now a full-fledged leader in the New York real-estate community. His unwavering optimism and the unusual success he had attained led everyone, Trump included, to believe that he possessed a Midas touch. "Part of it was fueled by his ego," said George Ross, "and part of it was what lenders were telling him. He felt invincible." If he needed $60 million, the bank gave him $80 million, even if the project wasn't worth $80 million. "There was a snowball effect," said Ross. "He felt he could take a project on and make it successful. He lost touch with reality." Ross did not mean that last thought negatively. Any man under those circumstances, Ross seemed to be saying, would have found it hard not to get swept away by such success.

By the late 1980s, Donald Trump was on a roll.

In February 1988, he acquired the Plaza hotel for $400 million and the Eastern Shuttle for $365 million—and renamed it the Trump Shuttle.

That fall of 1989, *Forbes* magazine noted that Trump was worth $1.7 billion.

Always in the back of his mind was making a grandiose statement, capturing front-page headlines, getting people to treat him seriously. To some, he seemed impatient, and indeed he had little patience for things that he considered a waste of time: making small talk, hanging around needlessly, getting bogged down in useless meetings. But he had a great deal of patience waiting for the right deal to come along. Never was his patience exhibited in greater quantities than in his attempt to develop one of the most valuable pieces of property in Manhattan: the 76-acre riverfront area along the Hudson River between 59th and 72nd streets that became known as Riverside South.

Though civic activists had hoped the property would be developed as a major urban waterfront park, Trump bought the 76 acres in 1974 with

other thoughts in mind. He was torn between building offices and apartments, but he later opted for apartments because, as a riverfront property, apartments seemed more appropriate. Even his patience ran out after
a time, and he sold the acreage, only to repurchase it in 1982.

TALLEST BUILDING IN THE WORLD

In time, he saw a chance to make a big statement. Aware that NBC, with
its 4,000-strong work force, was threatening to leave the city, early in
1985, Trump designed Television City for the Riverside property; it was
to include, at 1,670 feet high, the tallest building in the world, along
with a good deal of studio space for NBC. He was delighted to find that
reporters latched on to the "tallest building" notion; his announcement
that he planned to build the world's tallest building was a lead story on
Dan Rather's *CBS Evening News* that night.

Trump also wanted to build 6,000 to 7,000 apartments in six 70-story
towers, a rooftop park, a 2-million-square-foot suburban mall, and a
6,000-car garage underneath.

Critics remarked that he was, in effect, building a three-story-high
wall 14 blocks long that would divide the city from the river. The "wall"
would cast a huge shadow across the West Side, they argued, blocking
out light and wrecking the ambiance of the neighborhood.

"Every building casts a shadow, for God's sake," Trump shot back. "*I
want* (emphasis added) this job to be dramatic. I don't want it to be
contextual, blending into everything else. It shouldn't be like getting a
haircut and telling the barber 'I don't want anyone to know I've gotten
one.' I am competing here with the state of New Jersey, which is suck-
ing the lifeblood out of New York City. They're beating us up. Trump
City would take the play away from the development of the New Jersey
waterfront. There will be *nothing* (emphasis added) in New York to compete with Trump City!"

A New York planning official recalled visiting Trump in his office to
get a first look at the model for the site. "It was gargantuan in size. The
neighborhood groups hated it. It was terrible, really out of scale. It made
no sense." Mayor Ed Koch was also no fan of the project and, in the
spring of 1987, turned down Trump's proposed Television City. To
Trump, Koch was simply being spiteful after the embarrassment he had
suffered due to the Wollman Rink episode.

The Hudson River riverfront project had its critics. Roberta Brandes Gratz, a longtime West Side resident, was one of them. "His original plan was just so amazingly terrible, antiurban and a threat to the larger West Side, one of the most economically and socially vibrant neighborhoods in the country, it had to be stopped."

After years of watching the city make compromise after compromise on development proposals that she thought were inappropriate, Gratz had no confidence that the city would this time defeat Trump's proposal. "That's why I invited three couples for dinner to discuss a strategy for stopping the Trump plan."

Among their complaints, Gratz noted, was one that critics had aired against the Television City idea, "The project would create a wall between the West Side and the river. Its 2-million-square-foot mall would undermine the retail economy of the West Side, as well as other parts of Manhattan. And its 6,000 parking spaces would turn the West Side into a virtual parking lot, as well as create enormous traffic headaches on the West Side Highway."

To mobilize opposition, the dinner companions formed a civic group called Westpride.

Trump had no patience with Roberta Gratz and her colleagues at Westpride. At first, his inclination was to act aggressively against them, hoping they would go away. But the critics kept showing up at meetings and the approval process got bogged down, and Trump was ready to jump ship.

In the meantime, Westpride had gained support from some prestigious citywide civic groups. Together, they developed their own plan for the site, calling it the Civic Alternative. It would extend the street system, take down the elevated highway and move it inland, open up the waterfront, and create an avenue of residential towers with far fewer units than Trump had designed. The towers would still be large and would contain some affordable units, a remarkable addition to a luxury project. The beauty of this alternative plan, the residents thought, was that it removed the "Chinese Wall" effect along the river. It also required that a certain percentage of the park be built before Trump received a certificate of occupancy for each building. Roberta Gratz called this "the most revolutionary element of the agreement....Trump could not agree to build a park and then renege after construction was underway," the pattern followed by many developers around the city.

Trump realized that the fate of his project depended upon securing a truce with the civic activists. He agreed to meet with them. After the first session, the activists sensed how hard it had been for Trump to sit down with supposed enemies. But, feeling venom toward him, it was hard for the activists as well. Yet for all the venom, the activists had a grudging admiration for Trump. "I found myself very intrigued by him," acknowledged Sarah Kovner, one of the activists.

Trump faced a choice. He could carry on with his own plan, which included the tallest building in the world, a mall, resident towers, and a mall, or he could accept the Civic Alternative proposal. His closest advisers urged him to stick to his guns; but he thought the activists possessed the only realistic proposal. He decided to try to work out a compromise initiative with the activists.

Eventually, Richard Kahan became the leader of the civic groups and negotiated personally with Trump over several months. Kahan and Trump argued back and forth; then Kahan summoned leaders of the civic groups to hear his status report. Both Trump and the activists toned down their hostility toward one another and developed trust. "Trump began to realize that we were human," said Kahan, suggesting that this change on Trump's part was a big breakthrough. Ultimately, Trump and the activists agreed to forge an alliance, which was a unique partnership because it meant that an offending developer had aligned himself in a formal arrangement with his avowed enemies. That had never happened before in New York City.

With the negotiations a success, Trump could begin to build the largest private sector–initiated development in New York City—and the largest project ever approved by the New York City Planning Commission. The unique alliance between Trump and the activists had made it all possible.

On March 5, 1991, Trump and the civic leaders held a news conference and announced their agreement to move the West Side Highway inland, to build a 30-acre park that fronted the Hudson River, to build a series of apartment towers without breaking the street grid (instead of the 7,000 apartment units Trump had hoped to build, he settled for 5,600 apartments), and to include affordable units. Trump had compromised on his original plans. In a tribute to his negotiating skills, Sarah Kovner observed, "Whenever he compromises, it still becomes the biggest and the best in his mind."

Years later, at a meeting of the Riverside South Board that included Trump and the various civic groups, Trump confessed, "You guys have made my project better."

Gratz replied, "Someday, Donald, you have to say that in public."

He just smiled at her. "He always smiled when he didn't want to give you a direct answer," said Gratz.

But before the project could get off the ground, other sectors from the public voiced their opinions. On May 18, 1992, a seven-month period of public review began. A second group of West Side residents, who objected to Westpride's formation, continued their own battle with both Trump and the Civic Alternative coalition. Trump kept insisting that he would create 50,000 construction jobs and 5,000 permanent jobs, plus a great deal of tax dollars. He had some of the media on his side, along with union leaders.

Despite that support, the Community Board overwhelmingly (35 to 1) turned down the project. This might have seemed an insurmountable blow, but Trump took it in stride and simply approached Ruth Messinger, the Manhattan borough president. At first, they quarreled over how much low-cost housing to provide, but eventually, they settled on a figure. Trump was now willing to agree to a development of 7.9 million square feet (instead of 8.3 million).

Trump then had to get past the planning commission. One New York City planning commissioner from that time recalled spending hours with Trump, asking him to make compromises on the size of the project and other issues. "I did not find him unreasonable to deal with. Part of it could have been that it was a very vulnerable time for him, and he badly needed the project. He seemed on the verge of bankruptcy, and he was having troubles with his marriage. He was willing to compromise— but after the compromises, he still wanted to be able to say he got the biggest project approved."

After those negotiations, Trump secured the approval (12 to 0) of the planning commission. Following that, the New York City Council voted 42 to 8 to give Trump the zoning he wanted.

The $5 billion project, called Trump Place, embraces 30 acres of open space, 5,700 apartments in 18 residential buildings, 3,500 parking spaces, and 5 million square feet of commercial space. Ground was broken in 1997, and by July 2004, five towers had been completed and were occupied; two more buildings were under construction.

In June 2004, Trump called the Riverside project "one of the most successful jobs I've ever done. Part of its being so successful is that the buildings are so big. It is 10 million square feet, five times the size of the new Time-Warner building at Columbus Circle. That's big stuff. Yes, some people think the buildings are too big, but you can't knock me for that, right?"

Without calling them as such, Donald Trump began to develop three business strategies in the late 1970s and 1980s that became trademarks and guideposts of his entire career.

First, he wanted to make a name for himself.

And so, when he erected buildings, they had to be the biggest and the best, the most elegant, and the highest quality; they had to be efficiently managed.

Second, he wanted to market his persona, to turn himself into a brand.

And so, in naming his project Trump Tower and Trump Place and Trump this and Trump that, he had to make sure that his projects had the best possible reputations.

Hand in hand with these first two strategies went the third one: He wanted to attain celebrity status. He likes to deny that he ever pursued celebrity, and he is partially right. Sometimes, celebrity did come to him simply because of what he had achieved and the public way in which he conducted his personal and business lives. But if he did not pursue celebrity, he certainly enjoyed the fame and popularity that came to him. And he certainly did all that he could to nurture and widen his celebrity status.

With the Grand Hyatt, Trump Tower, and the Riverside South project, Donald Trump altered the skyline of New York City. He never spoke of building an empire; but as he moved from one real-estate project to another, as he bought airlines and hotels and organized a professional football league, he exhibited ambitions beyond Brooklyn and Queens—beyond Manhattan as well. When he gained some traction in the Manhattan real-estate world, he turned south to try to conquer another place where the money seemed to be his for the taking.

PART

III

THE VALUE OF CELEBRITY

CHAPTER

5

CONQUERING A
BOARDWALK

One day late in 1975, Donald Trump was listening to a news report on the radio about employees at Las Vegas hotels who were taking a vote to strike. With that news, the price of shares in Hilton Hotels, which owned two hotels in Las Vegas, plummeted.

Trump was baffled.

How could the stock price of an enterprise with 150 hotels be so adversely affected by a strike against just 2 of its hotels?

Soon he came up with the answer:

The two Hilton casino hotels in Las Vegas produced almost 40 percent of the hotel chain's net profits; in comparison, the New York Hilton, which Trump had always assumed was a great success, contributed only 1 percent.

Busy trying to put up the new Grand Hyatt in Manhattan, Trump had a sobering thought: Even if the Hyatt hotel project was a huge success, it would not be nearly the profit center of a casino hotel in Las Vegas.

He was far too inexperienced and far too underfinanced to even think of building a casino hotel in Las Vegas. But he had been following the burgeoning casino efforts in Atlantic City, 120 miles to the south of Manhattan. He knew that gambling for that resort town along the Atlantic Ocean had been put on the 1975 ballot.

Atlantic City was a latecomer to the casino industry.

Gaming had been authorized in the State of Nevada on March 19, 1931, and until the mid-1970s, that state had a monopoly on the business in the United States. Then on November 2, 1975, New Jersey voters, hoping to revitalize Atlantic City, once a proud family resort but very much a rundown city in the early 1970s, approved gambling for that town—and that town only.

In May 1978, Resorts International, formerly Hadden Hall, an Atlantic City landmark, became the first casino hotel established in the resort town. Resorts had purchased the hotel before the casino gaming law was passed, on speculation that the law would pass. It then refurbished the hotel.

Caesars was the second casino established in Atlantic City, a month later. Others followed. The casino hotel business looked promising. Shares in Resorts International shot up dramatically. Las Vegas casino hotel operators liked what they saw in Atlantic City, especially the fact that during midweek, as many people gambled at the New Jersey resort as on a New Year's Eve in Las Vegas. Steve Wynn, who had already had great success in the casino hotel business in Las Vegas, opened the Golden Nugget in Atlantic City in 1980. Harrah's, also from Las Vegas, opened a casino in the Atlantic City marina district that same year.

A BREATH OF FRESH AIR

To enter the casino hotel business in Atlantic City, one had to obtain permission from the New Jersey Casino Control Commission, an approval process designed to keep the negative influences (read: organized crime) that had infected Las Vegas from entering Atlantic City.

In that respect, Donald Trump was a welcome relief to the New Jersey casino regulators. First and foremost, he had no history of being connected to organized crime. "We thought, 'Oh good. We want to start to draw into this (casino) industry the big corporate legitimate types,'" recalled a New Jersey regulatory staffer. The first few applicants for casino licenses came from Resorts International, Caesars, the Sands, and Bally. The regulators had strong concerns about granting these operations approval to manage casinos in Atlantic City because, as another regulator noted, "they were involved in casinos in other jurisdictions and almost anybody who was had to at least have rubbed shoulders, if not be in bed, with mobsters. Trump was a breath of fresh air. He didn't have that taint that other companies did. We found that the first few applicants were mob connected. Not that they were crooked, but they rubbed shoulders with so many of these crooks."

Trump had no moral qualms against gambling. He thought it hypocritical of people to trade on Wall Street, which he regarded as the biggest casino in the world, and then object to casino gambling as if it were sinful. In his view, the only difference between Wall Street and casino gambling was that stock and bond traders wore suits and carried briefcases.

> *"Trump was a breath of fresh air. He didn't have that taint that other companies did. We found that the first few applicants were mob connected. Not that they were crooked, but they rubbed shoulders with so many of these crooks."*

In one sense, expanding his operations beyond Manhattan to Atlantic City kept Trump within his core competency: the real-estate business. "I've always felt," he said, "that the casino world to a large extent *is* the real-estate world." After all, striking similarities existed between erecting a Manhattan skyscraper and putting up a multistory casino hotel along Atlantic City's boardwalk.

But in another sense, becoming a casino hotel operator tested Trump's business skills in ways that were new for him, especially in marketing and public relations. The town offered him the chance to exploit his personal brand in an industry that had few brand names. That was intriguing to him. Bill Harrah was no longer around. Steve Wynn had yet to use his name for marketing purposes.

Some acquaintances advised Trump to steer clear of Atlantic City, arguing that the casino hotel business would not be that profitable and that it would only divert him from building up his Manhattan real-estate business. But he knew of the excitement swirling around the casino hotel industry, and he knew that people were flocking to the resort town.

He understood far better and far earlier than most just how valuable real-estate in Atlantic City would be once casino hotels were built there. He loved the heavy cash flow that was part and parcel of casino life, making Atlantic City seem a far more stable proposition than the volatile real-estate world of Manhattan. Casinos never lost money. (Later, when his hotel casinos did lose money, he took heat for not being able to make money in an industry that seemed to spew cash; the fact was that his casinos *made* money as well, but the heavy debt he had undertaken made his establishments profitless). Occasionally, someone who visits to gamble might get lucky and take the casino for a ride, but most of the time, the casinos came out ahead.

Donald Trump was not going to build casino hotels with his own money. He did not possess the kind of wealth needed for such a huge investment. He had to borrow the money from banks and other financial institutions.

But he chose a bad time to get interested in the Atlantic City casino hotel world, for in the late 1970s and early 1980s, interest rates had skyrocketed to astronomical levels. Moreover, anyone seeking financing for Atlantic City casino hotels found it extremely difficult to get the money. Casinos were considered very speculative, and in that new market, even fairly large corporate enterprises had a hard time raising the cash for the construction.

But Donald Trump was not an unknown quantity in Manhattan, and the banks there had been incredibly generous toward him after he had established a track record. When New Jersey regulators met with Trump, he brazenly told them he could easily raise a few hundred million dollars to purchase a casino hotel. The regulators remained skeptical. He was largely an unknown quantity to them. So they checked with the New York banks and were told that, indeed, if Trump asked for financing for Atlantic City operations, they would happily provide it.

The only trouble was that, Donald Trump or not, lenders were not keen on investing in the gambling business. This meant that he was forced to turn to junk-bond financing for the large investment required. Both because he employed junk bonds and because he invested so heavily, he had to pay exceptionally high interest rates. Those high interest rates eventually brought him close to financial disaster. A great deal of money flowed through his three Atlantic City casino hotels, but very little, if anything, got to the bottom line because of the high interest rates he had to pay.

Trump's plan, as he acknowledged openly in later years, was to siphon off the Atlantic City casino hotel profits and plow them into his New York real-estate investments, enabling him to expand his Manhattan holdings and benefit from the ever-increasing value of real-estate. He thought that this strategy was quite brilliant. Because the casino hotels that he owned were privately owned, it was all his money to spend as he wished. What he did, he suggested, was no different from the person who mortgaged a house and then invested money from the mortgage in the stock market. He had no investors or board of directors from whom to seek approval. "I owned the casino hotels privately. I heavily mortgaged them and took them public, and took all of that money and went out and bought a lot of real-estate in New York."

Trump was quite aware that he could have opted for building up the casinos. "I had a choice," he acknowledged. "I could have had a regular casino property and owned very little property in Manhattan, or I could have had an overleveraged casino company and bought up Manhattan." Had he avoided leveraging his Atlantic City assets, his net worth, he insisted, would have been substantially lower because "the value of Manhattan real estate went up many, many, many times, probably more than any other place in the United States." The value of casinos, meanwhile, has not gone up anywhere near such levels.

The conventional wisdom has always been that Donald Trump turned to the Atlantic City casino hotel market because he spotted yet another gold mine from which he would extract huge profits. That was only partially correct. In Atlantic City, he found a gold mine, and he certainly took out great profits. But in extracting huge profits from Atlantic City, Trump paid a price in other ways: Instead of using those profits to modernize and expand his casino hotels, he let his Atlantic City facilities tread water and eventually fall behind other more modern and plush casino hotels.

A BRILLIANT DECISION

Those who looked at what Trump did in Atlantic City thought he had acted reasonably. "Today, taking money out of Atlantic City and putting it into New York real estate looks like a brilliant decision: New York real estate is off the charts," said the managing director of a large investment bank that has done business with Trump. "He had limited resources, and you make decisions based on these limited resources."

The reaction in Atlantic City was equally benign. Residents did not think of Trump as a plunderer, but as a great benefactor for a city that, until the mid-1990s, had not been perceived as a particularly good investment. While other resort hotel companies stayed away, Trump's casino hotels created thousands of jobs in a city of only 40,000 people. In 2003, the total payroll for the three Trump enterprises was estimated at $300 million.

The Trump casinos also provided a new tax base and added to the luster of the city. In other words, he was a welcome addition, whether or not he siphoned off casino revenue for his other deals. "Donald Trump was viewed as one of the few individuals or companies willing to put dollars into this market," said Michael Pollock, editor of *Michael Pollock's Gaming Industry Observer*. A former editorial page editor of *The Press of Atlantic City*, Pollack is a former spokesman for the New Jersey Casino Control Commission (1991–1996).

Donald Trump kept his eyes and ears open and waited for the right moment to establish his own casino hotel in Atlantic City. It came in the winter of 1980, when he learned that a certain property located on prime land on the famous Atlantic City Boardwalk might be up for sale. He closed the deal but decided to hold up on construction until he secured a casino license from the State of New Jersey. To help him, he turned to New Jersey attorney Nick Ribis.

When the two men met for the first time, Trump liked what he saw and heard. He had to admit to Ribis that he was taken aback by how young the attorney looked.

"You know, I've never had a lawyer who looks younger than I am and can do the job that I need done. "

Ribis retorted, "Well, Mr. Trump, I've never had a client that is younger than I am who can pay my bills."

Trump stuck out his hand and said, "You're hired."

It took Trump until March 15, 1982, to secure the gaming license that allowed him to move ahead with putting up a casino hotel on a boardwalk site. In June, out of the blue, Trump got a call from the chairman of Holiday Inns, Michael Rose. He asked to partner with Trump in the casino hotel that Trump was about to build. Trump was taken aback. Rose's company already owned one successful casino hotel in Atlantic City, Harrah's at the Marina. Holiday Inns had spent a good deal of money to purchase a second site on the boardwalk, and Trump understood that this was where their next casino hotel would go up. Trump asked Rose why he wanted the partnership.

Well, said the Holiday Inns chairman, he was quite aware that Trump's enterprises came in on time and under budget. Rose thought Trump should go ahead and build the casino hotel, and Holiday Inns could manage it—a 50-50 partnership. They signed the agreement June 30, 1982. Sure enough, when the casino hotel opened on May 14, 1984, it was the first in Atlantic City to open on time and under budget.

The town was ready to welcome Trump with open arms. Atlantic City had eight casino hotels by this time. But the city had hit a dry spell, and the casino hotels were experiencing financial problems. "It looked like things had stagnated," said one Atlantic City veteran. "Donald Trump came along and said that he would build another casino at a time when nobody seemed interested in building another one. He was willing to come in and invest a lot of money into a town that needed a lot of investment. The local residents were happy to see him come and invest."

YOU DON'T WANT TO BE FORGOTTEN

The Holiday Inn was happy, too. Partnership with Trump, with his flair for branding and for getting media attention, looked like a smart move. A young man named Phil Satre, representing the Holiday Inns, had spent weeks with Trump in Manhattan and had watched a video of the new Fifth Avenue skyscraper he was building. Satre negotiated a 50-50 venture to put together the Harrrah's/Trump property in Atlantic City.

Satre had researched Trump thoroughly, discovering, to his delight, that Trump's name was associated with the cachet of well-built, luxurious high-rise residences in New York. But what really appealed to Satre was Trump's bluntness about the importance of getting into the newspapers. "As long as my name and picture are in the media, it is positive for me," he told Satre, "because the one thing you don't want to happen is to be forgotten."

When it came to choosing the new name of the casino hotel, Trump was at a decided disadvantage. He was still relatively unknown in Atlantic City, and he still had not attained success by branding his name on buildings in Manhattan. But Trump had some cards, too. Harrah's cared only that its name be first on the logo; it was happy to include the name Trump as long as he came second. So they compromised on the rather "tortured" (Satre's word) logo of Harrah's at Trump Plaza.

In the early 1980s, Steve Wynn was Mr. Atlantic City as well as Mr. Las Vegas. Wynn's Golden Nugget was the most important casino hotel in Atlantic City, outgrossing all others and generating more than $100 million a year in cash flow. Looking for partners, Trump naturally tried to interest Wynn in a joint venture. More than two decades later, Steve Wynn remembers the precise location where Donald Trump made his pitch.

It began when Diana Ross, one of Wynn's Las Vegas entertainers, phoned him to say that Donald Trump wanted to have lunch with her. Ross insisted Wynn join in. The three met at Le Cirque the next week. Trump talked at length of New York real estate and how he fit into that world. Wynn was overwhelmed, "I had never met anyone like him. He filled the space."

The lunch ended. Trump and Wynn left the restaurant and began walking. "Those eight blocks that we walked," Wynn said later, "were one of the most memorable experiences of my life."

It was memorable because this 37-year-old developer was about to make Steve Wynn an offer that shocked the normally unflappable Mr. Wynn.

Eager to gain more traction in Atlantic City, Trump was all too aware that, in addition to the Golden Nugget, Wynn owned a 14-acre site in the Marina district in Atlantic City. Adjacent to the site was another 14-acre site owned by Barron Hilton. Wynn hoped to build a casino hotel on his 14 acres that would be grander than the Golden Nugget along the Boardwalk.

THE MADISON AVENUE PROPOSAL

The two men walked south on Madison Avenue. Years later, Wynn recalled that they were walking on the eastern side of the street. Out of the blue, Trump blurted out:

"I've got a great idea."

He wanted to partner with Wynn on the 14-acre Marina site.

"Let's do it together. We'll call it Wynn and Trump."

The Trump pitch continued: "You know, we're real good at building buildings." Wynn nodded, not wanting to lead Trump on, but quite intrigued by the man's nerve.

"I could help with the design," Trump offered. "Marketing, that's really my bag." Wynn nodded again. He knew of Trump's marketing prowess.

"We could go 50-50," Trump concluded. "The world would love it."

A bemused Steve Wynn looked at Trump in disbelief. In Atlantic City, Wynn was high profile. Trump was a neophyte.

Wynn let Trump tackle the issue of financing such a project. The two men agreed quickly that finding money for such a project would be no problem.

It was Wynn's time to reply.

"Why do you think I need you as a partner?" he asked Trump. "Why would I want to go give up half the business? I'm the guy (he emphasized the last two words) in Atlantic City. You're the new guy in town."

"That's really a good question," Trump said, as if admitting that he had no ready answer.

Wynn was truly aghast at the man's *chutzpah:* Donald Trump wanted to put his name on a building that was still very much the dream and future establishment of Steve Wynn. To Wynn, although Trump seemed "sincere and respectful," it was the man's sheer nerve that made Wynn recall the incident so vividly more than two decades later.

By the time the two men had reached Madison and 61st Street, Trump was trying his best to give Wynn a reason to take the offer seriously. Trump suggested that Wynn would gain from the partnership because he (Trump) promised not to build another casino hotel at the Marina.

"Let me understand this," Wynn said to Trump. "If I let you have half, you'll forbear from being my competitor."

"Yes," said Trump.

Wynn was impressed by the deal. Years later, he said, "It was one of the most overwhelmingly self-confident presentations that any man ever made to me."

All Wynn said to Trump was, "That's very interesting." Both men knew he was simply being polite—and, in effect, saying no.

Wynn could not end the discussion without offering Trump some advice, "You've got to make a nickel on your own in the gaming business, and then we'll have parity." In other words, then the two could talk about making such deals.

Trump seemed to give what Wynn had just said serious thought. He hooked his arm on to Wynn's shoulder and looked down at him from his 6-foot-3 vantage point:

"That's a good point," he said quietly to Wynn.

With that, the conversation ended. The two men parted at Madison and 57th streets. Wynn returned to his office on Park Avenue. The first thing he did was to call his wife, Elaine, to tell her of his Madison Avenue conversation with Donald Trump.

Ironically, Steve Wynn never built a hotel casino on that Marina property. In time, he grew disillusioned with Atlantic City—or, more accurately, he grew weary of the Trenton regulators, who, in his view, imposed far too many rules on the gaming industry. He had been earning close to $100 million from the Golden Nugget for the previous six years, and he thought that the regulators, with what he thought was nitpicking, were keeping him from making even more money. In 1989, he sold the Golden Nugget for a reported $440 million and used much of the money to build the Mirage in Las Vegas.

Asked about the Madison Avenue offer to Steve Wynn, Donald Trump said that Steve Wynn's recounting of the incident sounded right to him.

Meanwhile, Harrah's at Trump Plaza opened in May 1984.

On opening day, Donald Trump predicted that the new casino hotel would be "the finest building not only in Atlantic City, [but] maybe anywhere in the world." Less than two years later, Trump bought out the Holiday Inns' investment and became the 100 percent owner. Trump's first acquisition in Atlantic City garnered much attention, not so much because Donald Trump was involved, but more because a new player with big bucks had come to town. So many people had tried to establish casino hotels, but they had proven lightweights, unable to execute or come up with the crucial financing. Trump looked very good indeed.

(In 1995, Trump Plaza fell under the aegis of Trump's new public company, Trump Hotels & Casino Resorts.)

Early in 1985, a second opportunity arose for Trump to take over a casino hotel in Atlantic City: The Hilton Corporation began building a casino hotel across from Harrah's in the Marina district. Harrah's had been one of the most successful of Atlantic City's casino hotels. At that time, Trump began hearing that Hilton was having difficulty trying to obtain a casino license. Indeed, in February, the New Jersey regulators decided that Hilton was unsuitable to hold a casino license because of the unsavory reputation of one of its executives. But the hotel was already in an advanced state of construction and was due to open in 12 weeks.

Hilton had spent $320 million and had hired 1,000 employees, but it had no choice except to seek a way out. Learning that the property was on the market, Trump bid $250 million. Hilton thought that was too low.

Trump sought the advice of colleagues. Most told him he was crazy to buy the property. But he wanted to become a major player in Atlantic City. He loved the profits and the glamour. He was willing to make the biggest gamble of his career. To come up with the needed financing, he would have to guarantee the sum personally, a first in his career. He was ready to go forward without stepping foot on the property.

He figured correctly that Barron Hilton would not sell the place for less than the amount he had put into it ($320 million), if only to avoid taking a loss and having to report the loss to shareholders. Trump closed the deal on April 27, 1985, paying Barron Hilton $320 million. Two months later, Trump opened the hotel. He called it Trump Castle and put his wife, Ivana, in charge as CEO for a salary of $1 a year. Trump had put his wife in an awkward position: She had to compete against the Trump Plaza! (In 1997, the casino hotel was renamed the Trump Marina.)

Two years later, in 1987, the two hotels—the Trump Castle and the Trump Plaza—were extremely profitable, among the top four casinos in Atlantic City. But they were not profitable enough to cover the debt payments that Trump had owed.

The large debt payments Trump owed for his publicly-owned Atlantic City casino hotels spoiled his ability to truly come out a winner on the Boardwalk. The Trump casinos did well but never well enough to cover the debt payments. The problem of paying off the debt loomed especially large for Trump at various stages of his business career: first in the early 1990s, when he courted financial disaster, and again in 2004, as he once again confronted a huge set of debt payments. In both cases, instead of selling the properties, he sought to restructure the debt.

Throughout the 1980s, Donald Trump was eager to expand his casino holdings in Atlantic City. The opportunity to acquire a third property arose in the middle of that decade.

By the mid-1980s, a multimillionaire named James Crosby owned Resorts International. When he died in 1986, television entertainer Merv Griffin and Donald Trump competed to buy Crosby's casino hotel. Meanwhile, next door to Resorts, Crosby had been putting up a magnificent new casino hotel in fits and starts, and it was little more than a distressed property at the time of his death. The project had practically brought down Resorts International; the company had spent a half-billion dollars over five years, and still the hotel was not complete.

Trump wanted that building as well. He decided that owning a third property would truly make him a major player in Atlantic City.

CREATING THE TAJ

In March 1987, Trump was able to purchase 12 percent in equity in Resorts International, Inc., for $80 million. He had planned to purchase the rest of the stock, but Merv Griffin made a much larger bid than Trump had expected. The two men entered negotiations. Griffin got the original hotel (which went bankrupt in 1990), and Trump obtained the unfinished adjacent casino hotel along with $12 million. It was estimated that Trump had to come up with another $525 million to finish the hotel. He persevered, hoping to open the casino hotel in the spring of 1990.

He planned to call the property the Trump Taj Mahal.

The decision to complete the Taj was a monumental one for Trump. It came at a time when some were questioning whether Atlantic City had truly benefited from the gaming business. After all, fully 20 percent of the town's population had departed since the 1977 referendum, and its crime rate was the highest in New Jersey. Half of the city's residents were on welfare. The 40,000 jobs the casinos had brought to the town had gone mostly to people who lived outside Atlantic City; new gambling taxes appeared to have had little effect on building up the resort town.

But Donald Trump saw the positives and played down the negatives. He would now have a casino that was the size of the Trump Plaza and the Trump Castle combined; its 51 stories (495 feet high) made it one of the tallest buildings in New Jersey.

THE TAJ GAMBLE

Key Trump advisers thought the Crosby deal was unsound, but Trump believed unreservedly that Atlantic City would turn around and that he would benefit enormously by being a primary player.

To make the Taj work, to pay off the enormous debt burden he had incurred, Trump's new $1.1 billion casino hotel had to attract far more gamblers than any other Atlantic City casino had thus far. Trump's interest payments on the Taj were so high that he needed a record-breaking $1.3 million a day in gambling revenue to make those payments.

Employing his marketing skills, he sought to distinguish the Taj from the other casinos by encrusting it with glitter and glitz. He put his name in red neon block letters atop the building; he covered the casino with candy-striped onion domes along with miniature gold-topped minarets. Large stone elephants stood next to the hotel's entrances. No other casino looked like the Taj.

No doubt, the Taj was meant to overwhelm the visitor: It had more than 3,000 slot machines and 160 table games, the elevators identified the 42nd floor as the 51st and the whole place had a pinkish glow. The opulent Scheherazade restaurant, with its pink chandelier, kept lists of the food and drink preferences of guests instead of offering menus.

Penthouse guest suites were named after such historical figures as Napoleon and Cleopatra. The 4,500-squre-foot suite named after Alexander the Great was great indeed and went for $10,000 a night. For that sum, a guest got a sauna, a weight room, a baby grand piano, and a steam room.

The opening of the Trump Taj Mahal, Trump's greatest project thus far, was set for April 1990. It was Atlantic City's largest and most expensive casino hotel.

The timing could not have been worse.

With the country in the throes of an economic recession, the casino industry was suffering from overcapacity.

For the Taj to succeed, Donald Trump had to operate what some on his staff were calling the Eighth Wonder of the World; he also had to make sure that outsiders fell in love with the place. He could not afford criticism. It would be a disaster for him, and he was willing to go far to quell any attacks on the place.

And so, when a Philadelphia-based gaming analyst named Marvin Roffman spoke pessimistically in public about the Taj Mahal's prospects, the mild-mannered "outsider" came up against the full fury of a very intimidating foe. Roffman recounted his tale of horror in a quiet, solemn voice one afternoon 14 years after the events that still bewilder him.

Marvin Roffman had acquired a reputation as one of the leading gaming analysts. He covered the gaming and food industries for an old-line Philadelphia brokerage house named Janney Montgomery Scott.

In July 1989, nine months before the opening of the Trump Taj Mahal, Roffman wrote a report that his firm published, entitled "Casino Gaming in Atlantic City: A Crisis Ahead?" Of the Trump Taj Mahal, he wrote, "Because this is a single-use structure, holders of its $675 million in first mortgage bonds have little to fall back on should the Taj not work. Certainly, it can't be made into a 'K Mart.'" Roffman had fired a shot at Trump, and the real-estate titan did not like it.

On March 10, a month before the Taj was due to open, reporter Neil Barsky of *The Wall Street Journal* interviewed Roffman, who said, "When this property opens, [Trump] will have had so much free publicity he will break every record in the books in April, June, and July. But once the cold winds blow from October to February, it won't make it. The market just isn't there. Atlantic City is an ugly and dreary kind of place. Even its hard-core customers aren't coming down as much."

> "When this property opens, [Trump] will have had so much free publicity he will break every record in the books in April, June, and July. But once the cold winds blow from October to February, it won't make it. The market just isn't there. Atlantic City is an ugly and dreary kind of place. Even its hard-core customers aren't coming down as much."

The article did not appear in the newspaper in the next day or two. Roffman dismissed the interview from his mind.

A few days after the *Journal* interview, Trump called Roffman to say:

"Marvin, I know that you're down on the Taj. But I want you to see it in its full splendor." Trump asked him to tour the property and then phone him to report; he was sure that Roffman would tell him that this was the greatest property he had ever seen. Two hours later, Donald's brother Robert, in charge of the Trump casino hotel properties, phoned Roffman to say he wanted to arrange for Marvin to tour the Taj. They set March 20 as the date of the tour.

GET OFF MY PROPERTY

On that morning, Roffman left his house in Philadelphia for Atlantic City without knowing that the *Journal* interview he had given ten days before had been published that morning. Roffman arrived at Robert Trump's office next to the Taj. Donald's brother walked toward the analyst. Roffman stretched out his hand. Robert Trump kept his hands at his side. His face was stern.

"I'm here to greet you," Robert began, his voice getting harsher, "and to tell you, get the hell off the property. You're no fucking good. You have stabbed our bondholders in the back. And my brother, all the things that he has done for you. How dare you make these statements?"

Marvin Roffman was taken aback.

He had still not seen or heard about the *Journal* article, so he had no way of knowing what Robert Trump was talking about. Innocently, Roffman said, "I think I ought to see it," of the Taj. He tried to calm Robert Trump down, to no avail.

"Get the fuck off the property," Robert screamed again. "Goodbye."

Walking over to the nearby Resorts International Hotel, a shell-shocked Roffman phoned his office and heard his secretary say, "Donald

Trump has sent a letter to the CEO (Norman Wilde) of the company, and you better get back here right away." Roffman first had his office fax a copy of the Trump letter to him, and he read it carefully:

Dear Mr. Wilde,

A number of months ago we spoke about Mr. Roffman's problems with Steve Wynn. I came to Mr. Roffman's defense even knowing that he is considered by those in the industry to be a hair-trigger and, in my opinion, somewhat unstable in his tone and manner of criticism.

Today, Mr. Roffman states in THE WALL STREET JOURNAL that "Atlantic City is an ugly and dreary kind of place. Even its hard-core customers aren't coming down as much. When this property (The Taj Mahal) opens, he will have had so much free publicity he will break every record in the books in April, June, and July, but once the cold winds blow from October to February, it won't make it. The market just isn't there."

For Mr. Roffman to make these statements with such definity (sic) is an outrage. I am now planning to institute (sic) a major lawsuit against your firm unless Mr. Roffman makes a major public apology or is dismissed. For a long while I have thought of Mr. Roffman as an unguided missle (sic). His statements about the Mirage have proven false, and his statements about the Taj will prove false.

You will be hearing shortly from my lawyers unless Mr. Roffman is immediately dismissed or apologizes.

Sincerely,
Donald J. Trump
Cc: Marvin Roffman

Returning to his office, Roffman feared that his bosses might fire him on the spot to avoid the Trump lawsuit. Roffman doubted that Trump had any legal basis for the lawsuit, "but the way he operated, was he would always threaten lawsuits and...a lawsuit has to be defended, and this becomes extremely expensive, and the way a lot of people win that legal action can wear you down."

Roffman heard Edgar Scott Jr., co-chairman of Janney, say, "I should fire you on the spot. How dare you make those disparaging comments about Atlantic City? You know we have an office there. What are our clients going to think?"

He had never seen Scott so angry.

As for Trump's demand for a public apology, Scott had made clear that Janney Montgomery Scott had never publicly apologized to anyone since starting its business in 1837.

Scott told Roffman that the condition for his continuing to work for the firm would be never to talk to the media again, a kiss of death for any analyst. Roffman received at least one call from a journalist each day, sometimes as many as ten. He would get no more bonuses, and he was being put on probation until the end of the year.

Roffman was asked to respond at once. He asked for a delay until 2 PM the next day, at which time he agreed to Scott's three conditions. Scott then got Donald Trump on the phone.

What kind of apology did Trump want, he asked?

Trump laid down two demands:

First, Roffman had to call the *Wall Street Journal*'s managing editor (then Norman Pearlstine) and tell him "that the son of a bitch Barsky misquoted him."

Second, Roffman had to write a paper stating that the Taj Mahal would be the greatest success ever. Trump would make sure the paper got published.

Scott decided to write the paper himself. He showed it to Roffman and asked him, "Can you live with this?"

Roffman responded, "Look, Ed. This is an endorsement. These bonds are going to go bust." Still, Roffman reluctantly agreed to sign the paper. That night he could not sleep. The next morning, he wrote a letter disavowing the entire paper and sent it to Trump.

When the firm found out about the letter of disavowal, Roffman was fired on the spot.

The director of research at the firm, Jim Meyer, told Roffman as he escorted him out the building, "Marvin, a little friendly advice: Keep your mouth shut about this or you'll never work in this industry again."

But the story got out quickly. When a *Philadelphia Inquirer* reporter made a routine call to the analyst that day, Roffman told him, "I may not be working here anymore." Then, hearing the entire story from Roffman, the reporter published it the next day.

Trump had not gotten an apology, but Roffman was fired. So Trump did not file the threatened lawsuit. Roffman, however, filed suit against both Trump and his bosses.

He accused Trump of wrongful discharge and tortuous interference with a contract, as well as defamation of character. The litigation was not easy: In November 1990, Trump's attorneys put Roffman through a deposition that lasted five days a week, eight hours a day, for an entire month.

In the case against his bosses, the New York Stock Exchange arbitrators granted Roffman $750,000.

As soon as the arbitration matter was resolved, Trump settled with Roffman, who was about to take the case against Trump to federal court. "It took me three hours to read the document that Trump's lawyers had drawn up for me to sign," Roffman recalled with a laugh. He was forbidden to discuss the terms of the settlement. He was not barred from discussing the entire incident.

Donald Trump had always loomed large in Roffman's eyes as a marketing genius and a promoter, but he held little respect for him as a casino hotel operator; even Trump's behavior that led to Marvin Roffman's dismissal did not eradicate completely the respect he felt toward Trump. Roffman set up a business, Roffman Miller, Inc., a Philadelphia-based investment advisory firm, with partner Peter Miller. At first, they had trouble finding work, but were eventually extremely successful.

Four years later, Roffman went to Trump, not as a beggar looking for a handout, but to get him to invest in a casino mutual fund that Marvin was exploring. Trump said no, he was not interested; Marvin did not hold it against him. He was, after all, a forgiving man, even if Donald Trump was not always one.

Trump was much more forgiving when it came to Steve Wynn.

By 2004, Donald Trump and Steve Wynn had become good friends. They visited one another and were given personal tours of their respective properties. The rivalry that had existed in earlier days in Atlantic City, now strongly denied by both men, had become a thing of the past. In 2004, Trump barely mentioned their old differences. Wynn downplayed them as insignificant.

But back in the late 1990s, the tiff was tense enough. Dating back to 1995, Steve Wynn had thought of building a three-casino complex near the site of the new Borgata casino hotel (which opened in July 2003). He planned to partner with Circus Circus Enterprises and Boyd Gaming Corporation.

Wynn asked Atlantic City to help him cut certain costs. Donald Trump fought him tooth and nail, and lost on all counts. Trump believed that he was Mr. Atlantic City at this stage. Wynn had long ago left the scene. There was room in the resort town for only one of them, so Trump believed. The stakes were high, and it was not clear how the Trump-Wynn feud would play itself out.

"It was as bitter a public feud as you could see between two public titans," said Joe Weinert, the casino industry reporter for the *Press of Atlantic City* from 1996 to 2004.

As Wynn sought more relief from the State of New Jersey for his planned complex, he had a harder time getting it; meanwhile, Trump kept gnawing at him, hoping to get him to back down and get out of Dodge.

In January 1998, Wynn decided to scuttle the partnership he was forging with Circus Circus and Boyd, and go it alone.

Trump was elated.

In Wynn's decision to scuttle his partners, Trump saw hope that Steve Wynn would lose the public's confidence, thus weakening his efforts to proceed.

THE NAME-CALLING BATTLE

Joe Weinert decided to do a sidebar to the main story of Wynn dropping his ex-partners, hoping to get comment from both Wynn and Trump.

When Joe Weinert phoned Trump for a reaction to Wynn's decision, he listened as Donald shouted into the phone, taking pleasure in the crisis surrounding Wynn, calling Wynn a rather colorful name (which Weinert printed) and urging the reporter to run a headline that would say Trump had been right all along about Steve Wynn.

Weinert then phoned Wynn: "Steve, what's going on? Donald just called you a scumbag for this." Wynn, far calmer than Trump, used an equally quotable phrase about Trump, calling him a "forgettable blowhard."

With both men's view of the situation, Weinert then sat down and wrote his eight-paragraph article, reflecting the worst moment of the Trump-Wynn feud.

The article began, "Donald Trump was in his glory Tuesday: bashing Steve Wynn.

Weinert then wrote, "Trump said the decision by Mirage Resorts, Inc., to void casino-development deals with Boyd Gaming Corp. and Circus Circus Enterprises, Inc., shows that the Mirage organization and its chairman are greedy and cannot be trusted.

"I told you so! I told you what this scumbag would do. I knew this is exactly what was going to happen. I guess this is why I'm a rich guy," an excited Trump said. "Those guys at Boyd and Circus must feel like fools because they allowed their names to be used through this entire process, but they have a great lawsuit against Wynn. But the key to this is, I told you so. That should be the headline of your article," Weinert quoted Trump as saying. (Actually, Trump said "goddamn article," but the word *goddamn* was removed by an editor.)

"That's Donald," Wynn responded calmly. "You're stuck with him. You have my sympathies. He's a forgettable blowhard. He can talk all he wants. We'll get down to building buildings and running casinos, and we'll see what he's made of. He gets a chance to substitute action for talk. We'll see how he does." (Six years later, Joe Weinert noted that whereas Trump was very worked up on the phone, Steve Wynn was quite calm and composed, even soft-spoken.)

The article went on to note that Donald Trump had, for more than two years, fought Mirage's proposed casino development in the Marina District. Trump claimed that the company had been given unfair subsidies, including a free 150-acre casino parcel from the city, new legislation to recoup some cleanup costs of the casino site, and a connector road to the site funded mostly by the state. Trump filed four lawsuits to halt the project.

Wynn's response, the article went on, was to bring a $150 million antitrust suit last fall. Mirage announced the week the article appeared that it had hired well-known architects Frank Gehry and Philip Johnson to design its larger, 4,000-room casino hotel in Atlantic City.

Trump noted in the article that Johnson's last project was Trump International Hotel & Tower in New York.

The article concluded, "Donald Trump flapping his jaws at us is like the breeze blowing off the ocean—nothing," Wynn said. "He seems to be petrified. I don't know why; maybe he does. It's the sound of a hysterically frightened man. Based on what conclusion, only he knows. Maybe he's right to be scared."

In an unfortunate footnote to the whole Trump-Wynn tiff that week, Joe Weinert's story was printed on the first day of a lengthy road trip by the National Gambling Impact Study Commission, which decided to start in Atlantic City. One commissioner was distraught that the article appeared at a time when Atlantic City and the gaming industry were hoping to put themselves in the best possible light for the commission.

In the end, Wynn decided not to build the complex, a victory of sorts for Donald Trump. Going through a number of incarnations, the Wynn project eventually led to the creation of the Borgata.

As quickly as tempers had flared between the two men, the unpleasant episode came to an end, and eventually Trump and Wynn found a way to repair the damage.

Though the Atlantic City properties proved a constant challenge for Trump, if only because he could never draw down the heavy debt he had assumed on them, he refused to walk away from them—though, at times, it must have been tempting.

For not walking away, he earned much good will from Atlantic City residents and from New Jersey officials, who were pleased that someone like him was such a key player in the resort town. "The regulators love Donald Trump," said Mark Brown, Trump's man in charge of his casino properties. "They know what he's about. There is no bullshit about him. He's the number one real-estate developer in Manhattan. He has golf courses all over the country. That's what he's about. There are no shady things going on.

"Today's casino world is made up of just big companies. The old Bugsy Siegel days are gone. Gambling is very accepted everywhere. Donald Trump is the clean, fresh face. Las Vegas is dying to have him. But it probably won't happen for another three to five years because the money has to go into Atlantic City first."

Meanwhile, the Trump properties in Atlantic City continued to produce cash. From the $48.1 billion in gambling revenues in Atlantic City in 2003, the 12 Atlantic City casinos earned profits of $4.88 billion—or 10.7 percent. Of that sum, Trump's gambling revenue for 2003 was $1,094,997,999. Of course, the cash flow did only so much good when stacked against the huge debt payments Trump had incurred: In 2003, 85 percent of the operating cash flow of Trump's casinos went to servicing his debt.

Given the debt and the difficulties associated with reducing that debt, some had the sense that Trump did not have his heart in Atlantic City. The more hands-on casino hotel operators assailed Trump for not being as intimately involved in all aspects of the business as they had been. These operators pointed out that Trump ran his casino hotels as part of his larger real-estate assets in New York and elsewhere. "He doesn't have the visceral reaction and association to this business that you will see if you sit down with [various Las Vegas casino managers]," said Phil Satre, the Chairman of the Board of Harrah's, Entertainment, Inc., in Las Vegas.

"We're all deeply involved in the daily functioning of our business; we're meeting with employees, entertaining customers. We are directly involved at a very, very intimate level, and Donald is not. One reason: I don't think it fits the makeup of his personality. His associations have been more tied to New York and the New York media. I think his view of this business is that it's a bricks-and-mortar business. He can put his name on it and can get value out of it, but he doesn't have the same commitment of time and passion about the experience of the customer in his casinos. For him, it's a sidelight business.

"My view of Donald," said Satre, "is that I don't consider him to be an operational threat to us in operating our casinos, but I do recognize and I think it's obvious that he understands how to leverage his name in making assets more valuable, a show, beauty contest, casinos. They would be far less successful without his name attached to them."

Even if the criticism against him—that he had not involved himself heavily enough in his casino hotels—had been valid, he had derived great benefit from his Atlantic City properties. Those properties had contributed to the growing belief in the mid- to late 1980s that Donald Trump had a Midas touch. But lurking behind the rosy picture was a dark side that, until the late 1980s, had been concealed.

When the darkness struck Donald Trump, it hit him hard, for it appeared to threaten all that he had built.

CHAPTER

6

FALL AND COMEBACK

Project by project, acquisition after acquisition, newspaper article after article, Donald Trump was becoming a celebrity. He seemed to have everything going for him. "To be young, blond, and a billionaire," *Playboy* wrote fawningly of Trump in its March 1990 edition. Young he was, a mere 43 years old when the magazine wrote those words. Blond he was (and blond he remained, even in 2004, at the age of 58, thanks to hair coloring). And a billionaire he was, as *Forbes* put his net worth at $1.7 billion in 1989. As the 1980s progressed, he was on his way to becoming a true celebrity; less because of business success and more because of the way he visibly played the role of a billionaire.

> *"To be young, blond, and a billionaire,"* Playboy *wrote fawningly of Trump in its March 1990 edition.*

At every turn, he deployed a strategy of making news. He kept arguing that his projects were the biggest and the best. He hoped that Trump Tower would be the greatest building in the world; that the Trump Taj Mahal would be the greatest casino in the world; and that when he built a television tower for NBC along the Hudson River, it would be the tallest building in the world. He understood the news business and knew that his creating the biggest or the best of anything warranted coverage, perhaps even front-page treatment.

His specialty was to do what no other business figure was prepared to do or was capable of doing: In his building projects, he sought to defy convention, and in his personal life, he ran against the grain by allowing large audiences to peek into his life and learn what it was like to live the life of a billionaire.

ONE BIG FAIRY TALE

Until Trump, billionaires were almost always reclusive, unwilling to permit their privacy to be invaded. He had neither the patience nor the temperament to spend a great deal of time in one of his homes or on his newly purchased yacht. But he was eager to show off his acquisitions to friends. He took acquaintances on tours of his yacht. He invited friends to join him on his jet plane and helicopter; special high-voltage friends could even borrow the jet or the chopper. He shared the high points of his billionaire existence with friends in almost daily phone conversations, boasting of his latest conquest, whether of the cement or the feminine kind.

He wrote candid memoirs, naming his friends and his enemies and explaining his negotiations, sometimes down to the last penny. Though he claimed that he minded the barrage of publicity surrounding the break-up of his marriage to first wife Ivana, he actually relished even the salacious invasions of his private life, boasting to friends that no other business figure had ever been such a constant object of media attention.

His life in the 1980s seemed like one big fairy tale: He had swept into the Manhattan real-estate world with landmark buildings such as the Grand Hyatt and Trump Tower; he had opened three hotel casinos in Atlantic City, making him a major figure there. In all that he did and all that he tried to build and sponsor, there was always the strong hint of glamour and glitz. He completed the problematic Wollman Skating Rink. He staged some of the biggest heavyweight boxing fights in Atlantic City. He bought the third-largest yacht in the world and one of the world's most famous hotels, the Plaza; he purchased an airline shuttle; and just to keep himself busy, he sponsored a television quiz program and a long-distance bicycle race. No wonder *Playboy* affectionately called him "the most daunting entrepreneur since the Astors, Vanderbuilts, and Whitneys."

The media wrote that he seemed to have a Midas touch, that he could do no wrong when it came to Manhattan real estate or the Atlantic City casino world. He, too, began to believe that he was infallible. As late as 1989, he saw evidence that everything was still going well for him. He purchased a midtown Manhattan property from Harry and Leona Helmsley for $70 million, only to sell it soon thereafter at a $110 million profit!

He had chosen two industries—real estate and gaming—that seemed to print money for him, real estate even more than casinos. Getting caught up in the buying frenzy of the 1980s, he thought the frenzy worked in his favor. Each new initiative enhanced his reputation, no matter how much money it brought him. He knew—and the banks that had been his main supporters certainly knew—that his entire business empire depended upon a healthy economic environment. As long as the economy rode on all cylinders, he would do just fine both in real estate and casinos.

But if the economy soured and he generated much less revenue from real estate and gaming, Donald Trump would suddenly look very fallible indeed. For he had structured his finances so that he had invested little of his own money in his projects. He had turned to the banks for loans, and the banks had willingly loaned him all that he had asked for—and more. As long as his businesses generated strong revenues, he had no trouble making his ongoing debt payments. But without robust revenues, he could land on his face. He did not allow himself to think such morbid thoughts.

Two events in the fall of 1989 were precursors of the trouble that lay in Donald Trump's path.

The first happened that October.

The construction of the billion-dollar Trump Taj Mahal casino hotel had been taxing his nerves. It was due to open the following April, but the project was running behind. Trump depended on several senior executives to get the job done. Then disaster struck. On October 10, 1989, three of his top gaming executives took a helicopter for Atlantic City. Trump had planned to join them on the journey but changed his mind. The three executives, Stephen F. Hyde, Mark Etess, and Jonathan Benanav, were killed along with the pilot and co-pilot when the chopper crashed in Lacey Township, New Jersey. Trump grew despondent. Suddenly, his business career seemed to pale when compared to the tragedy in Lacey Township.

Meanwhile, disaster of another kind was swirling around his personal life at Christmas that year. Already by then, the press was monitoring the break-up of his marriage to Ivana with rarely seen glee and zeal. The media had a field day upon learning that Ivana had a stormy confrontation with Marla Maples on the top of the slopes at Aspen that Christmas. *The Trump Affair: Don Juan* was the headline in the *New York Daily News*. Some writers described the Ivana-Marla encounter as the most well-documented marital confrontation in history.

A helicopter crash in October, a wife and girlfriend going after each other at Christmas—could it get any worse for Donald Trump?

The answer was yes.

Late in 1989, the Northeast was feeling the effects of a recession. Business travel slowed abruptly. Manhattan real estate dried up. People stopped going to casinos. And here was Donald Trump planning to open the largest casino in the world the following spring.

The plummeting value of his real estate made it that much more difficult for Trump to pay off the debt that was coming due in 1990: "I was in deep trouble, obviously. I owed a lot of money, and the real estate markets collapsed, so all of a sudden I had x dollars of debt and I had x dollars of value. One day I had the same debt, and I had value down to here." (He moved his hands downward.)

If he could not meet the debt payments, his entire empire could collapse. The banks and other financial institutions that had so willingly thrown money Trump's way during the 1980s would, it could be assumed safely, simply take over those properties. Not even Donald Trump, for all his persuasive powers, could keep the banks from descending on his properties if he was forced into bankruptcy.

In the past, the banks wanted Donald Trump on their books. They needed him as much as he needed them.

He had been able to persuade these banks and other financial enterprises that by putting his name on an asset, the value of the asset increased. They bought into his argument. Accordingly, the banks skirted the usual lending guidelines and requirements for collateral. "In the late 1980s, every lender wanted to lend money to Donald Trump," observed Alan Greenberg, chairman of the Executive Committee at Bear Stearns. "They wanted him on the books. They heard other banks were doing it. And other banks were making a lot of money. It was a mark of distinction to have him on the books. It was a mark against you if you weren't doing business with him."

But that was in the past.

The situation had changed. The banks' generosity had given way to a new hard-hearted approach that could spell financial disaster for Trump.

SUDDENLY VERY VULNERABLE

He was all too aware of banks that had swept down on newly bankrupt business figures; no matter how much they had begged, no matter how many tears they had shed, the businessmen got nowhere with the banks. True, some of these people had been arrogant and contemptuous of their bankers, snootily making fun of them for making much less money than they did. Grovel as they might, these businessmen got nowhere with bankers, who could only enjoy what for them was payback time. Trump promised himself that he would do as little groveling as he could toward his own bankers.

He was Donald Trump—and he would bounce back. That was the argument he planned to use with his lenders.

Still, he could not be certain how the banks would behave. Suddenly, Donald Trump seemed very vulnerable.

The day of reckoning for him came on January 1, 1990, when the bottom fell out of the real-estate market: "I was in deep trouble. I owed billions and billions of dollars to banks." He owed, in fact, a total of $9 billion to a consortium of banks. It was a sum that defied imagination. Yet here he was, the one-time man with the Midas touch whose properties had suddenly lost all of their value. He still owed the money. He still had to make those annual debt payments. The next payment, for $73 million, was due in June.

> *The day of reckoning for him came on January 1, 1990, when the bottom fell out of the real-estate market: "I was in deep trouble. I owed billions and billions of dollars to banks."*

Not to make the payment ensured bankruptcy. It was not a word that Donald Trump wanted to contemplate.

These were horrible months for him: He was forced to watch as his name and his problems were splashed all over the newspapers. One day, it was a story about his faltering relationship with his wife, Ivana; another, it was about his faltering relations with his banks. Some days, the newspapers ran stories on both events. The man who felt he could not get enough publicity now felt that the media was giving him inordinate attention. Surely there were others whose fortunes were being affected by the recession. The media found little interest in those others, though. Trump was a celebrity, and his fall was all the more enjoyable to watch. He became the poster boy and the most famous casualty of the growing recession.

In later years, as he plowed through the lowest moments of his career in the late 1980s and early 1990s, Trump tried to make an honest assessment of what had gone wrong.

He knew it was facile to blame an entire economy for his troubles, or to blame the lack of tourists at his casinos or the shrinking prices for his real estate.

He knew, better than everyone else, that he had been just as much at fault. He had felt business was easy. After all, he had made all that money without seeming to work very hard at it—at least, so it had appeared to him. Because everything had been going so well for him, he had gotten a little lazy: "I was doing so well that, at a certain point, it seemed too easy." The banks were spoiling him. They were giving him all the money he wanted to do anything he had in mind. "He confused brains with a bull market," said GE's John Myers, the president and CEO of GE Asset Management. "That's easy to do sometimes. He was spoiled with his earlier success."

In the late 1980s, a major business magazine did a story saying that everything Trump touched turned to gold. "I started to believe that." He began to think that he could leave others to run his various businesses and go off and have a good time. The whole exercise was fun while it lasted: "I was going to Paris to the fashion shows, for the girls, not for the fashions. I was doing things that were wild and good and cool and fun."

As Trump stepped up his purchasing of businesses and baubles, he chose not to worry what might happen to him if storm clouds appeared. So confident in his own business skills was he that he left the daily operations of his businesses to subordinates.

I WASN'T THERE

On reflection, he openly admits that he spent far too much time in the late 1980s away from the office, neglecting various business initiatives that, he is confident, would have been completed had he been around. He did not admit as much, but news reports drew the conclusion that he was, in fact, carrying on a secret affair with a young model/actress named Marla Maples.

On one occasion, while in Paris, he allowed his subordinates to handle a big lease. But it never got signed. At the time, their failure to close the deal did not bother him that much. He figured he would get the lease signed when he got back. Later, when things turned bad, he remembered that incident all too vividly as the classic example of how he had screwed up, how he had not kept on top of things, and how he had paid a very heavy price. "If I had been there, there's no way they wouldn't have signed the lease. But I wasn't there."

In later years, when he analyzed what had gone wrong, he put it all down to losing focus. When he kept his focus, he did well—simple as that. The cynics attributed his business acumen to riding good markets, but Trump thought differently: "I always made money in down markets. I made a lot of money in the early '80s—even in the '70s, when the markets were terrible. But at the end of the '80s and the very early part of the '90s, I wasn't nearly as focused as I am now in 2004 or I was before."

Why had he allowed himself to lose focus?

First, he was overly competitive. He wanted to win.

Second, he got bored too quickly.

He lost patience quickly with the deals that he made. His solution was to search for more deals. To others, such behavior smacked of avarice, but not to Trump. He was built not to savor the asset, but to enjoy the struggle for the asset—and that meant he had to strike and then move on. "For me, you see, the important thing is the getting ... not the having," he wrote in his 1990 book, *Trump: Surviving at the Top*.

He had, so it seemed, adopted the same attitude toward women. He admitted as much in his now-famous 1990 interview with *Playboy* when he refused to say whether his marriage to first wife Ivana had been monogamous. It was a telling nonstatement. A simple "yes" would have placed him in the same category as all faithful husbands or faithless husbands who lie to their wives. By not answering "yes" to the question, he appeared to confirm the numerous media reports that he had been carrying on an affair with Marla Maples.

GIMME THE PLAZA!

Two weeks after the *Playboy* interview, Ivana consulted a divorce lawyer, hired a publicist, and spoke to gossip columnist Liz Smith. Ivana wanted a good portion of her husband's fortune. She was looking for $2 billion. The $25 million provided for her in the 1987 prenuptial agreement look paltry to her.

The figure Trump had in mind was $10 million.

The media smelled blood. "Gimme the Plaza!" was one headline.

What did any of this have to do with Trump's struggle to avoid bankruptcy?

A good deal, as it turned out. Trump understood the nexus all too well.

Here he was about to appeal to his bankers to let him off gently. Yet at the same time, his wife was running to the media expressing the hope that he would turn over a good part of his fortune to her.

How was that going to sit with bankers who felt they had first claim to the Trump fortune?

Trump's line of defense was the prenuptial agreement. Ivana might try to overthrow it in the courts, but Trump was confident that the courts would side with him.

For Trump, the marital tiff had to be resolved if he was going to resolve his financial difficulties. "I know firsthand," he wrote in his 1997 book, *Trump: The Art of the Comeback*, "that you can't come back if you're spending 100 percent of your time fighting with a spouse for your sanity and financial life."

Trouble was brewing for Trump that same March 1990 in his battle to remain solvent.

He was forced to declare for the first time that he might not be able to make a debt payment—specifically, the $43 million he owed on the Trump Castle.

Until then, he had never missed a payment. Until then, the casinos had provided enough cash to service his debt. No longer was that true.

A spark of hope surrounded the glorious opening of the Trump Taj Mahal in April. Atlantic City had another casino hotel, this one the largest and most expensive ever built in that town. Trump was especially optimistic about the prospects of the hotel, so much that he personally guaranteed a $75 million loan. Yet to meet interest payments on the hotel, the Taj would have to generate $1.3 million a day, an unimaginable amount until then.

The spark quickly faded as the Taj was mired in problems of its own that kept its profits down.

Meanwhile, of the $9 billion that Donald Trump owed banks and other financial institutions, that included $975 million that he had guaranteed personally.

Donald Trump had his back to the wall.

Other men in his position might have set off for Mexico—or the nearest roof.

But at the worst moments, he felt no real sense of depression. Throwing himself off the roof of Trump Tower was simply not in his arsenal of business strategies.

Other men might have assumed that it was simply impossible to imagine coming up with the billions of dollars required to calm the increasingly agitated bankers.

But Trump did not believe in running away from battles.

On many occasions when he had launched a business initiative, close advisers had told him that he was crazy, that he would never succeed, that the odds were stacked against him, and that the powers that be held all the cards and he held none, or nearly none. He was too young, too inexperienced, too this, too that.

He listened—and then he pressed ahead. And when all was said and done, he overcame the obstacles; he built his buildings, and his closest advisers watched in awe at how he had defeated the odds.

Trump saw himself in very much the same position in early 1990.

The banks might have a good reason to foreclose on his empire. But he was not going down without a fight.

He knew that he had some things going for him.

He had his name. He had his reputation. He had his celebrity. His buildings might have lost their value. The economy might be falling apart. But nothing had happened to his name or his reputation. He was still as famous as ever. People still wanted to live in buildings with the name Trump on them. People still wanted to gamble in his casinos. Unlike others who were truly worth nothing when their assets lost value, Trump looked at what he was going through as a very temporary setback. He kept calling it a blip. All he had to do was convince the banks and the other financial institutions to look at his situation in the same way.

Meanwhile, he was not throwing in the towel.

He vowed that he would never allow himself to fall into bankruptcy. He would not give up. He had a reputation to that effect. Those closest to him knew he was a fighter. The *New York Post* columnist Cindy Adams noted, "If you set Donald Trump down in the middle of the Mohave desert, he will open a soft-drink stand. He will never go down."

Trump would not let himself fail. His choices were to retreat and give up, or to battle harder than he ever had in his life. He chose to fight.

He needed to come up with $73 million in debt payment by June 15.

The problem was, he simply did not have the cash.

In 1989, *Forbes* had put his fortune at $1.7 billion. Now in its May 14, 1990, edition, it ran a cover story estimating Trump's fortune at only $500 million.

Why couldn't he just sell off some of that net worth?

He could have, but "it would have been throwing good money after bad, and I didn't want to do it," Trump explained. "That was one of the reasons I survived and others didn't. "

By early June, Trump's struggle had intensified. The bankers were less than forthcoming. His efforts to sell or refinance his holdings had gone nowhere.

And those debt payments hung over his head like an ominous storm cloud: $350 million a year, or almost $1 million a day—way beyond what his cash flow was at the time. He had no idea where he might find the cash to make these payments. Only two of his holdings, the Grand Hyatt and the retail segment of Trump Tower, stood any chance of making a net profit.

THE IMPORTANCE OF BEING FIRST

To survive, he figured he had to move quickly.

He knew the way bankers felt. They would be kind and generous toward the first ones who showed up at their door.

But if Trump was too far back in the queue, the bankers might be less forthcoming. So he did not want to be 50th or 100th in line; he wanted to be first.

Speed was essential.

He raced to his bankers and let them know that he wanted to deal. In his view, no decision he ever made had been as important as this one— to seek an early deal with his lenders.

He sensed that most of the bankers with whom he had dealt did not want him to fall. If he fell, the bankers would have egg all over their faces for lending so much money to one person. If he were allowed to fall, the bank would get nothing back on its loans, creating a self-fulfilling failure for everyone involved.

So Trump believed. But he could not be sure. He was concerned, and he was right to be concerned.

Some bankers proved outright unsympathetic to him.

One trader with a bank that was dealing with Trump's corporate bonds in the late 1980s noted, "It wasn't so much that the bankers worried about Donald Trump because if he went down, people didn't care. The concern was much more that he would default on the bonds and there would be a cascading waterfall effect: Somebody with a big position in junk bonds would go under, unable to make his margin payments on other calls that he's leveraged. It could have conceivably filtered through the market significantly and trickled down from one investor who has a lot of junk bonds to lots of other investors."

Accordingly, Trump could not guarantee that bankers friendly to him could withstand the pressure from less friendly types who wanted to tighten up their finances, to put the screws on Donald Trump, to press him to make those debt payments.

To make sure the bankers fell in line, Trump played his strongest card. He reminded the bankers that, given the chance, he would be able to build his business into an even bigger one because he alone possessed the brand name of Donald Trump. "He never threw in the towel," said George Ross, one of his senior attorneys, "because he never had to. He was Donald Trump. People were willing to invest in Trump the brand, Trump the man. He did not succumb because the brand still stood for something."

Howard Lorber, a close Trump acquaintance, noted that the banks were in for a good deal of money, so they had the feeling that it was better to work it out rather than force Trump into bankruptcy: "His name was on everything. That was a concern. If you have an asset and part of it is the Trump name, what good is it to tarnish the name? Why beat him up? It became self-serving to work it out so that you don't tarnish the name. That was the big advantage he had; having that brand name was terrific."

Trump knew that the banks needed him to succeed. The best way for him to succeed was for him to maintain a high-profile pose. He might not have liked the derisive nature of the publicity he was attracting, but at least he knew that it kept his profile high. So he did little to stop the media from writing about his personal life.

As June 15 approached, Donald Trump needed to secure a deal with his lenders.

He called his bankers together for a meeting in his conference room and admitted that he was in serious financial trouble.

He needed another $65 million.

He insisted on a five-year breathing space. No bank could lay claim to him until June 30, 1995. That meant the banks had to defer all interest and principle on loans for that five-year period.

The bankers could not believe what they were hearing.

Here was someone who owed the bank money—a good deal of money—who was effectively saying, "I'm sorry, but this is no longer a good deal for me; I want you to scrap our agreement, give me a five-year time-out to improve my financial situation, and forget about the debt payments I owe you for the next five years."

Trump put additional teeth into his argument by threatening to tie up his lenders in court for years with litigation. He would, of course, drop the legal threat if they agreed to the $65 million line of credit.

To anyone else, the bankers probably would have not given the time of day. They would have said, "We are sorry for your problems, but you made an agreement with us and you must honor it. If you don't, we have no choice but to take over your property."

But the bankers were smart enough to realize that foreclosing on Trump flew in the face of logic. Yielding to Trump's demands meant allowing him the chance to get over his financial problems so that he could eventually pay his debts. Foreclosing on him meant never getting any of those debts—ever.

Though the bankers understood that Trump had a gun to their heads—and they did not like that—they caved in.

The banks agreed to Trump's terms with four days to spare.

Trump told acquaintances that his goal was to "survive until 1995," a phrase he repeated frequently. "I knew," he said almost a decade later, "that if I could survive until 1995 and hold on to most of my properties—which I did—I felt the market would come back, and it did."

What helped him through this period was "an incredibly positive attitude": "I didn't crawl into a corner. A lot of people do. They crawl into a corner and they die."

Years later, Trump called the agreement "one of the best deals I made," for it provided him with the liquidity to pay the banks and make other good deals.

He had come to the banks just in time. "Another year down the road," he recalled, noting his good fortune, "the banks were unwilling to do with others what they did with me."

Unquestionably, Trump's celebrity insulated him from the wrath of his bankers.

When asked later, Trump had trouble admitting that he had gotten by on the strength of his celebrity. To him, being a celebrity was a double-edged sword, so he could not talk about the positives without mentioning the negatives.

Celebrity, he insisted on pointing out, was a mixed blessing. Yes, it was a good thing to be a celebrity because it enabled him to win a five-year moratorium from the banks: "It gave me negotiating power with the banks because they felt the name was very important."

But it was a bad thing because "I got carried every day on the front page of every newspaper, whereas if I were a normal person, no one would have given a shit. It would have been just another story because the real-estate markets crashed for everybody—not just for me."

In the end, the banks had reacted not only to Trump's celebrity, but to his proven track record. They loved the idea that when it came to loaning money to someone, Trump had been a safe bet in the past. He had built his buildings on time, he had come in under budget, and, to top it all off, by attaching his celebrity name to his buildings, he had added luster and value to the properties.

Most business leaders eschewed power and fame, fearful that whatever publicity they attracted might well be negative.

Trump had a completely different take on the value of power and fame. He understood that becoming a celebrity meant attracting publicity that was both positive and negative.

He did not like the negative publicity, but he could live with it, knowing that there was great value in just being a celebrity. As he was able to demonstrate in the early 1990s, his celebrity helped to insulate him from a complete collapse of his financial empire.

Although Trump was not pleased with the negative publicity surrounding his failed marriage, it still made him a figure to whom people paid attention. "What Trump found is that, as a result of the fame and publicity, he was much more bulletproof than other businesspeople who have just power," said Paul Levinson, professor of communications and media studies at Fordham University. "If something goes wrong with your power, you're out. But what publicity does is [make] you supported by the viewers; you become a commodity almost regardless of what you do."

Though the banks insisted that he live a less lavish life, both publicly and privately, they let Trump decide which parts of his luxury life to retain and which to scuttle. He never believed that he had led a lavish life, so, in his view, the whole exercise of "cutting back" was not that much of a hardship for him. Still, to give the appearance of spending more conservatively and to bring in needed cash, he sold a number of properties, including the Plaza Hotel, the Trump Shuttle, and his yacht. He made clear that his banks never told him what to sell; it was clear, however, that some things had to go as part of his new, less wealthy lifestyle. The media reported that the banks had ordered him to sell specific items, but Trump contests that view: "It was never part of the agreement; it was part of the understanding. I told the banks that I was going to work to sell some properties; they didn't say which ones I had to sell."

His great triumph was that he did not have to declare bankruptcy. Avoiding that catastrophic step at the time is one of Trump's proudest business achievements. He watched as other business figures fell by the wayside and knew that he might have fallen, too.

He was able to keep most of his businesses alive and functioning. He kept the casinos, the West Side Riverside project, and many other assets.

Trump understood from his bankers that he needed to appoint a chief financial officer.

Until now, he had effectively been his own CFO. The banks insisted that this practice had to stop. There was to be no more "truthful hyperbole" surrounding the financial health of the Trump Organization. The very professional and solid Steve Bollenbach was named to the CFO post.

The media reported at the time that Trump had to limit his personal living expenses to $450,000 a month in 1990, $375,000 a month in 1991, and $300,000 a month for 1992. Trump insisted that this report was inaccurate and that he was never put under any expense constraint. "Give me a break," he said in the fall of 2004, explaining why no one would have imposed such figures. "I don't live on $450,000 a month." Imposing such a ceiling on his spending "would have made the banks look like fools. How could you tell someone driving a cab, Donald Trump is in trouble with the banks, but the banks are only letting him spend $450,000 a month? I had to be cool. I wasn't supposed to be crazy. But there was no specific number. I spent much less. When that $450,000 a month figure came out in the media, the banks had a fit because they looked like idiots." He assumed that one of his "enemies" leaked the incorrect information to the press.

The banks wanted Trump to sell his Palm Beach property known as Mar-a-Lago more than any other because, as Trump recalled, "the symbolism was horrible. I owe the banks a lot of money, and I'm living weekends in Palm Beach, Florida, in the most expensive house in the United States," worth $250 million. But he never sold it.

Trump was able to avoid selling the Palm Beach estate by convincing the banks that he could draw cash from the place by subdividing it.

One day in the early 1990s, in what he later called a "fit of bravado," he jokingly told the same bankers to whom he owed billions of dollars, "Hey, it's Friday afternoon, I think I'm going to jet on down to Mar-a-Lago." No sooner did he utter the first few words of the sentence than he realized he should not be making such a comment. "I shouldn't have been saying this because it's rubbing their faces in the dirt." He quickly noticed how the atmosphere in the room had gone from friendly tones to ominous and dead silence. "There were bad vibes in the room," Trump remembered.

Trump quickly revised his thought, telling the bankers that he was actually going down to Mar-a-Lago to subdivide the property into individual lots so that he could pay the bankers back with all the cash that would come from these mini-deals. Trump's revised utterance produced, he said later, "a great lessening of tension." To get along with the banks, Trump moved ahead with subdividing Mar-a-Lago, but the town then disallowed the arrangement. By the time the town had reversed itself on the issue, now permitting the subdivisions to go ahead, Trump no longer cared about subdividing. Realizing that a private members-only club would have higher value than a subdivided property, Trump turned Mar-a-Lago into what he had always wanted: his own private club.

The first hurdle was cleared. But there would be more. Trump was by no means out of financial trouble.

One New Jersey official who spent time with Trump at this juncture found him filled with worry. "I wouldn't say he was gloomy, but he wasn't his vibrant self." He still faced personal bankruptcy. The whole process of extricating himself from further financial difficulty might prove lengthy.

The next hurdle for him came toward the end of 1990.

On December 17, 1990, another bond payment was due to the institutional investors who held the debt on bonds for Trump Castle.

The sum owed was $18.4 million, but Trump was short a few million dollars.

Help came from a familiar quarter: Donald Trump's father. "He did it as a favor to me," Trump said.

One day, Fred Trump showed up at the Trump Castle with $3 million.

He purchased chips in that amount but did not head for the gambling area. He walked out of the casino.

His son Donald suddenly had an infusion of cash with which he could make the debt payment.

Fred was fined $50,000 because he was not licensed as a financial source for the casino.

Though his son still owed billions of dollars, the $3 million infusion from Fred Trump was "sort of a vote of confidence. I was in trouble. People would go up to my father that maybe didn't dig me or didn't like me, but they sort of said, 'Your son is in trouble.' They said it in a gloating way." Showing great confidence in his son, Fred insisted that his son would not fail because Donald did not know how to fail.

Thanks to his father, Trump had cleared a second hurdle.

More, however, remained in his path. He was still at a very low point.

Walking along Fifth Avenue with Marla Maples, he saw a man across the street in front of Tiffany's, holding a can. "That man is wealthier than I am," Trump said to Marla. She looked at him as if he were crazy.

"What are you talking about?"

Trump continued, "That man across the street is worth $900 million more than I am at this moment."

"I don't understand. He's not worth $900 million."

"No, let's assume he's worth nothing. I'm worth minus $900 million."

Donald Trump had been rescued once by the banks, but there was no guarantee that he would be able to count on the banks again. The one image that remained embedded in his mind was of one particular visit he made at 3 AM on a cold, snowy night to the offices of his bankers, where he personally negotiated over the phone with Japanese bankers to allow him to preserve his crumbling financial empire.

The year 1991 seemed like it would be no better for him than the previous one. The banks were all over him, and once again, he had to run to them hat in hand. Though the banks in the end agreed to see him through his ordeal, Trump knew he was at a low point in his career.

His businesses had $9.2 billion in debt, of which Trump had guaranteed nearly $1 billion personally.

On March 26, 1991, a day that Trump later called "by far the worst moment of my life," both the *New York Times* and *The Wall Street Journal* ran front-page stories on his financial crisis. The stories implied that his career was at an end. The phones had stopped ringing. Close friends did not know what to say to him. No one was calling about new deals. Then he got a phone call from Ivana. He was at first pleased: She was calling, he thought, to wish him well. Instead, she was calling to say she was willing to give up her court battle with him if he would give her $10 million at once plus all the other assets owed to her via the prenup.

In the end, Ivana buckled, apparently sensing that the prenup was, as Trump argued, iron-clad. She received a $10 million check and assets worth another $15 million.

When he could not make the necessary debt payments, in July he was forced to put the Trump Taj Mahal into bankruptcy.

Time after time during this crisis, the media was prepared to write Trump's epitaph. Here, for example, is *Business Week*'s opening paragraph of a 1992 story: "Donald Trump. The name is a punch line now, associated with the worst of 1980s extravagance, egomania, and greed. Once, the world marveled at the scope and mastery of Trump's megabuck deals. Today, he's widely regarded as a washed-up real-estate mogul who has been stripped of his once lustrous possessions."

But Trump proved resilient. No matter how difficult and embarrassing it was to fight with the banks, he did so, believing that as long as he was left with a part of his once-vaunted business empire, he could return to glory.

Still, the early 1990s were a dismal time for him. With each book that he wrote, he devoted a chapter to an hour-by-hour account of a week in his life, but when it came to 1990 and 1991, he chose to skip over those years—with good reason. There were too many incidents that he simply did not want to expose to the public light.

One of them concerned his close friend Howard Lorber. At one stage, Trump approached Lorber to borrow a sum of money to get over some short-term debts. "He needed some money for something," said Howard Lorber, "and I lent him some money at a rather high rate of interest which he paid back quickly; not a lot of people were willing to lend him money at that time. He was getting ready to take the casinos public, and he needed some money for lawyers or accountants. It was in the millions of dollars, not hundreds of millions of dollars; we talked about collateral. I was happy to do it. He paid it back in six months because it was high interest and he was in better shape. It never became public. I trusted his integrity. I always thought he'd do the right thing."

Finally, by 1993, Trump began to see some light. He had reduced his personal debt of $975 million to just $115 million.

After the recession ended, his Atlantic City casinos picked up steam, and Trump began to see some of that marvelous cash flow again. In 1995, he took the casinos public, raising $2 billion in two separate public offerings, using a good deal of that to repay previous liabilities.

By June 30, 1995, Trump was debt free.

If he had taken his success for granted in the 1980s, he was unwilling to do so now. In the mid-1990s, he savored his return to stability with far more enthusiasm than he had ever mustered for his earlier successes.

By 1997 Trump was, he said, worth more than $3 billion, though *The Economist* put it at $2.5 billion. Whatever the actual figure, Trump was worth more than he had been before his debacle. His public company carried $1.7 billion in long-term debt, but Trump no longer had any personal debt. He had learned a valuable lesson.

Donald Trump's celebrity had helped him through the worst financial crisis of his career. But to remain famous, Trump needed to turn media coverage of him to his advantage. That was no small trick.

PART IV

THE NURTURING OF A NAME

CHAPTER

7

STUDENT OF THE MEDIA

Most business leaders shun publicity for what they believe are the best of reasons.

Their corporate cultures encourage teamwork, not ego-boasting, and they do not want to seem as if they are trying to burnish their egos.

It is hard to imagine most other business leaders engaging in the kind of personal marketing that has become the trademark of Donald Trump. Most CEOs are eager to downplay their own personal accomplishments and want to make sure that the rest of their teams get due credit for what the company has achieved. Many business leaders run publicly held companies. The last thing they want to do is say something in the media that offends their shareholders.

For Donald Trump, this is never an issue: He has less than 1 percent of his net worth in his public casino hotel company, so there is less chance of his hurting his shareholders.

WHY CULTIVATE THE MEDIA?

Most business leaders do not understand the media, nor do they trust the media to report on their companies accurately or sympathetically.

To most of these leaders, cultivating the media makes no sense. Indeed, they view getting involved with the media one big negative.

Real-estate developers, Donald Trump excluded, are especially reluctant to seek attention for themselves. For one thing, they know they have an uphill battle, given their negative reputations. They are seen as landlords, and the very term *landlord* is pejorative. Landlords are seen as easy targets of the media, people who have made a great deal of money but seem penny-pinching.

This is what makes Donald Trump so unique—so different from business leaders in general and real-estate developers in particular.

He harbors none of the fears or suspicions toward the media of other business leaders. He does not regard the media as his enemy. He sees most members of the media as potential allies.

By developing good relations with the news business, Trump believes he will gain popularity and acceptance.

Howard Rubenstein, one of the most influential public relations executives in the United States, handled Donald Trump's public relations efforts in the early 1970s when Trump first burst onto the real-estate scene. Rubenstein wound up working on and off for Trump for 30 years. Rubenstein remembered that he had run Donald Trump's very first press conference, which was at the rail yards at 34th Street. "He was somewhat hesitant. We rehearsed it somewhat, but after that he was flying high. He did well. He's a natural."

Other business leaders don't want to take the heat of negative publicity by using Trump's technique of openly cultivating the media. "Most businessmen try to be low key," says Rubenstein. "They say, 'Gee, I expose myself so much if I'm available all the time, if I hype everything around me.'"

For those who don't know how to handle the media, says Rubenstein, the whole experience can be very dangerous: "You can hurt yourself dramatically."

OKAY WITH ALMOST ANY STORY

Donald Trump is not low key. His colleagues gently chide him for being a kind of press addict. His long-term aide, Norma Foerderer, joked with him that a microphone was his cocaine. Putting it slightly differently, Bear Stearns's Alan "Ace" Greenberg told Trump one day, "You better fire your PR people. Your name hasn't been in the papers in the last two days." Foerderer and Greenberg, both great admirers of Trump, still picked up on one of his cravings. "I almost think he's okay with any story about him," said Howard Rubenstein. "The recognition that he gets is remarkable for a businessman. It's as important to him as money. He can always get money."

No one did a better job of keeping his name in the public light for so long. He paid a price for being so good at public relations. He wanted the media to focus on his buildings. But he was so accessible and so visible and so controversial that the media preferred to write about him personally rather than professionally.

Putting it slightly differently, Bear Stearns's Alan "Ace" Greenberg told Trump one day, "You better fire your PR people. Your name hasn't been in the papers in the last two days."

Had he wanted, he might have curbed the media's appetite simply by avoiding personal controversy. That meant not divorcing his wives. But on each occasion, the marriage collapsed and he saw no way of avoiding divorce.

He certainly wished the media would have focused on his business, not his personal life, but he understood the value of *all* publicity, so he rolled with the punches.

He believed that every day that his name was in the newspaper was a day he might sell an apartment or draw customers to his casinos. He understood that his "15 minutes" would one day come to an end, and he wanted to keep his name in lights for as long as possible. Others might tire of seeing their names and faces in the media, but Trump shared no such concern. He genuinely believed there was no such thing as overexposure.

He knew that he would pay a price for wanting so much attention, a price that most others in business were unwilling to pay. He had to reveal to the media and the general public more of the personal side of his life than any business executive ever had. He granted a lengthy interview to *Playboy* and appeared a number of times on *Larry King Live*. He wrote book after book. He willingly explained why his marriage to first wife Ivana broke up, why he insisted upon prenuptial agreements with his wives, and what he really thought of his billionaire assets (he liked the struggle to acquire them more than their actual use). He cheerfully berated Frank Sinatra, Malcolm Forbes, and any journalist who printed an anti-Trump comment. Most business executives would discuss their wives and children only under threat of a gun. Donald Trump constantly talked of his immediate family in public, disclosing detail after detail of his conversations with his ex-wives and children.

Yet if attracting publicity required him to be candid, he did not seem to mind. As long as people wanted to hear him speak, as long as journalists sought interviews, as long as publishers wanted him to write books, he saw no reason to be tight-lipped.

Even when he got negative publicity, Trump seemed to understand its value. Negative publicity, as he puts it, "makes you hotter, crazy as that is. I'm not advocating bad publicity because I don't like it at all, but the thing I've learned over years of doing this stuff is that it makes you angry for the day, but (after a while) you hardly remember what they wrote about you. It's gone, gone."

When one of the New York newspapers gave his marital difficulties front-page coverage day after day in 1990, he boasted to a friend that no other business figure could get such front-page treatment for so long. On another occasion, when the press got wind of a story concerning Marla Maples that could have proven very negative for Trump, he called up a public relations executive to let him know that TV crews had gathered at Trump Tower.

"Do you want me to come over and get rid of the crews," the PR man asked, assuming that was why Trump had called.

"No," was Trump's reply. "I just wanted to tell you the crews were outside. That was all."

In other words, Trump was not calling for help; he was calling to boast.

It would have been far more upsetting to Trump if he had discovered that bad publicity affected his business adversely. He constantly worried about that, but often he found that the negative publicity bestowed on him an aura of celebrity that defined him and gave him an advantage in negotiating business deals. That was the case when Trump began a relationship with John Myers, the president and CEO of GE Asset Management, which bought and sold real estate, among other things.

In the early 1990s, Myers' unit had taken back through foreclosure the deteriorating Gulf & Western building in Manhattan. Myers did not want to sell the building, given the weakness of the real-estate market. When he asked developers to bid on the property, all but one would have forced GE to sell the building too cheaply.

Donald Trump was one of the bidders. Myers, who at the time was running the real-estate portfolio for GE Asset Management, knew of him only through the media, and his first impression was not overly positive: "He wasn't the type of guy who I thought would fit in with a GE partner. He was too visible; he had had very visible financial problems.

He was on his ass at the time. I thought he was too litigious for us. That was the image."

Trump's proposal seemed the most attractive: It included hotel condominiums and a high-class restaurant. Myers was still reluctant to do business with Trump because of his reputation, but then he spoke to an adviser to his GE unit who told him, "Don't believe what you read in the papers. This guy conducted himself honorably in negotiations with me." Myers was persuaded, but he knew that Trump was no ordinary developer.

By way of illustration, Myers recalled visiting some Trump-owned sites with Donald, emerging from a limo and heading for a newsstand. Trump picked up a *New York Post* that carried a headline in which Marla Maples was quoted as saying the best sex she ever had was with Donald Trump. "This is what sells condominiums in New York," Trump said to Myers, brushing off the headline as if it referred to someone else's sex life.

Unlike others in the business community who are dreadful in their public relations, Donald Trump is a master at PR. He feels that he needs to be. Building up a positive image in the media is, for him, a primary business goal.

More than the money, more than his assets, he wants acceptance and recognition—and it is the media that confers those things on business leaders.

He understands that better than most others. Hence, he has made a point of becoming a student of the media. He knew that he could not get the media's attention by seeking out journalists to interview him. That would seem overly aggresive. And so he chose not to phone journalists on his own. It annoyed him if someone seemed to suggest that he cultivated the media through his own personal initiatives. Journalists sought him out, he made clear. When they did, he had to make sure they sustained their interest in him.

To get the media's attention, Trump understood from the start that he needed to create extraordinary products with the hope and expectation that the media would take notice of them. "If it can't make the front page of the *New York Times*, I don't want to buy it," he often said when thinking about the kinds of acquisitions he wanted to make. Ultimately, not every Trump building had to earn front-page coverage; but he certainly wanted whatever he was doing to generate some news coverage.

> *"If it can't make the front page of the New York Times, I don't want to buy it," he often said when thinking about the kinds of acquisitions he wanted to make.*

RUNNING HIS OWN PR SHOP

To get the media's attention, Donald Trump also understood the value of taking charge of his public relations. No one else speaks for him, explains him, or issues statements in his name. He has no interest in letting others do his PR for him because, as he correctly believes, no one can do a better job of presenting Donald Trump to the public than he can.

Doing his own PR requires time and patience—and Trump is willing to devote a good deal of both in making sure that he gives the media what it wants and needs. Routinely, business leaders like to take questions from journalists and authors on the big questions related to their businesses. Trump does as well. But where he differs is that he happily takes questions on the smallest details of his business and personal lives. The media usually takes such fact-checking questions to a spokesperson. In the case of Donald Trump, one goes to the man himself. He is comfortable with that.

Trump not only takes charge of all questions about himself, but he makes the lives of journalists and authors easier with his willingness to talk candidly and at length about almost anything and everything. Journalists and authors constantly encounter public personalities with demonstrably large egos, but no one in the business world outdoes Donald Trump's reverential referencing of himself. The plain, simple fact is that he loves to talk about himself—to journalists and pretty much anyone else as well.

In one 20-minute phone conversation with the author in May 2004, he managed to get into the conversation the following items about himself: that the ratings for *The Apprentice* were sky-high; that the last few years had been the best in his business career; that he was selling apartments like crazy; that he was the biggest real-estate developer in New York; that he had recently been inducted into the Hall of Fame of the Wharton School at the University of Pennsylvania, which was now the hottest business school in the country; that he had been asked to be the grand marshal of the Israeli parade down Fifth Avenue in a few days; and that he planned to start 90-second daily commentaries on politics, business, and news over 300 stations via the Premiere Radio Networks, a subsidiary of Clear Channel Communications.

During the course of the day, Trump talks to countless people on the phone, and to many of them, he gives an update on the latest great successes in his personal career. In 2004, practically anyone who picked up the phone to Trump listened to an opening monologue on how well *The Apprentice* was doing.

RESPECTING THE WRITTEN WORD

No one talks about himself more than Donald Trump; and no one writes about himself more than he does. He has written book after book on what it's like to be Donald Trump. He says that he writes his books to make money; but there's obviously more to it than that—much more. The fact is, he doesn't need the money from his books—no billionaire has to rely upon the royalties from a book, even a best-selling one. So, why does Donald Trump write these books?

One reason: Of all the vehicles of communication available to him, writing books appeared the best one for beating back his critics and explaining to a large audience why he deserved its respect. And when the first one, *Trump: The Art of the Deal*, became a huge best-seller when it was published in 1987, Trump was more than happy to write more such business memoirs. The first Trump memoir held the number one spot on the *New York Times* best-seller list longer than any business book since the 1984 memoir of Lee A. Iacocca. Trump noted that it was the best-selling business book of the decade, with more than three million copies in print.

Most business leaders wrote no more than one memoir, but Trump wrote five (only Charles Schwab, head of one of the country's largest financial services firms, has written as many). The book world was, indeed, in his word, "seductive" and he loved seeing his name and his books in bookstores. "It's a cool thing. It's one of the very cool feelings." When asked why he wrote these books, he said it was because "they sell like hotcakes" and because "I get a great kick of looking at my name on top of all the lists and telling everyone else to go fuck themselves."

> When asked why he wrote these books, he said it was because "they sell like hotcakes" and because "I get a great kick of looking at my name on top of all the lists and telling everyone else to go fuck themselves."

Another reason for his book-writing: his undiluted respect for the written word.

He knows that his reputation has been built to a large extent on what print journalists have written about him; he lives in fear that others will write negative books about him and that after he is gone, those negative books will help form the general consensus about him. He writes his books, so it seems, as a way of supplying the world with as much written material on him as possible, in the hope that posterity will rely on his books—and not the negative tomes—in determining his ultimate reputation.

Trump has been pleasantly surprised to find that his books have been huge best-sellers, giving him an incentive to publish the next one, and the one after that. He wrote his first book, *Trump: The Art of the Deal*, when he was only 41 years old, young for someone to be writing a personal memoir.

At first, he argued that he was not writing these books to make people rich, but that was in the late 1980s, when he was accused of being greedy and hedonistic. As he gained sympathy for his artful financial comeback in the early 1990s, he promoted himself as someone who could make others rich. And so he shouted it from the rooftops: Read my book and you'll become rich. One of his books, published in early 2004, is even called *How to Get Rich*.

By 2003, he had written three books (*Trump: The Art of the Deal*, 1987; *Trump, Surviving at the Top*, 1990; and *Trump: The Art of the Comeback*, 1997). But in 2004, three more were published in his name (*Trump: How to Get Rich*; *Trump: The Way to the Top: The Best Business Advice I Ever Received*; and *Trump: Think Like a Billionaire: Everything You Need to Know About Success, Real Estate, and Life*), surely some kind of record for most books published in one year by a business figure.

Each time a book appeared, Trump behaved as if the publisher forced him into the deal, this from one of the shrewdest negotiators around. His advances were so high, he suggested, that he could not say no. It was no wonder that Random House kept returning to him to ask for one more book. His books sold like hotcakes.

As candid as he is—both in his interviews and in his books—some subjects are off-limits. Surprisingly enough, the women in his life is not one of these subjects. He often brings up his past and present relationships without being asked. But the one subject on which he offers few specifics has to do with his finances. He will happily give the big picture, such as how much he is worth at any given time ($6 billion, he says, in the summer of 2004). But he won't identify every last one of his properties or how much each is worth. Such intelligence is far too useful to too many people, he insists, and because his net worth is 99 percent private, he feels no obligation to get explicit.

Writing books was not enough to win Donald Trump the recognition he was seeking. From the start, Trump understood that he needed the print media as his ally in his search for attention. He needed to be able to convince journalists that he was worth writing about, that he was not simply someone who was "braggadocios" (his word), and that he had substance behind him.

To get those messages across, he had to go to school on the media. He had to learn what would make the media sit up and pay attention. He understood—and this was an advantage that he had in being wealthy—that he could always pay thousands of dollars and get an ad in the *New York Times* promoting one of his properties.

But the number of people who would read a newspaper story about a Trump property dwarfed those who would read such an ad: "I've always felt that a story is better than an ad. If I'm building whatever building, that story, a nice story, is in the *Times*. If I took that same space and doubled it and paid the *Times* $60,000 for an ad, people would go like this, next page, they wouldn't even read it. Yet they read every word of that story, and I sell a lot of apartments because of that story. And it costs me nothing other than an interview that lasts for about a half-hour. Now I do that because instinctively I'm a businessman."

THE VALUE OF BEING AVAILABLE

He also learned how to behave around journalists. He sensed that he was better off speaking candidly and openly to the media than appearing secretive and mysterious. He understood how important it was to be available when the media called—and he made it a point of taking phone calls from journalists without forcing them to do what was standard practice in other major businesses: making them get a hold of some public relations executive first to request the interview.

All one needed to do was dial the phone number of the Trump Organization and ask for one of Trump's assistants; often Trump would get on the phone right away, with an immediacy that startled most journalists. There he was, sounding friendly, offering colorful quotes, and getting in the latest news about his business empire. To be sure, he moved conversations along. He had to. There always seemed to be someone on hold waiting to speak to him on the phone. Once, Donald Trump asked Mark Brown, the man in charge of Trump's casino hotels, why Brown felt he needed a public relations person on his staff. "I'm my own PR machine," Trump told him, adding that no one can tell the story better than he can. Brown picked up the hint and began taking on some of the PR responsibilities himself, speaking directly to reporters.

Natalie L. Keith, editor-in-chief of *New York Construction*, was one of those startled journalists who got to speak to Trump far more often than she had expected. She could not get over how approachable he was. After all, she was the editor of a relatively small news outlet. "I could get him on the phone. That was unbelievable, working for a rinky dink publication like I was, that was not the *New York Times*. There were a lot of developers in this town who wouldn't talk to you, certain developers who were very press-shy. They didn't want publicity."

But Trump did. And so he talked to the Natalie Keiths of the world as well as the big-shots at the *Times* and at the television networks, when other real-estate developers were not nearly as forthcoming. Keith remembered trying to write about a certain real-estate project that was going up on Lexington Avenue that was to house the Bloomberg news organization. "We were a construction magazine, and we wanted to write about this project, but we couldn't get past first base with them. The real-estate company was tight-lipped; they didn't want to talk about what they were doing. It was the complete opposite of Trump. He loves publicity."

Trump made sure to give journalists a good deal of time, sometimes spending hours with them in person at interview after interview.

He spent apparently massive amounts of time with *New York Daily News* celebrity interviewer and syndicated columnist Glenn Plaskin for the March 1990 *Playboy* interview, who got Trump to "sit down with him over a period of nearly 16 weeks."

Trump was so friendly to the media that journalists cut some slack with him. Whereas other potential newsmakers who exaggerated and embellished as much as Trump did would not get the time of day, the media listened to his "truthful hyperbole," understanding that he was overstating the case on most occasions, but then reporting what he said, making sure to question some of the hyperbole.

But the reporters came back for more because, even though Trump did exaggerate, there was usually enough substance behind his hyperbole to justify doing news stories about him—and because Donald Trump was so good at cultivating the media. "What all CEOs have in common," says real-estate executive Pam Liebman "is a great passion for what they are doing. You have one real-estate conversation with Donald, and you are drawn into his passion, whether he's just bought a piece of land, a building, a golf course. He may be the world's greatest salesman. He draws you in because he believes in what he's saying. Some people will say it's not all true, but enough of it's true that it matters."

There was more to Donald Trump than the verbal excess. If that's all there had been, the media would have gone away a long time ago.

He had, PR veteran Howard Rubenstein recalled, "an extraordinary flair": He knows what a good picture is; he knows what a good story is. He understands the workings of media. And he understands what will create a headline: his social life, all his dating, and all the column items about him. He looked at his own PR in context as a whole unit." Rubenstein is not sure where Trump learned all this. "I didn't teach it to him. He might have learned some things from me. I'm glad he didn't go into competition with me. He would have had the best PR firm in the country."

Trump never feared the media the way Rubenstein's other clients did, nor, in Howard's view, did Trump make many mistakes in his handling of PR. He never let a crisis get to him. He never gave the impression that the media's questions were too tough for him to handle. And he always tried to stay on the good side of journalists, calling them and complimenting them when they had written favorably about him or when they had written something positive about the gaming or the real-estate worlds. Mike Pollock, the former editorial page editor of *The Press of Atlantic City*, had to admit that the tactic was effective. "No self-respecting professional journalist would ever say, myself included, that being complimented by someone is going to influence how you write about that person, but I would argue that, at a subconscious level, it has an enormous impact."

Joe Weinert had been a sportswriter for *The Press of Atlantic City* before he became its casino reporter in 1996. He got to know Donald Trump very well and phoned him frequently. "He can control an interview. I think of myself as hard-nosed, let's stick to the facts. He rushes you along. He says what he wants to say. You try to come back with a question. But he'll say, 'Good. Got to go. Be good.' That's how he always ends it. He won't answer a question that he doesn't want to. If you get back to the question, he says we'll get back to it. He likes to say this is off the record, but you can use it. He means just don't quote him. I would say, 'Donald, I don't want it off the record. If you want to call this guy a jerk, it has to be on the record." And sometimes he would go on the record and call the guy a jerk. My typical phone call with him was only four minutes long. Most were in the two- to three-minute range."

Even Small Newspapers Count

Trump was deft at winning many in the media over to his side, Weinert noted: "Short of some journalist calling him a child molester in print, I don't think he sees any media as bad media. He loves to talk to the media."

As part of his strategy to talk with all kinds of media, big and small, he took a strong interest in what a relatively small newspaper, such as *The Press of Atlantic City*, wrote about him. If the newspaper wrote something he was not happy about, he would pull the newspapers from his hotels' stores. But in general, he felt a need to deal with the newspaper. "He felt that there was no such thing as a newspaper being too small for him," said Mike Pollock. "Anything that can start at the local level can always escalate larger."

The media found Trump an odd fellow to figure out. They liked his quotes. They liked his bluntness. They liked his accessibility. They liked that he said what was on his mind. He did not hold back. He might have seemed slightly different from other businesspeople, with his long, swept-back golden hair; his loud, booming voice; and his constant effort at self-promotion. But somehow he pulled it off. "He's a great actor," said Joe Weinert. "And he has a great sense of humor. You don't quite take him seriously. He's a cartoon character; he's self-deprecating enough to pull it off. He's like a NASCAR race. You're waiting for the accident to happen, and it's fun to watch. But ... the accident doesn't happen. He is like so operating near the edge. "

Yet for all his charm and all his understanding of the media, Trump discovered that the media was willing to write only so much about his business achievements.

By allowing his personal life to become such an open book, he made it that much easier for the media to steer clear of his business side and to focus on the controversies that erupted from time to time, especially in his relationships with women.

He might have avoided the controversy, but only if he had not divorced his first wife—or his second, for that matter—and only if he had avoided the public spotlight in the presence of a seemingly endless series of beautiful women.

He did the job of making news so well that the media flocked to him. He knew that setting himself up as a target for the media would bring negative as well as positive coverage, but he accepted that because he believed fervently that even the negative publicity was good business for him.

He could live with the bad publicity because, as he noted, "people forget about bad publicity very quickly." A negative article about him "bothers me for the day and maybe even for the week, but after that it's over. ... It doesn't have any impact."

In flocking to him, the media still did not know what to make of this man. He appeared to have certain abilities as a real-estate developer: He had a fingertip feel for what constituted high-quality building; he prided himself on executing, getting things done, and bringing projects in on time and under budget. He had turned himself into a real-estate and casino hotel operator; he had amassed a fortune. But no major business figure of the era had become fodder for the tabloids as Donald Trump had.

The more Donald Trump appeared in the gossip columns, and the more he trumpeted his own glory, the more convinced the media became that he should not be taken seriously and should not be thought of as a major business figure. Trump, of course, thought courting the media would bring him celebrity and acceptance. It certainly brought him celebrity. But it brought him little affection within the media.

HARD TO AVOID

He was simply too in-your-face. He tried too hard to convince journalists that he was the greatest guy around. Sometimes journalists, weary of the Trump assaults but too polite to ask him to cease the overtures, came up with devices to get around his in-your-face tactics. *Fortune* magazine, for instance, noted that when it was putting together a list of billionaires on one occasion, Trump had called so often to show that his net worth was higher than what he thought the magazine planned to write that *Fortune* assigned an intern to field his calls.

Still, the media found Donald Trump hard to avoid.

He was simply too big a celebrity—and journalists knew that audiences loved to know the ups and especially the downs of celebrities.

Pete Hamill served as editor-in-chief of the *New York Post* for five weeks in 1993. He vowed, upon taking up his new post, that he was not going to cover gossip as much as the newspaper had before, nor was he going to put Donald Trump in the paper. He had tired of seeing Trump's face in the *Post*; he saw Trump as little more than a shrewd promoter, and he was not going to be caught up in the media frenzy toward the man. He did not ban Trump from the newspaper, but he did require that Trump do something to appear in its pages. And so the Trump stories slowed down considerably. But Trump was too attractive a figure to the media to be tossed aside for good. After Hamill was fired, Trump stories came back in the newspaper with a great rush.

Even when he was on the losing side of an argument, as he was in hoping to build the tallest building in the world, he managed to generate a good deal of publicity for himself.

In 1983, after purchasing the Television City land along the Hudson River, he announced that he planned to put up the tallest building in the world on the site. "It means a lot to everyone to have the tallest building in the world," he would constantly tell Ruth Messinger, then the Manhattan borough president, to which Messinger replied, "Honestly, Donald, I can't find anyone who thinks it's important that New York be defined as having the tallest building in the world."

Trump never built the tallest edifice in the world, but the debate surrounding the issues found its way into the media quite easily.

He understood that his divorce from Ivana in the early 1990s was bound to generate negative publicity about him: "If a man leaves a woman—and I never left for another woman—unless the man wants to totally denigrate the woman he's left, which I did not want to do, you cannot come out ahead. There's nothing you can do PR-wise."

He found all media attention surrounding the breakup of his marriage dehumanizing; he did not like it at all that he was made out to be egotistical and greedy; it annoyed him that the media looked upon his dissolving marriage as entertainment, not a source of sadness.

Indeed, he dislikes any seemingly negative publicity about him.

UPSTAGED BY PRINCESS DIANA

And when he feels the media has slighted him, he wants to tell the world. One day in the late 1990s, his good friend Alex Yemenidjian, the chairman of the board and CEO of Metro Goldwyn Meyer, was in Manhattan on his way to a meeting. Suddenly, Donald Trump called and implored him to come over urgently to his office at Trump Tower, "If you have five minutes, I have to show you something."

Trump sounded mysterious, and the MGM boss was intrigued.

Entering the lobby of Trump Tower, Yemenidjian saw many people gathered around a man signing books. It was Donald Trump doing a book signing.

Trump looked up from the crowd and spotted his friend.

"What are you doing here?" Trump asked him, seemingly forgetting that he had summoned the MGM chairman.

"You told me to come over," the rather startled Hollywood man replied.

Suddenly, Trump remembered his invitation: "This isn't what I called you to come see."

The two men went upstairs to Trump's office on the 26th floor.

"Look at this," Trump said, thrusting a copy of one of the day's newspapers into Yemenidjian's hand. There was a tinge of disgust in Trump's voice.

"Can you believe it?"

Alex Yemenidjian looked puzzled. So Trump continued to explain:

"I was supposed to be on page one, but because of Lady Di, I ended up on page three. This is crazy."

"Donald, relax," Alex urged him. "Who cares?"

Donald Trump cares, that's who.

Donald Trump does not say outright that it does not matter what the media writes about him, as long as it spells his name right: But he does say, "I believe that good publicity is far better than bad publicity. But the amazing thing is, the bad publicity has not hurt my business."

Once he realized that bad publicity did not affect his pocketbook, Trump was ready to share all facets of his life with the media, understanding that the more the media knew of his billionaire lifestyle, the more it would write—which would only add to his luster.

For the media to write stories about someone like Trump, it had to gain access into his personal life. Trump was all too happy to reveal those "secrets" to an eager bunch of reporters.

And so one learned what he thought...

- About his wives: He disliked first wife Ivana discussing business with him at the end of the day; he liked second wife Marla behaving like a good housewife should.
- About anyone who called him Donny: He hated it.
- About travel: He is not crazy about long-distance travel.
- About small talk: He cannot stand it.
- About attending parties: He is lukewarm to the idea.
- About exercise: He dislikes it, though he plays golf regularly.

He had no trouble criticizing Frank Sinatra in public for the way he treated women, or of assailing an in-house attorney for asking for a raise at the wrong time, or of maligning most of the Manhattan contracting industry by saying that he trusted only 20 percent of them.

Rule number 1 for most CEOs is not to talk about their personal lives in public. Rule number 2 is not to reveal their attitudes toward other public figures.

Accordingly, Jack Welch, the former chairman and CEO of GE, would never publicly criticize another company or business figure. Nor would he disclose the names of his close family members to the media and authors. The public relations executives who escort journalists and authors in to see Microsoft chairman Bill Gates feel no need to suggest in advance to a journalist that there be no questions about Bill's relations with his wife and children; interviewers know intuitively Gates will likely deflect all such questions.

But Donald Trump has no difficulty answering questions about his personal life, about what he thinks of other public figures, or about his ex-wives and children. He has made these aspects of his life part of his persona, and he accepts the fact that the media will want to know the latest on these personal aspects.

Trump's willingness to reveal many private aspects of his life makes him a big fan of the media—which needs good quotes, a good story, and all the fresh news it can muster on New York's celebrity crowd. What makes Trump such an alluring figure to the media is his willingness to behave in public in ways that would be abhorrent to all other business figures.

No CEO in America would go on national television and talk about whether he was wearing a toupee. But Trump knows that his own rather unique hairstyle has become a trademark and that helps people identify him. So when Trump appeared on *Larry King Live*, he seemed quite pleased to let King grab his hair to show that it was real. Most CEOs would rather put a gun to their heads than get so personal in front of the media.

No CEO would grant a lengthy interview to *Playboy* magazine. Trump did.

No CEO would perform in comedy skits on "Saturday Night Live." Trump did.

No CEO so happily flaunted his wealth as did Donald Trump.

When he was asked by the *Playboy* reporter if it wasn't embarrassing to flaunt his wealth, he might have denied such flaunting. But he did not. He justified his wealth, noting:

There has always been a display of wealth and always will be, until the depression comes, which it always does. And let me tell you, a display is a good thing. It shows people that you can be successful. It can show you a way of life. *Dynasty* did it on TV. It's very important that people aspire to be successful. The only way you can do it is if you look at somebody who is.

And he was quite willing to be that "somebody."

Unlike so many other business figures, Donald Trump lived for the media. He understood that appearing on television and on magazine covers conferred on him celebrity status, and he was very comfortable with that. Once, while stuck in traffic in his limo, with all hell breaking loose—shouting, horns blowing, tempers flaring—he decided to step out of his limo and stand in the middle of the traffic. He wanted to test his personal celebrity.

At first, there was silence (he couldn't have liked that). But then as the drivers and passengers realized who the person was on the street, they began to shout:

"Donald."

"It's the Donald."

"Hi, Donald."

It's hard picturing a Jack Welch or former IBM CEO Lou Gerstner pulling such a stunt—and equally as hard imagining that anyone would have recognized either one.

Others contemplating such a stunt might have worried that no one would have recognized them. But Donald Trump did not have that problem. He was very good at making himself into a true celebrity.

For anyone truly surprised at how much of a celebrity Trump had become, there was that Gallup poll taken in the spring of 2000 that gave Trump a 98 percent recognition rating, a much higher score than all others polled: Bill Gates and Ross Perot also scored in the high 90s, but Jack Welch, Warren Buffett, Steve Jobs, and Ted Turner were much farther down in the poll.

Just how much of a celebrity Trump was came home to Howard Lorber, a leading New York business figure and close friend of Trump's, when they were together attending a boxing match between Lennox Lewis and Mike Tyson in Memphis, Tennessee. It was June 2, 2002. Trump flew Lorber and a bunch of gamblers in his plane to the fight.

As they entered the arena, Lorber watched as hundreds of people rushed over to them to secure Donald Trump's autograph. Nearby sat actor Denzel Washington. Only a handful of people approached the actor.

Lorber felt bad for Denzel. Then the actor did a strange thing. He, too, approached Trump—and asked him for an autograph.

"Now I've seen everything," Lorber thought to himself.

Lennox Lewis easily won in eight rounds to retain his world heavy-weight title. But Lorber's memory of how the fight turned out was far less vivid than of Denzel Washington asking Donald Trump for an autograph.

When he entered a crowded room, Trump seemed like a combination of rock star and presidential candidate. He did not simply walk into a room; he strode in as if the cameras were rolling, all pointed at him—and often they were. He raised his hand as a greeting or made a "V for victory" sign as if he were a general back from the wars. It never seemed to bother him that all eyes were fixed on him. He relished the idea.

All of his juices were flowing in June 2003 when he walked on stage at the Trump Taj Mahal for the celebration of his 57th birthday. This was his casino hotel. It was his birthday. And he was the star of the evening. He could not have been happier.

He took the stage with self-assured confidence, looking as comfort-able as any actor on a Broadway stage. Waving his right hand continu-ously toward the fawning crowd, Trump said he was overjoyed at being at his birthday party. He was used to throwing out superlatives, and tonight was no different: He was standing in the greatest hotel in the world, he insisted, surrounded by the greatest people in the world.

A ROLE HE HAD COME TO LOVE

He began to give money away, a small payback to an audience of gamblers and revelers who felt something magical in Donald Trump's presence. They wanted to touch him, to get his autograph, to gamble away their incomes at his casinos. His characteristic bluntness, one of his more attractive features to the millions who idolized him, forced him to admit into an open microphone that maybe it was not so legal to dis-pense money in this way; but then, reverting to his I-can-do-anything-I-want mode, he dismissed the issue with a "Oh, what the hell. Only in a casino can I get away with this crap."

He continued to dispense the money.

The "birthday bash" allowed him to do what he wanted to do most: project an image of a man of remarkable achievement who had built the best and largest buildings in New York City and who has taken Atlantic City by storm, the greatest of the casino moguls.

Trump was playing a role he had come to love, that of the superstar on center stage, standing before his loyal, fawning, loving audience. He was playing other roles as well: that of the super salesman, the supreme marketer, the public relations whiz—all wrapped into one.

It was a wonderful look into the life and celebrity of Donald Trump.

In the early 2000s, Trump's careful tending of the media was paying off. The overwhelming majority of media coverage of Donald Trump was positive, focusing on *The Apprentice*. Some journalists did lengthy background pieces on Trump's career, but none was damaging. If anything, the articles made him seem more complex, more powerful, more human, and, thus, more interesting. Scanning the media, Trump liked what he saw: "I haven't had too many people attack me recently," he said in the summer of 2004. "The people I thought of as my enemies are giving me very strong grades, now where six or seven years ago they would have really hit me."

Still, Trump tried to be a perfectionist, and that meant striving for 100 percent warmth from the media. He loved it when newspaper articles pointed out his achievements. But he could not let go of articles that seemed negative to him. Unlike many business leaders who simply ignored negative publicity about them or their companies and did not fight back, Donald Trump attacked every time he found himself unjustly treated in the media.

Some of his worst altercations have been with the editors and reporters at the business magazines.

He could not understand why anyone in the media attacked him. The most reasonable explanation that he came up with was that they were jealous of his wealth.

Such arguments baffled journalists.

"You wonder why he would have this insecurity," said *Forbes* senior editor Larry Light. "He's rich, good-looking, tall, not some wimpy little kid who got kicked around in junior high school. It's beyond me. I've always heard he was insecure because he was an outer-borough guy; the rich grandee families, the dynasties looked down at him as a parvenu, but so what? You can overcome that. New York is not the landed gentry of England of Jane Austen's time."

There was, so it seemed, a tension between Trump and the business media that had to do as much with his braggadocio and bluster than with his billions. Reporters and editors can get used to men and women of wealth, but they have far less tolerance for those who flaunt their wealth, as Trump seemed to do at every turn. And they have less tolerance for those who seem to be concealing their true wealth. After all, the editors and reporters believe they are in business to identify the actual finances of people and corporations as a basis for comment and analysis.

And so the editors and reporters at the business magazines were not great fans of Donald Trump. Their voices and their body language betrayed their true feelings. They wanted to show that Trump could not get the better of them. They were independent of his charms and persuasions. As if to demonstrate the point, one editor picked up a document that Trump had just sent him, Trump's latest effort to convince the editor that he was a very important and very wealthy man, and cheerfully threw the piece of paper into the wastebasket.

A key point of contention between Trump and the business media was whether, as he claimed in 1992, he had made the kind of financial comeback to warrant major coverage. Trump contacted *Business Week* senior editor Chris Welles, who said he would put a reporter on the story. He assigned it to Larry Light.

Trump gave reporter Light a bunch of numbers, but Light dug around and found other sources who contended that Trump was still heavily in debt to the banks. In the article that Light wrote, he explained why Trump had not made a comeback yet, but he predicted that he would in due time. Light thought it was a balanced story. Trump was angry but did nothing to protest.

I WILL SUE YOUR ASS OFF

In 1993, Larry Light wrote a story about a deal Donald Trump was making with a Japanese man with a crime-ridden past to resurrect a hotel and call it the New Japan. Trump saw Light's one-page story and hit the roof. Picking up the phone to Light, Trump demanded to meet with editor-in-chief Stephen B. Shepard. "I'm going to sue your ass off," was all Trump said to the reporter. That night, Larry Light said, Trump left an unpleasant voicemail message on his home telephone.

A meeting was set the next morning between Trump and Stephen Shepard. Before the meeting, Light played back the voicemail message to Shepard and a *Business Week* attorney. Shepard could not believe that it was Trump on the voicemail.

Upon arriving at *Business Week*, Trump delivered as yet unfiled legal papers accusing the magazine of defamation. For three and a half hours, Trump berated *Business Week's* coverage of him. Among his charges: Larry Light was jealous of him.

"Why would I be jealous of you?" Light asked Trump.

"Because," Trump reported, "I am so wealthy."

The meeting concluded with the *Business Week* attorney warning Trump, "If you want to sue us, it's your right, but know this: If you do, we'll demand disclosure of all your finances in court."

That was something Trump apparently did not want to happen. The matter faded away quickly.

Walking out of the meeting, Shepard turned to Light and suggested, "That was Donald Trump on your voicemail."

A year later, still at *Business Week*, Larry Light was editing the "Upfront" section of the magazine. He wrote a brief article entitled "Donald Ducks Another Bullet" for the July 31, 1995, edition.

Light wrote: "Donald Trump has scored another one. The New York–based developer and casino operator had $115 million in personal bank debt come due on June 30. *Business Week* has learned, though, that the banks have granted him three extra years to pay."

"Say what you want, Trump is a master at giving himself breathing room."

It was, Light wrote further, an "open question" whether Trump could have raised the $115 million by selling other properties, as Trump contended he could have.

Trump asked for another meeting with Larry Light. This time, he did not threaten to sue. He simply complained that Light was out to get him. He did not suggest that Light had been wrong. It was Trump's way of putting the magazine on notice. The editors observed later that few business figures complained as loudly; and few demanded meetings with editorial staff—and got them. While denying that his antics intimidated them, the editors knew that Trump was a continuing presence hovering about any story they would write.

For reporters from less powerful organizations than *Business Week* or *Forbes*, Trump's ability to threaten reporters and editors with lawsuits proved quite intimidating. One reporter who covered Trump extensively noted, "He has far more control of the media than a lot of other tycoons do. It's his litigious nature. He really does view things in a zero sum game in a way that others don't. He's willing to go to the mat even if it doesn't seem it's worth his time. Even if a newspaper wins a lawsuit against him, you still have to pay the legal bills. Everyone knows the stories of people who were fired for trying to point out what they thought was the truth about the man."

Howard Rubenstein was certainly conscious of Trump's grousing with the media. If other clients decided to attack the media in Trump-like fashion, Rubenstein quickly suggested to them that this was not the best way to deal with the media. But he made no such comment to Trump.

To Rubenstein, Trump was unique:

"His handling of PR created a new approach to PR that I have not seen; I have not one other client that does that. Donald doesn't follow the normal pattern of response that most executives follow who are afraid of the media. He's not afraid of them. A lot of these executives are afraid if they complain, the beat reporter or whoever is reporting it will take revenge, however subtle. Revenge can be just shading a story, just maneuvering a story around, just not covering someone or something. I've seen some people insult a reporter who then says, 'Okay, if that's the way you want it, don't bother calling me anymore.' The reporters don't say that to Donald."

Trump sees red when he thinks the media is out to show that he is not as wealthy as he claims.

He feels that he has good reason.

From the moment his business empire nearly collapsed in the early 1990s, Donald Trump needed the media to show that he was still alive and kicking, that he was on his way to a comeback, and that his businesses were moving steadily from the red to the black.

If his financial empire was threatened with demise, so was his status as a celebrity—and he could not let that happen. To maintain his celebrity status, he had to be thought of as a multibillionaire.

But his eagerness to advertise himself as one of the world's richest men collided with his deep-seated need for privacy in his financial affairs.

On the one hand, to convince the media that he was superrich, he would have to disclose all of his holdings.

On the other, however, he was not required to divulge all of his holdings—only the less than 1 percent that was wrapped up in his casino hotel world.

I'M WORTH MORE THAN YOU SAY

The dilemma was never better reflected than in the long-standing battle he waged with *Forbes* magazine to persuade the magazine that he was indeed a superbillionaire.

Over the years, Trump fought aggressively to have *Forbes* magazine show him off in the best possible light. That's why he had a running battle with them, arguing that they were not describing his wealth in large enough terms.

On May 14, 1990, *Forbes* did a cover story on Trump titled "How Much Is Donald Trump Worth?" *Forbes* put the figure at $500 million, less than a third of his worth the year before, according to the magazine. "This we can say with confidence," *Forbes* wrote. "His net worth is nothing like the $3 billion *Business Week* magazine estimated three years ago and has dropped considerably from our own 1989 estimate of $1.7 billion."

Trump balked.

He accused the magazine of undervaluing the Plaza Hotel, the Trump Shuttle, and the Riverside South project.

But there was little Trump could do at that stage. With the *Forbes* cover story, word spread fast. Donald Trump was on his way out. As evidence that his best days were over, he did not make the *Forbes* list for the next few years.

But by 1996, Trump had made a financial recovery, and he was busy calling the new man in charge of the *Forbes* 400 list, Peter Newcomb. Trump wanted the new editor to put him back on the *Forbes* list. With the cutoff for the list at $450 million, Trump insisted he had more than $500 million in assets. So, according to Newcomb, he was eased back on to the 1996 list in the number 373 spot, appearing for the first time in seven years.

"Since, then," said Newcomb, "I have taken an extremely cautious approach in evaluating his net worth. If I relied on Trump, he'd be on the list at $6 billion." It was difficult to evaluate Trump's true net worth, said Newcomb, because most of his properties were tied up in partnerships and profit participation deals: "It's a hard empire to value. Normally, when we look at real-estate guys, they own the building. We find out what a building is worth, how many square feet there are; we find out how much debt he has against the building. But Trump has these profit participation deals—he might have a 20 percent equity stake and he might get 20 percent of the profits. How do you capitalize that?"

However complicated it was to evaluate Trump's real worth, he had only one goal, and that was to seem as rich as possible. And so he was on the phone to whoever was running the list at *Forbes* with updates on his worth. He often sent articles as well that demonstrated what he felt was the true size of his wealth. *Forbes* got calls from others about the list, but they called to say that *Forbes* had missed out on someone who should have been on the list.

Only Donald Trump called to say that the magazine should have valued his fortune higher. "Most of those who call us don't want to be on the list, or they say, 'I'm too high,'" said Larry Reibstein, the assistant managing editor at *Forbes*. "Only Donald Trump says we have him as too low."

In the summer of 2004, Trump tried to downplay his long-standing tiff with *Forbes*, perhaps because the magazine in 2002 had ranked him 92nd, with $1.9 billion, noting, "It wouldn't quite be *The Forbes 400* if The Donald didn't disagree with our net worth estimate."

The news was even better for him in 2003 when the magazine credited him with a fortune worth $2.5 billion. These figures made for a mellower Donald Trump: "I know I'm worth much more than that. But that's okay. That's not exactly serious." Indeed, as he pointed out, being ranked the 73rd richest man in America wasn't bad. "*Forbes* says I'm worth $2.5 billion. That's a lot of money, and I'm relatively young (at 58) to be on that list."

Trump said he has learned to live with *Forbes* not evaluating his fortune higher. "Worse things have happened."

By September 2004, he was eagerly awaiting the 2004 list, having heard from someone that the magazine had evaluated his fortune at an even larger figure. When the list was announced, Trump had dropped a notch to 74th, but his fortune had risen to $2.6 billion.

Trump still insists he's worth $6 billion.

He is quite aware that he is, at least in part, responsible for *Forbes* setting his fortune at a much lower figure.

He acknowledges that he keeps the details of much of his fortune close to his belt. "They don't know everything I own, and in a lot of cases, I don't want people to know everything I own."

One reason: If the tax authorities knew that he owns a certain piece of property, the land gets assessed at a much higher value and he has to pay much higher real-estate taxes.

A second reason: Trump sometimes wants to purchase property adjacent to his, but if the owner of the land next door learns that Donald Trump is bidding on the property, the owner automatically increases the price drastically, knowing of Trump's wealth.

Of his attempts to buy adjoining property, Trump says frankly, "If you're trying to assemble something, the worst person possible to own an adjoining piece of property and be the assembler is Donald Trump. So I'll put things in a corporation. Sometimes I'll have people go out and claim to be the owner of the land to try to buy the adjoining piece. So there are things I can't talk about."

Ultimately, he has a lot to talk about. He makes a point of talking a great deal—about himself, about his financial empire, about the next great deal he is about to announce. For Donald Trump has learned the value of promoting himself, of working hard to get himself covered in the media. He has learned how to turn himself into a brand, another aspect of his business life that makes him unique. We turn to the branding of Donald Trump next.

CHAPTER

8

BRANDING A NAME

In figuring out what makes a business leader successful, one normally looks at his leadership secrets, business strategies, and management styles.

One also asks, is he a good speaker? Does he articulate the company's policies and initiatives clearly? Can he get employees to fall in line behind new programs? Does he have the personal skills to sell his company's products?

What's never asked is, does he know how to promote himself?

That question is never asked because no CEO is expected to promote himself. The CEO is expected to promote the company's products.

For the most part, the leaders of the nation's major corporations consider themselves too humble and too modest to link their own name with their products. Jack Welch would never rename General Electric as the Jack Welch Company; nor would Bill Gates rename Microsoft as the Bill Gates Company. Wall Street would laugh, or frown, or wince—or all three.

Donald Trump openly names his products after himself and markets his name as synonymous with his products: his luxury residences, his casino hotels, and so on. He insists, as well—correctly, as it turns out—that using his name on his company's products enhances their value.

He thus engages in the ultimate marketing chutzpah—the branding of his name and the branding of Donald Trump—and he has had great success with this unusual business technique. He knows that the name without his celebrity would have little worth. Accordingly, Trump works hard at nurturing his celebrity, knowing that the greater his celebrity is, the more value his name has when attached to his buildings and casino hotels.

> *"All of us know how to put up a building," says Richard Lefrak, who has built his share of buildings in Manhattan and its surroundings. "Donald was the only one who created a luxury brand name. That's a big distinction between him and everyone else. He not only made a brand name, he made a luxury brand name, which is harder."*

Others in the real-estate industry are especially bemused by the branding techniques of Donald Trump. "All of us know how to put up a building," says Richard Lefrak, who has built his share of buildings in Manhattan and its surroundings. "Donald was the only one who created a luxury brand name. That's a big distinction between him and everyone else. He not only made a brand name, he made a luxury brand name, which is harder. He did it by the sheer force of his personality."

Among the best-known brands in America are Coca Cola, Microsoft, Disney, and Nike. They are instantly recognizable. Customers easily identify the products behind the brands, and their products monopolize markets.

Donald Trump has done much the same in branding his own name. He has widespread recognition; the name Trump signifies high-quality luxury residences and slick, flashy casino hotels. And, if only because he seems so one of a kind, he drowns out all other competition.

Trump has done well at branding himself in part because he has watched other celebrities take their turn at personal branding—and many of them have failed. He points out that Britney Spears tried the restaurant business, but it bombed.

CREATING A PUBLIC PERSONA

No other business leader has worked as hard as Donald Trump to create a public persona—an image, if you will—and then enlisted that public persona in furthering his career. He is relentless at it. He never seems to stop promoting. It is as if self-promotion were part of his DNA. "He has never missed an opportunity to promote whatever he's doing," says Phil Ruffin, owner of the New Frontier hotel in Las Vegas.

Trump takes great pride in the fact that very few celebrities can put their names on almost anything and do well. He can think of only three: Oprah Winfrey, Tiger Woods, and Donald Trump! He could have added to his list Martha Stewart, who successfully branded herself, merging her name with her products; but her career took a nosedive in 2004 when a jury convicted her of all four counts of obstructing justice and lying to investigators about a well-timed stock sale and sent her to jail for five months.

When someone picks up the phone to Trump, he never misses an opportunity to plug his latest initiative.

The phone caller is peppered with all sorts of rhetorical questions:

"Did you see that article in the *New York Times* talking about the great ratings for *The Apprentice*?"

"Did you hear that I just announced that I'm building a spectacular luxury residential tower in Las Vegas?"

"You know that I'm going to put together the greatest deal in the world for my casinos?"

Only after listening to such questions can one begin the business at hand with Trump.

Trump's appreciation for self-promotion—one can call it the marketing of Donald Trump—stems from his belief that others might sing as well as Frank Sinatra or play golf as well as Jack Nicklaus, but they often fail to catch on because they do not know how to attract public attention. "You need to generate interest, and you need to create excitement," Trump wrote. In the same way that he mistrusts outside consultants, he disdains public relations consultants. They are outsiders; he trusts only himself to do the job.

Trump has created three different identities for himself. He is at different times—or occasionally at the same time—Donald Trump the person, Donald Trump the head of a business empire, and Donald Trump the brand.

In this sense, he is quite unique among American business leaders.

Only he is engaged in promoting himself as a brand.

Conspicuous, seemingly ubiquitous, Trump sometimes seems as if he were the only business figure engaged in self-marketing.

Certainly, of all the other business leaders, he has been the most visible, the most exposed, and the most publicity-conscious.

> *One of his big admirers is GE's John Myers: "His name stands for extravagance, but it also stands for quality. In New York, if you say, 'I live in a Trump building,' that means something."*

Some business executives think Trump takes his style of self-branding too far and wince at his in-your-face antics. Others admire him for creatively exploiting his name and turning it into a commodity. One of his big admirers is GE's John Myers: "His name stands for extravagance, but it also stands for quality. In New York, if you say, 'I live in a Trump building,' that means something. It means it's generally a quality product. We felt that having his name on one of our buildings gave us an incremental $50 a square foot."

Whatever others think of him, Trump is very good at branding himself and getting value from that exercise. He might well be the most successful self-promoter in the business world. Through his intense and aggressive efforts, he has elevated self-promotion to a critical business strategy, and no one does it better.

He attributes his success in branding to the same micromanaging that he employs in other facets of his work, whether it's negotiating or public relations. In marketing himself, he takes on marketing and sales functions that routinely belong to a CEO's subordinates. He micromanages because he is convinced that no on else can manage the promoting of Donald Trump better than Donald Trump.

To get a feel for Trump's self-marketing, walk along the Garden Level of the Trump Tower, which is one floor below the lobby. One shop is selling *The Apprentice* T-shirts for $24, "You're Fired" T-shirts for $19, "You're Fired" tank tops for $24, and "You're Fired" baseball hats for $22.

In the lobby near the front door is a photo of Donald Trump with his latest book, *How to Get Rich*. Next to that photo is the award given to Trump by the American Academy of Hospitality for his "commitment and adherence to the highest standards in building and hospitality." Next to the award is a billboard with a beautiful woman in front of the Trump Marina of Atlantic City. In the fall of 2004 *Conde Nast Traveler* chose the Trump International Hotel and Tower in New York City for its best hotel in North America award.

Exiting Trump Tower, one could find further employment of the Trump name on nearby buildings. Indeed, one might have thought there was a Trump building every few blocks: Trump Place at 180 Riverside Boulevard, Trump World Tower at 845 UN Plaza, Trump Palace at 200 E. 69th Street, Trump Plaza at 167 E. 61st Street, Trump International at 1 Central Park West, and Trump Parc at 100 Central Park South.

The T-shirts, the baseball caps, the Trump photos, the banner, the hotels—all of it was part of Donald Trump's ongoing campaign of self-promotion, his ongoing effort to market himself.

Trump believes fervently that using his name as part of a project's name makes eminent business sense. He was certain that using his name brought in extra dollars. Real-estate brokers agreed with him. Pam Liebman recalled that her Corcoran Group had sent brokers overseas when the Asian market was buying a good deal of residential space in New York. "They could go just with Donald's name. They could sell properties from floor plans." Some of those Asians, she said, might have been nervous about buying Manhattan properties sight unseen without the Trump name attached to the properties. "They might be nervous that the product wouldn't be finished on time, etc. But they knew if Donald Trump put his name on the building, he wasn't going to run away."

Of course, putting his name on so many buildings might backfire. Trump insists there are plenty of buildings he owns on which he does not place his name. When Trump seemed to be running for the presidency in 1999, Larry King noted facetiously that if he won, he would rename his new residence the Trump White House.

What are the ingredients of Trump's self-branding?

First, there is, above all else, the force of Donald Trump's personality that makes him, in the phrase of his sister Maryanne, "a legendary promoter." She contrasts her brother with her father and herself. "Dad was not into flash or dazzle. He was a very

> *"We don't dazzle. Donald dazzles. He really has the whole package."*

left, right foot kind of person." She is the same way; she says, "We don't dazzle. Donald dazzles. He really has the whole package." Even his competitors, people such as real-estate executive Steve Witkoff, president of the Witkoff Group, call him "magnetic," adding that "he has an ability to capture people. He's got such a commanding presence."

It is indeed a commanding presence, at the size of some professional basketball guards, 6 feet, 3 inches tall; a solid build; that shock of blond hair; and a slow, almost methodical gait. He requires most people—those under his height—to look up at him. That automatically gives him an advantage. Then there is the brusqueness in his speech. He speaks passionately about almost everything. Almost every comment a visitor makes elicits a strong reaction from Trump. So, when someone raises a subject and he replies with silence, it is jarring. On occasion, he shouts—to a nearby assistant to fetch a document or to reach someone on the phone. He does not just shout; he erupts, and a visitor is taken aback. That is his commanding presence and his dazzle.

He seems constantly in motion. He does not leap from his desk and walk around his office, not that kind of constant movement. It's more that he's always doing something, gesturing with his hands, reaching for the phone, looking for some article, reaching for his Diet Coke. "He's such a volcano of activity," says Richard Lefrak, "that it generates this excitement or charisma. A lot of his charisma derives from that energy."

He's also very shrewd. "He realizes," says Lefrak, "that no matter what he says, some of it is going to stick." Part of that shrewdness is an uncanny ability to make people believe that what he says is true, even as he engages in what he loves to call "truthful hyperbole." Even his closest friends know that he exaggerates, but they forgive him for it because they know he's not far off the mark, and he can be awfully persuasive.

THE CARNIVAL BARKER

Alex Yemenidjian, the head of MGM, winces just a little when he's told that Trump tells everyone that he is the biggest star in Hollywood, based on *The Apprentice*. "He's the not the biggest star in Hollywood—he is the biggest star in reality television. But Donald can make everyone believe that he is. That's all that matters." Tony Schwartz, who co-authored *Trump: The Art of the Deal* with him, winces even more in describing Trump's artful inventiveness: "Donald's style when it comes to the truth is creative and very much a part of who he is. He's a carnival barker. He's a P. T. Barnum. The truth is for university ethics professors."

Usually, braggarts come off as offensive, heavy-handed, and unpleasant to be around. "With Donald," says Yemenidjian, "you never feel he's offensive. Even if he's bragging about himself, his properties, it's light, comical, never taken very seriously. One of his big advantages is that people like him a lot. If people like you, that's half the business."

One reason people take to Trump is his ability to get them on his side.

He is great at flattery. Even he knows that he can talk about himself for only so long without turning people off. So, he tries to make a visitor to his office or a caller on the phone feel very important. That makes it harder not to warm up to Trump and become loyal to the Trump brand.

He knows how to push all the right buttons.

He will tell women they are beautiful. He will tell men they are handsome.

He will use the word *legendary* to describe business associates. He will send newspaper articles to friends when their names appear in the press. He will tell a writer that he has just seen a great review of one of his books.

Of course, the ultimate flattery is to be invited along on one of the trips he makes on his 727 jet or his helicopter. For Trump to spend a few hours or more with someone on the plane or the chopper is his way of flattering the person. He's saying, "I think you're important enough that 15 or 30 minutes with you just won't do."

He is, as his sister says, the whole package because when he promotes himself, he has something to sell. Builder Richard Lefrak notes, "Fifteen or twenty years ago, there was a lot of noise [with Trump], but today there's a lot of substance."

It is the very force of his personality that makes him such a great salesman. Some insist that Trump could have made it big in various professions because he knows how to market and sell so well. "He could have been an unbelievably successful guy on Madison Avenue," observes Albert N. Greco, professor of communications and media management at Fordham University in New York, "because he knows how to sell so well. He could have been a tremendous success on Wall Street, selling stocks and bonds, because that is what he does—he sells."

A second ingredient that explains Donald Trump's success at self-branding is his ability to deliver the goods.

Only if there is substance, only if the person has the goods to back up his words, truthful hyperbole and all, can someone seek to self-brand. As Trump suggests, "You can only promote if you got the goods." Nothing illustrated the point better for Trump than the world of boxing; in his view, no other fighter promoted himself as well as Muhammad Ali.

Why was that?

Because Ali had the goods: "I've watched a lot of guys come into the ring with a far better line of bullshit than Muhammad. They look sharp. They look great. And then they get knocked on their ass. You know what? The bullshit doesn't mean a thing as they carry the guy out."

Muhammad Ali was different. He did his "I am the greatest" thing, and he pulled it off because he won in the ring. He had the goods, so he could self-promote and sound credible.

Trump knows all too well that, without the goods, his name would not be famous, nor would he have much of a business. To show that he delivers the goods, he notes that Mar-a-Lago in Palm Beach was named Best Club in the World by the American Academy of Hospitality Services, that Trump International Tower and Hotel is one of only three hotels in the United States to earn five stars from Mobil for both the hotel and the restaurant, and that the Trump International Golf Club has been called one of the best courses in the world.

I HAVE THE GOODS

Noting that, like Muhammad Ali, "I have the goods," Trump says, "I have the best buildings. I have the best locations." His mind skips to a New York builder who, Trump says, can't understand why his buildings sell for half of Trump's. Trump knows. The man simply doesn't have the goods.

"I recently looked at a building he built—the worst pile of shit I've ever seen: little tiny windows, very expensive. He didn't save on the money, a very expensive building. It looks like it was built in the 1920s, but a cheap 1920s replica. And little windows, cheap window frames. Everything is bad. And then he goes around saying, 'That fucking Trump. Why the fuck does he get more money than me?' This [New York builder] is a crude, loud, boisterous guy with absolutely no taste. He's a smart, tough business guy, but it drives him crazy that I get double the price per square foot than he does. And I look at his building, and I can tell you why: He doesn't have the goods. He doesn't know how to do it."

To Trump, all the truthful hyperbole in the world will not get him very far unless there is substance backing him up. Had the media discovered that Trump was *only* truthful hyperbole, they would have ignored him a long time ago, condemning him to an obscurity he would have labeled as hell.

But the media credited Trump with having substance. One former British journalist noted that, in the late 1990s, when he mentioned to colleagues and analysts that he was interviewing Trump for a story, he was warned that Trump tended to exaggerate or even fabricate data. "In the course of several interviews, "said the former journalist, "Trump did indeed quote numerous facts and figures, apparently off the top of his head. All [but one] subsequently turned out to be accurate."

He was, in the words of Hollywood executive Kirk Kerkorian, "a closer." He got things done. And the media responded to that. Trump had, said public relations expert Howard Rubenstein, "a history of excellent achievement. So the media would talk to him. They would be friendly toward him at every step of the way. If he had been just a bag of wind and didn't build all those wonderful things, the media and others would not have treated him so well."

To Rubenstein, it was Trump's foresight and perseverance that led to his building successes, and the media responded favorably to such traits. "Look at what he's accomplished with the Riverside South project. I had other clients who tried to develop that site for years. They couldn't get to first base. Donald put it over after a gazillion years of everybody trying to build that housing. How he built it, I'll never know, but he did build it."

He might deal in superlatives, notes senior Trump attorney George Ross. "But he does what he says he's going to do. He says he's going to build a building and get more money for it than anyone gets in the City of New York—and he does. People in the industry think there's some gimmick—no one can get those prices. But they don't like him because he says what he's going to do and then goes ahead and does it. The Wollman Skating Rink is a classic example."

It is Trump's ability to deliver the goods that compels his close friends to believe that his technique of self-branding will endure. "You're Coco Chanel," *Conde Nast*'s Steve Florio told him. "A hundred years from now, people who did not know what Coco looked like will know what her brand was all about. You have the ability to sustain a quality brand the way Chanel did."

The third ingredient in Trump's arsenal that explains his self-branding success is his playful—some say charming—disregard for what is true, or what is precisely true—and then getting away with that disregard for the truth.

He has gotten very far, indeed, on branding himself through a form of exaggeration that he good-humoredly calls "truthful hyperbole." Few business leaders are allowed to get away with what he does—seemingly whimsically, but systematically enough that it is a dominant part of his personality.

Every other business leader is held to a far higher standard when it comes to telling the truth. Reporters interviewing business figures who constantly improve upon the truth about their companies get shot down without being cut much slack. When Donald Trump engages in truthful hyperbole, the reporters certainly ask him if he's really telling the truth, but they do not cut him to shreds. The reporters tend to regard his disregard for the precise facts as a charming, almost irrelevant feature of his personality.

PLEASANT LITTLE EXAGGERATIONS

In giving a name to his lack of truth-telling, it is as if Trump feels pride in expanding on the truth. He finds nothing wrong with the practice; he is simply playing up to people's fantasies. In one of the most candid passages in the five books he has penned, he wrote in *Trump: The Art of the Deal*, "People may not always think big themselves, but they can still get very excited by those who do. That's why a little hyperbole never hurts. People want to believe that something is the biggest and the greatest and the most spectacular. I call it truthful hyperbole—It's an innocent form of exaggeration—and a very effective form of promotion."

In short, he's saying that he is doing everyone a favor by his pleasant little exaggerations, and we will come to appreciate him for it.

He has been caught saying the following:

- That he owned 10 percent of the Plaza hotel, when he meant he had the right to 10% of the profit if it was ever sold
- That he was building a "90-story building" next to the U.N., when he meant it was a 72-story building that had extra-high ceilings
- That his casino hotel company had become the largest employer in the State of New Jersey, when, in fact, it was eighth largest

He constantly speaks with such passion and certainty that few dare to challenge him.

He insists that he is the greatest builder in New York, that his buildings are of the highest quality in the city, that the Trump Taj Mahal is the greatest casino hotel ever built, and that he is the biggest star in Hollywood.

"He liked to schmooze the press," observed Daniel Heneghan, who covered the casino industry from 1979 to 1996 for *The Press of Atlantic City*. "We always knew that there were plenty of times he was exaggerating. He said the Taj Mahal was the greatest thing that ever happened.

Maybe his kind of exaggeration was so well known and so well accepted that you knew that it wasn't really the truth, but it's a promoter's hype and Donald Trump is a promoter and he had hype." Heneghan's favorite example: Trump liked saying the Trump Taj Mahal had 52 stories, even though floors 3 to 13 did not exist.

Those who do their research on any or all of Trump's statements find a good part of them to be true, but a certain part to be exaggerated. When journalists pick apart some of these statements, Trump goes ballistic. When he engages in truthful hyperbole, he seems playful; but when someone challenges him on such hyperbole, he is anything but playful.

He wants to be known as the biggest and the greatest, and he is not interested in anyone casting doubt on his assertions.

In the early 1990s, when it was clear that he had to put his business-es in order, the banks insisted that he appoint a chief financial officer; it was the banks' way of saying they wanted to deal with someone other than Trump, someone on whom they could rely for accurate data.

After Trump took his casino hotels public in 1995, the bankers, who were seeking to attract investors, gently hinted to Trump that it would be better if others in his organization made the pitches to potential investors. "If you're an asset manager," said a gaming analyst, "and you're thinking of investing tens of millions of dollars, you want facts. You don't want celebrity. You don't want to be blinded by celebrity. You don't want your junior people running for autographs. You need people who can answer questions precisely. Donald talks in generalities. And he's not always precise with the facts. So to get him out of there would help the cause."

A BRILLIANT CON MAN

Not all of the media gave Trump a pass when it came to his truthful hyperbole. One cynical journalist who covers him on a regular basis suggests that behind the PR and the truthful hyperbole is a very different person, one that most journalists did not want to investigate too deeply. "He is a cool guy," admitted the journalist, "but big deal. Cool people don't necessarily make you money. That's why his PR is so good. I think the reason he does so well is that he dates very young, attractive woman. He's an older guy with an awful haircut. He owns lots of stuff. He gets along very well with people at banks who see his spotty but decent bank record and still say, 'I want to do business with this jet-setter with famous friends.'

"But he's got hotels that haven't been upgraded in 13 years. No one's privy to Trump's private stuff. But we know that his publicly traded company has never posted a profit. And in Atlantic City he's so cash strapped, he can't upgrade the hotels. He's the same tacky guy he was 15 years ago putting his name on 3-foot-high buildings. There's nothing discrete about Donald Trump. Bill Gates is discrete. You don't see something called the Gates building. You don't see other older business leaders going out with beautiful young women. But who's more successful? Who's more of a star? Who got the television show?"

As sneering as this journalist is toward Donald Trump, such venom has had no effect on the man. If all journalists thought like this cynical one, Trump would have been a mere footnote in business history, not the resilient, creative titan he has turned out to be. Indeed, others in journalism, claiming to have their eyes just as wide open as the cynical journalist's, are forgiving of Trump's flaws—perhaps because they feel that so much of what he says is close to the truth, if not the truth itself.

Accordingly, Trump possesses a solid group of defenders from the very institution that supposedly cherishes the truth the most: the media. "He's not purporting to be Mother Therese," argued Cindy Adams, the gossip columnist. "He's not purporting to be anything beyond what he is. He is what he is. He's a high-class, Wharton-educated, brilliant con man. And I think he's the best at it."

It is one thing for a gossip columnist to forgive Donald Trump for his playing with the truth. But no less a magazine than *Fortune* wrote, "No one's saying that Trump ought to be held to the same standards of truthfulness as everyone else; he is, after all, Donald Trump." With a Cindy Adams and a *Fortune* magazine in one's corner, it is no wonder that Donald Trump feels no guilt over stretching the truth.

Not everyone can be a Donald Trump, exaggerating the truth and being admired for it. But not everyone wants to be a Donald Trump if it means acting in that manner. Steve Wynn has been one of the dominant figures in the gambling industry and one of its greatest promoters. He has watched Donald Trump over the years, known him personally, fought with him, made up with him, and, in 2004, spoke frankly about what he thinks of Trump's self-promotional efforts.

Trump is unique, says Steve Wynn because of his "blatant self-promotion and his almost comical use of hyperbole, making an art form out of bragging."

Such bragging, as Wynn points out, is a very dangerous thing to do, a very risky business. "We as a culture admire modesty and understatement."

Wynn takes a more traditional approach to marketing. "I think the product speaks for itself. My orientation has always been that if you can build a better mousetrap, it will amplify itself. You can whisper. I guess I picked that up from my parents. Long before I met Donald Trump in my 30s, my personality and values had been formed.

"So I never considered doing what he did. He built buildings that he sold that depended on selling the sizzle. In a sense, I did. I didn't sell and walk away. I had to make sure my businesses kept working. I built operating businesses that had to continue. The jury was always working. I never got to walk away." Wynn could not afford to tell everyone too early in the game that what he was building was going to be the greatest. The standard for him was higher than it was for Donald Trump. In Wynn's case, "You damn well better keep your mouth shut until you got it done."

For Trump, it was different, Wynn explained. "Trump is like a man who has a product to sell. He puts a price tag on the product, and you buy it, and then he goes and does another product. I have to sell it every day. That introduces an element of humility. I have to worry about keeping the promise."

Other reasons existed why Trump could engage in truthful hyperbole and not be roundly attacked. Real-estate executive Tom Barrack, a close Trump acquaintance, explained that the slice of society in which Donald Trump moves, the world of the New York sophisticates, could forgive a business magnate exaggerating his worth, knowing full well that he was worth less than what he said: "When Donald Trump says, 'I'm worth $5 billion,' the New York sophisticate doesn't take it seriously."

That, in a perverse sort of way, might make it easier for Trump to exaggerate, knowing there's little cost to such hyperbole.

But a more compelling explanation for the gentility displayed toward his flights into exaggeration is his reputation as an honest businessman. "He might be accused of using too much creative hyperbole," says Howard Rubenstein, "too much press agentry, but I've never heard him accused privately or openly of being dishonest—never once."

It is in Trump's nature not to be bothered when people call him a self-promoter. He'd rather be known as a great builder than a great promoter, but he understands why he's gained a reputation for making his name into a brand. "He wouldn't take offense at that, "says Trump attorney David Friedman. "He would say, 'What's your point?' He understands what he's doing."

One more explanation for Trump's success at branding is the bold, high-risk way he uses his name for branding.

This kind of business strategy—relying upon one's very own name to serve as the marketing device—is indeed risky business. Customers can turn against all Trump products if one of his Trump-named buildings fails.

Trump says he is careful to use his name only on high-quality buildings, suggesting, "People know that if it's a Trump building, it's the best location, which it is, it's the best fixtures, best windows, the best window frames. You can buy windows for one-fourth the cost of quality windows and they're good; they're going to last for a period of time. But they're going to leak in three years. You can almost predict the day they are going to leak. I build the best, I build on time, I build on budget."

Using his name to sell real estate and putting his name on a building set Donald Trump apart from other real-estate developers who did not want to risk their reputations on boldly using their names as marketing tools.

Many of the top Manhattan real-estate developers were happy with a tiny plaque near the front door indicating who they are. These low-key promotional efforts contrast sharply with the gold-lettering Trump uses on the outer facade of Trump Tower.

LASER-BEAM CONSISTENCY

Some real-estate developers were concerned for their own personal security and that of their families. They did not want photos of themselves or their families in the newspapers. They enjoyed walking the streets of Manhattan without bodyguards. They did not need the personal satisfaction of seeing their name atop a building.

"I don't care for it, "said Richard Lefrak, whose father, Sam, did put his name on his buildings. "I'm not sure I would want to put my name on a building. I'd rather have the product speak for itself, to be honest." The middle-income or upper-middle income tenant with whom he deals "is not interested in finding out how big my yacht is or how many seats my plane has," he said "They only want to know if they can cover their rent or pay for their gas. Why do I have to make an issue of myself? All I need to do is provide a safe, clean place that is a good value for the money. My tenants don't have to read about what I do after hours. But they read about what Donald does, and he gets a premium for his name."

Lefrak shakes his head in bemusement at how Trump pulled off that one. Peter Newcomb, senior editor at *Forbes*, is mystified by how Trump gets people to pay higher sums. "The thing I don't get," Newcomb said, "is why his buildings fetch premiums. I can't explain it. Some have nice views. But why is he so popular? People are fascinated by him. He's not just making it up. I'd like to think he's creating it. But go down to the communities; they love him."

Although some admire Trump for marketing himself so aggressively, they would still not follow in his marketing footsteps. "Sam Lefrak used his name very well," noted Fred Wilpon, principal owner of the New York Mets and a prominent real-estate executive, "but not with the same flamboyance or the same laser-beam consistency of Donald Trump." Wilpon suggested that Trump added his name because the name Trump added value to a building.

But Wilpon would never put his own name on a building. "I didn't have to. If putting my name on a building had been value added, I might have. I don't do any publicity in my businesses that doesn't have a business purpose. I'm not interested in personal publicity. There's no right or wrong. Some people have used their name, but I don't know of anybody who has used the name so consistently and as effectively as Donald Trump. That's not to say that others don't do buildings of a similar kind just as well. I could name ten other people who do just as well."

Every once in a while, Trump encounters someone who feels strongly about using a name other than his for one of his buildings. When Trump purchased a golf club in Bedminster, New Jersey, in 2002, it had been called Lamington Farm. Ashley Cooper, from whom Trump had bought the property, wanted to keep the name because it resonated with the history of the place.

"Ashley," Trump said to him, "outside of this 20-mile area, Lamington Farm means nothing to people, but my name will help generate an enormous amount of publicity. It will also show that the quality really will be there; it will help in our marketing and membership."

Cooper at first was not convinced, but in the end, he was won over when the club was able to ask a $200,000 one-time membership fee with

$13,000 membership dues annually, making it one of the most expensive golf clubs in the United States.

Real-estate executive Lou Cappelli saw the Trump name power up close when he partnered with Donald Trump to build a high-rise project in White Plains. When Trump agreed to join Cappelli in building a 35-story luxury condominium tower project, they agreed to call it Trump Tower at City Center. The name worked magic. "I've got so much more interest already," said Cappelli. "People want to live in Donald Trump's buildings because they might see him. They buy a condo for a million dollars because they might see him." Some ask if Trump plans to live in the building.

Cappelli is impressed. "Companies spend hundreds of millions of dollars to brand their names. He's effectively branded his name and added celebrity status to it to the point where people want to be around him, to live in his buildings, to gamble in his casinos, to visit Mar-a-Lago, to be in *The Apprentice*, or to play golf with him."

When other real-estate firms were branding their company names, Trump was making his company and his name synonymous. Only someone such as Trump, with his personality and his eagerness to be such a public figure, could pull it off. As Cappelli noted, "When your successes and failures are in the public eye, when your divorces are in the *New York Post*, when it's publicized that your bonds are due at your casinos, it isn't about the company—it's about the person. That's a very scary thing. You have to have tremendous balls to be able to say, 'I'm going to take the accolades and take the hits.'"

Trump did not put his name on all of his buildings. He might have liked to, but for good, solid financial reasons, he knew he should not. "I have a lot of real estate in New York that doesn't have my name on it. But it's not real estate you'd put your name on. I own a lot of little parcels all over. I have strategic parcels all over, which I love doing because it's all a chess game, when you get right down to it."

The final "secret" to Trump's success at branding is the knowledge he brings to the subject. He has a fingertip feel for finding ways to promote Donald Trump the brand.

Trump's one-time adversary, Steve Wynn, views Donald Trump as a master of marketing and merchandising. "Have you known anyone who has created a brand name with as much enlargement as this man? Not in my lifetime. In the short period he's done it, and in spite of struggling in gaming, his name in New York is a household word."

THE POWER OF TELEVISION

Trump has established his name as a brand "with more positives than anything else," contended Wynn. "His kind of self-promotion is very easy to dislike; it's controversial to thump the table so blatantly on your own behalf. He got away with it. He managed to finesse it."

Public relations executive Dan Klores, who helped Trump with public relations in the past, called him a natural-born promoter. He was back in the 1980s, and he is in the early 2000s. "The only thing that's different," maintained Klores, "is the power of television. Trump is now a bigger hit than ever, and it's validated by television. [Television] enabled Donald to truly become a popular cultural icon. America looks for heroes, and Donald has become one of them."

Trump's technique, Klores explained, was to make his name synonymous with high-end living. "If he could do that, people would buy apartments, go to Trump Tower, rent hotel rooms, and shop—and they would believe. He was a genius at that."

He seemed to have an instinctive knack for marketing. When he announced on October 8, 1999, on *Larry King Live* that he was forming an exploratory committee to run for president, Larry asked who his vice presidential candidate would be. Oprah, Donald answered, indicating that he had not thought about it very much. Maybe he had not, but if Trump had run for president—and if Oprah had agreed to be his sidekick—he would certainly have garnered media attention—and perhaps a few votes.

He knew the marketplace better than most.

"It didn't matter," asserted Klores, "[whether] someone took exception to his taste, his style, or even the idea that he was a braggart. It just didn't matter because he understood his marketplace." He understood those who could afford a multimillion-dollar apartment in Trump Tower and those who came to shop at the high-quality stores on the ground floor. He understood the gamblers, those who came by bus for a day to Atlantic City and the high rollers who might get a chopper right back to New York if they lost a large amount.

Trump was always trying to understand the marketplace—and to create a stronger connection between customers and the Trump brand name.

Larry Mullin certainly knew the value of the Trump name. He did everything he could to give casino customers in Atlantic City the chance to come in contact with Donald Trump the person—and, at the same time, Donald Trump the brand.

In the spring of 2004, he was the executive vice president for marketing at the Borgata Hotel Casino & Spa. Sixteen years earlier, he had met Trump for the first time when Mullin was hired in 1988 to work at the Trump Castle and stayed on there as director of customer development over the next year. From 1990 to 1995, he was vice president of casino marketing at the Trump Taj Mahal.

Late in 1995, Mullin started his second tour with Trump Marina as senior vice president of marketing, and after four years, he was promoted to president and chief operating officer.

Trump wanted to attract customers and, on one visit to the Castle, wanted to know why Harrah's was doing so well with its slot machines. The table business at the Castle and Plaza was good, but not the slots.

"How do we get these customers?" Trump asked Mullin.

Mullin thought a moment and then said, "You have to treat them as good as high rollers."

One way was to give these high-end slot players a place of their own, just as high-end table players had a place of *their* own.

Without Donald Trump to pay attention to them, the high-rolling slot players might have drifted to another casino.

Mullin suggested the idea to Trump, who asked what it would cost. One million dollars, Mullin said. "Do it," said Trump. Thus, the Monte Carlo Casino was created at Trump Castle, a private room with 75 slot machines for high-end players. "It gave me instant credibility," Mullin recalled. "I had been able to get the owner of the place to pay attention to the customers."

Mullin had another idea for exploiting Trump.

"You have to let some of the slot customers go on your boat (the Trump Princess). It's important to make them feel as welcome as the table customer."

Mullin said the slot customers "like you, but they don't know you." He suggested having a party for the high-rolling slot players. The next time high-rolling slot customers showed up for a weekend at the Trump Castle, Trump invited them aboard his yacht for a one-hour cruise. Access was very limited.

Trump hosted the party, and everyone took photos with him. Mullin recalled, "He was an icon then, bigger than life in Atlantic City. Other than Steve Wynn, there wasn't a personality in gaming that people could identify with. There was no personal icon, only Steve and Donald. So people really wanted to meet Donald."

And why did they want to meet Trump? It was because he had established himself in their minds as not just a person, but as a brand.

It was not only that Donald Trump had a keen sense of self-branding. He was quite prepared to do the most outrageous things to market himself. One only had to watch the *Saturday Night Live* program on April 3, 2004, when Donald Trump served as host, or observe the Friar's Club Roast of Trump on October 15, 2004, to appreciate how willing he is to parody himself or be mocked—all to garner maximum public attention.

Sometimes, Trump worked behind the scenes to promote himself and his products. In late 1987, Random House was about to publish Trump's first book, *Trump: The Art of the Deal*. Dan Klores, working in public relations for Trump at the time, had an idea of how to promote the book. He convinced Trump to take out full-page ads in four major U.S. newspapers: the *New York Times*, *The Wall Street Journal*, the *Los Angeles Times*, and the *Washington Post*.

In the ads, Trump attacked American foreign policy, making him sound more like a presidential candidate than a real-estate developer or casino manager. That was precisely the idea Klores had in mind. Soon after the ads, Klores planted the idea in the media that Trump was thinking about running for president on the Republican ticket. He then arranged for Trump to visit New Hampshire, where the presidential primaries were due to take place in a few months. Naturally, the media asked Trump if he was running for president, to which he replied that he had not made up his mind. "He didn't run," said Klores, "but it was probably the greatest book promotion of all time."

A decade later, again Trump appeared to be running for president. He and others were stunned to find that a poll in the *National Enquirer* had put him first in a race for president, thus catapulting him into a possible candidate for the presidency.

It was, said GE's John Myers, not a real presidential campaign; it was an effort at brand building. "His view is any time he gets his name in lights or in the newspaper, that's brand building, that's publicity." He was able to garner a good deal of publicity just by letting people know that he was considering a presidential race.

Appearing on *Larry King Live* on October 8, 1999, soon after that poll, Trump was still stunned. Here he was in first place in a poll: "I haven't even started campaigning yet. Now, maybe when I start campaigning, I'll do worse. Perhaps I shouldn't campaign at all, I'll just, you know, I'll ride it right into the White House." But when polls showed him dropping in popularity, he dismissed the whole exercise as an unserious effort. "I didn't consider it long."

He considered it long enough for someone to prepare publicity photos of him for a possible presidential campaign. One showed him on the phone to a world leader with then girlfriend Melania Knauss draped in an American flag across his desk, gazing up at him. Trump winced when he saw the photo: "This is over the top, even for me." The photo never saw the light of day.

All he had done, he said later, was to give a speech in New Hampshire as a favor for a friend, and everyone thought he was running for president. He kept the "campaign" going for two weeks. "But I wasn't running. I love what I'm doing."

People such as Henry Kissinger told Trump that he should run for president. "He always thought I would win," Trump recalled. Others said he should run, too. But he didn't want to give up doing what he loved, building buildings. "I have a lot to lose," he told Larry King. "I'm the biggest developer in New York by far...I'm building 90-story buildings all over the place...And we're doing great. I'm the biggest developer in the hottest city in the world right now."

In the summer of 2004, asked how he would have felt had it been possible to make a serious run for the presidency, Trump replied, "It's not my thing. I think I'm too honest in many respects." He laughed. "I have great respect for a great politician. It's not easy to be a great politician. But I think I would do a good job [as president]."

Trump certainly appeared to have many of the traits of a politician. People recognized him on the street. Most of those who met him seemed to like him. Some worshipped him. He had charisma. He was a household name. He thought his popularity and celebrity stemmed from being antipolitical, "maybe more because I don't necessarily say things that are so correct. If you look at *The Apprentice*, as an example, I'm not very politically correct on the show."

Unquestionably, his self-marketing worked.

"His great strength," said Deutsche Bank analyst Andrew Zarnett, "is that he's an amazing marketer. When you ask someone what the Trump name means, they know it means fancy, high quality, big, opulent, and expensive. He's been able to take that great marketing skill and wrap it around his business.

"The proof of his success is that he gets the highest prices for his real estate. He also gets the highest golf-membership fees because he has a brand that people want to be associated with. That's a great business skill. He is a celebrity, and people want to be associated with a celebrity. He's been able to create many products, but the biggest one is the one around his name and his image."

In New York Attorney General Eliot Spitzer's view, Trump "has transformed himself and his name into one of the most identifiable brands in the world": "He's not Coca-Cola, but he knows how to capture the imagination of the public—and, more than that, you can be villainous or a hero and still have the public associate good things with your name. With Trump, people think of high end, quality, and a certain degree of flamboyance. He is obviously partly a showman. If Jack Welch is the quintessential manager and Bill Gates is the quintessential innovator, then Donald Trump is the quintessential deal maker, and part of deal making is marketing, flamboyance, and self-promotion."

Ultimately, Trump's self-marketing led to his being selected to host a new kind of reality-television program, one that concentrated on business. The show required someone who had great business success and a larger-than-life personality. Such a combination was unique within the business community. Mark Burnett, the creator of the show, chose Trump to host the show because only he possessed that combination.

Part of the reason Trump seemed so good at self-promotion was that other business figures were not very good at it; they felt uncomfortable on television, squeamish about appearing on magazine covers, and generally mistrustful of the media. Jack Welch rarely appeared on television during his two decades as chairman and CEO of General Electric. Nor did Microsoft's leader, Bill Gates, who preferred to appear before large high-tech industry gatherings. It was no accident that hardly anyone outside of the business world could name the CEOs of most major companies.

Some of these business leaders genuinely believed that the less one appeared in public, the fewer press conferences over which they presided, and the fewer magazine covers they appeared on, the more powerful they would seem. These business leaders sought power just as much as Donald Trump did; they simply thought the best way to pursue it was by adopting a low profile. Talking to journalists was out of the question, for that would lead to getting quoted in the newspapers, and powerful people, in their view, simply did not get quoted in the media. Powerful people operated behind the scenes, affecting and making decisions, and they acquired their power by the very fact that they operated out of the spotlight.

Trump faced none of these problems: He genuinely believed that publicity was worth pursuing because it brought the celebrity that enabled him to achieve business success.

He had no desire to operate behind the scenes.

THE TRUMP FACTOR

Even as he approached iconic status around America in 2004 and sensed how popular he had become, he worried that it was for the wrong reason. He complained that too many thought of him as a genius at promoting but not at building magnificent buildings: "I believe that I'm given too much credit as a great promoter, which isn't a terrible thing, and not enough credit as a great builder. When people say I'm the greatest promoter, that should be a compliment; but I'm not complimented by it. I hate it because a promoter indicates to me I did a great job when I didn't have the goods."

He believes he had the goods, and ultimately he wanted to be known for having those goods. It pained him when people overlooked the anguish he went through to put up those buildings: "They don't know about the fighting and the plumbing contractor that I have to beat to shit. They don't know about the roughest fucking contractor in the world. Then they say: 'Trump's such a great promoter.' It has nothing to do with promotion. I actually get credit for being a good promoter because of what I build. Then it becomes successful and they think it was a great promotion."

The fact was that Trump had a small army of supporters who believed he was a great builder—period.

They appreciated his eye for location; his instinct for what property could be bought cheaply and turned around. Sure, he laid on the glitz. Sure, his buildings were shinier and gaudier than other structures. But it was precisely the shine and the glitz that attracted the high-spenders, those who insisted on living only in a Trump building. Certainly, some believed that Trump's buildings were monstrous and ugly, but plenty of others flocked to become residents, paying the highest prices in the city. Real-estate brokers in the city called the premium he got because people wanted to live in a Trump-named building the Trump Factor.

PART
V

SUDDENLY, A HOUSEHOLD NAME

CHAPTER
9

THE PERFECT MATCH

Donald Trump had been preparing his entire career for a starring role in some undefined capacity.

He had yearned to become a Hollywood mogul but chose real estate. Yet even when he became a real-estate developer, he made clear that one of his primary business strategies was to put show business into real estate.

It bothered him when people said that he pursued celebrity—but he certainly yearned to be famous, and when he became famous, he wanted to become even more famous.

Always searching for the next big project, always demanding of himself to be the biggest and the best, he cleverly positioned himself for whatever next would come along, hoping that it would spread his name and that it would give the name Trump an even greater aura than it presently possessed.

In his wildest dreams, however, he could not have dreamed of finding a vehicle to indulge his personal and business pursuits in quite the way that *The Apprentice* allowed him.

The television program not only kept his name in the media; it provided him with the best publicity he had ever enjoyed. By offering so much free and exciting exposure, the program offered Trump the chance to brand his name in ways that went beyond what he had thus far been able to do. And by attracting whole segments of the American audience who had never heard of Donald Trump, he was able to achieve a kind of supercelebrity that had until now been beyond his reach, even when he was exceedingly famous.

Now, with *The Apprentice*, he had truly become a household name.

A FREE COMMERCIAL

Thanks to *The Apprentice*, it was as if Trump had been handed 60 minutes of free commercial time to air a Donald Trump commercial—but it was even better than that: He was getting paid—not that much at first, at $50,000 an episode for the first series—but, eventually, he was paid millions of dollars per episode. Even better than the money, he was getting praised to the hilt. Movers and shakers who had simply counted him as a friend or an acquaintance now boasted of their close friendship to him. Some rather shamelessly heaped praise on him, relying upon the same truthful hyperbole that had once been his almost unique stratagem.

Hoping to attain a kind of supercelebrity had been the recurrent theme of Donald Trump's business career. That was why he became a student of the media, why he sought to brand his name, why he entered the Manhattan real-estate world, why he sought membership in Le Club, why he hoped to alter the New York skyline, why he hoped to make a name in the Atlantic City gambling world, why he wrote best-selling business books, and, just as important, why he attempted to forge a business empire of hotels, airlines, and professional football teams.

Before *The Apprentice* came along, Donald Trump had achieved a good deal of fame. He was far more recognizable than most CEOs. Many more people knew his name—even knew what he looked like. Had there been no television program in 2004, Trump might have had to suffice with that kind of recognition. He might have had no choice.

He had achieved most of his popularity in an age when television was just coming of age, before newspapers and magazines turned business figures into larger-than-life cultural heroes. It was the power of television that finally offered him the chance for superstardom. Television, after all, was the medium that established stardom in the popular culture, more than radio, more than the Internet, perhaps even more than Hollywood (if only because television personalities appear in people's living rooms far more regularly than actors appear on movie screens).

Now television was there to provide Trump with the kind of platform he had been missing throughout his career. No guarantees existed that television would like him, nor were there any assurances that a mass audience would flock to watch him.

But at least he now had the opportunity. If he succeeded, the fame he had attained in the past would pale before the supercelebrity that would come his way.

The show began in the mind of a young entrepreneur, Mark Burnett, who had come to the United States from England with no money but plenty of enthusiasm. He had been a member of the British Army Parachute Regiment and had a lengthy career producing unconventional outdoor competitions.

It took him until 2000, but he finally made his mark with the television phenomenon, *Survivor*, the first truly big reality show that offered contestants a chance to engage in a highly publicized experiment in social Darwinism, competing for food, shelter, friendship, and $1 million.

One day, while Burnett was walking along Venice Beach in Los Angeles, a lawyer skated by him on roller blades, shouting, "Hey, you want to be a big businessman? Read this book." He then handed him Donald Trump's *Trump: The Art of the Deal*. Burnett had never heard of Trump, but he read the book and became a huge Trump fan. He quickly read Trump's other books. He decided that he must meet this man.

A week later, Burnett sought a meeting with Trump. After the success of *Survivor*, he had another idea for a reality show. It would be set against a jungle that was every bit as wild and risky as the backdrop for the *Survivor*: New York City. Burnett decided that Donald Trump was ideal to host the show. Trump's ability to make a great deal of money and his resilience in the face of financial difficulty appealed to Burnett: "That says a lot about someone's character." But perhaps what truly convinced the entrepreneur about Trump was his fondness of the limelight. "He is the only executive who doesn't mind publicity," said Burnett, suggesting how much of a plus it was to find such a person.

Burnett got up the nerve to approach Donald Trump at the Wollman Rink in New York's Central Park, raising his idea for the show on the spot. Trump was eager to listen to what he had to say. Burnett had been the producer of the hit TV reality show *Survivor*, and his idea was to make Trump the star of a businessman's *Survivor*.

CHARISMATIC BILLIONAIRE

Trump had not known Mark Burnett until Burnett confronted him at Wollman Park, but, as he got to know him, Trump liked Burnett's reputation in the television world.

They spoke for 45 minutes. Burnett made his pitch. He liked what he saw with Trump in person. He came through as the same fellow Burnett had liked so much in *Trump: The Art of the Deal.* "I found," said Burnett, "that he makes very fast decisions, doesn't waste time, and operates largely on his instinct."

What especially appealed to Burnett was the "showman" in Trump. "All business leaders have to have a certain amount of showman in them, and Donald certainly has a great marketing and show touch to him. I'm sure he has made better deals on the strength of his personality than if he had been very quiet. Not all wealthy people have the showy personality.

"Trump is not an entertainer. He is a charismatic businessman. He's a great communicator. If Donald wasn't that showy and flamboyant, I wouldn't have asked him to be my partner. You can't have someone worth a few billion dollars be a wallflower and have nothing to say. It wouldn't work with this kind of program. You need a billionaire who is charismatic and communicates very well."

Trump obviously liked what he saw (and heard), too. He loved the idea that he would get to star in a program that showed New York City as the vicious business jungle that he felt it was. When Burnett suggested the program, Trump made some adjustments in the idea. As the meeting ended, he shook Burnett's hand and said, "This is going to be great. Let's do it."

Burnett's idea, to be sure, was not the first offer for Trump to appear on television, but his notion had an appeal to Trump that other television offers had not. In the past, when television networks sought out Trump for reality programming, he cringed at their insistence of leaving television cameras rolling in his office as he negotiated deals: "I can't do business that way. I'm not Anna Nicole Smith."

When launching the show, Trump and Burnett formed a company and shared in the ownership, 50-50.

With Burnett's vehicle, Trump would not have to do business "that way." There would be no Anna Nicole Smith moments for him. The Burnett-conceived program called for Trump to pit teams of contestants against one another in business projects, with the team that earned the most money remaining on the show. In the series, Trump would fire one member of the losing team each week. At the end of each

60-minute show, Trump faced the contestants across a huge conference table. Flanking him were two of his top executives who serve as board-room judges advising Trump: senior counsel George Ross and Carolyn Kepcher, chief operating officer and general manager for the Trump National Golf Club in Briarcliff Manor, New York, and the Trump National Golf Club in Bedminster, New Jersey.

At the end of the series, the one person left among the 16 contestants would emerge as the winner and become an apprentice to Donald Trump for one year at a $250,000 a year salary, helping to run one of his projects.

The show was taped, but the conversation between Trump and the contestants—his asking tough questions of the losing team, why they had failed, and so on—was entirely unscripted and offered a glimpse into how a real CEO might challenge his executives to explain why certain deals soured.

Donald Trump asserted in retrospect (after the huge success of the first *The Apprentice* series) that the networks were eager to scoop up the Burnett/Trump program. However, Robert Wright, vice chairman of GE and president of NBC, said that his first reaction upon hearing of Burnett's proposal was "Let's think about it." Even with Trump and Burnett, "it was going to be a tough show to be a hit."

Certainly eager to work with Murk Burnett after his success with *Survivor*, Wright had the normal fears of a television executive when presented with an untried initiative: "I thought this would be something that could be screwed up pretty badly because Mark Burnett didn't have a template."

Compounding Wright's nervousness was the unfortunate "reality" that reality television had a large failure rate.

(Later, after the show was a success, Trump decided that he was pleased that no one had told him what a huge failure rate shows of this kind have. If he had known, "I wouldn't have done the show because I don't want to fail." Had *The Apprentice* died of low ratings, the media would have written one front-page story after another about how the mighty Donald Trump had fallen—so he feared.)

HOW BAD COULD IT BE?

Despite the high failure rate, Wright was confident, given the track records of both men: "I figured, how bad could it be?" In the end, NBC decided to bid for the show. "We cannot decide not to bet," said Wright.

"Otherwise, we don't have a business." Wright figured the odds were in favor of the show because "Donald is a tireless promoter. Burnett is a great producer, and we at NBC are great at promotion."

Jeff Zucker, president of the NBC Universal Television Group, was immediately attracted to Burnett's proposal because of his own background. Burnett had pitched the show to NBC in Los Angeles, where network executives welcomed the idea with certain coolness. The Florida-born Zucker, however, knew of Donald Trump and knew his reputation in Manhattan: "A lot of people didn't understand the magnitude of Donald Trump, which maybe you can only do if you're a New Yorker."

Spending much of his adult years in New York, Zucker understood Trump's ability to generate interest in the media and in the public at large. Some NBC executives argued that Trump was too much a staple of the gossip columns to pass for the highly respected business titan that the host of *The Apprentice* was meant to be. But Jeff Zucker found Trump's blend of "gossip, social, and business" just the unique mix that would appeal to television viewers: "There's no other businessman like him and very few other social figures like him."

To those at the network who argued that Trump was a has-been, Zucker retorted that anyone who read the New York newspapers every day, as he did, knew that Trump was very much a major presence: "Some assumed that he was the playboy businessman of the '80s who was past his prime, but they woefully underestimated how big a draw he still was."

With Wright already signing off on the idea, it was Zucker's decision. He wanted to sign Burnett right away.

Trump decided to go with NBC because it had been producing his Miss Universe, Miss USA, and Miss Teen USA pageants quite successfully for some time.

No one had any sense of how well Trump would do as host of the show. That explains why at first Burnett planned to use him in the first 16-episode series, hope that it would be successful, and then pick some other well-known business figure, such as Microsoft's Bill Gates, Virgin Group owner Richard Branson, or the Dallas Mavericks owner Mark Cuban, to take over the hosting for the next series.

Trump had been, in many ways, training for the role his entire career, honing his skills as a businessman *cum* entertainer so that he had become the most intriguing billionaire in America. Though the odds seemed low, perhaps the chance now existed for Trump to truly make it big.

Without knowing the high failure rate for such shows, Trump had his own doubts that the show would succeed.

Would the public want to watch a flamboyant, controversial billionaire who had less than a stellar reputation among the media—and watch him week after week?

Would potential viewers who had cringed at the scandal-ridden corporate life of America in the early 2000s want to watch a show set, in part, in a corporate board room?

Would women watch a show hosted by someone who had a reputation for womanizing?

Finally, would television viewers want to watch behind-the-scenes maneuvering in the business world?

But Trump prided himself on being a prudent risk-taker, and much seemed attractive about *The Apprentice*, not the least the glamour and excitement surrounding national television.

He remained cautiously optimistic: "Everybody figured it would do fine and then go off."

When friends suggested to Trump that the show would be a runaway success, he made a face, as if to say, "You must be kidding." He simply did not believe that the world was ready for Donald Trump the television star—much as he had always hoped it would be. Rick Hilton, son of Barron Hilton, grandson of Conrad Hilton, and father of Paris Hilton, suggested to his friend Donald Trump that he would become even more famous by virtue of the program.

"I'm already famous," Trump countered.

"You're going to be even more famous."

Gradually, Trump grew excited about appearing on television. He took Steve Wynn on a tour of the studio he was building on one of the lower floors of Trump Tower. He showed Wynn where the kids would sleep and shower; Trump told him about the idea of the show, and he showed him the board room that had been mocked up.

"You're going to do this?" Wynn asked him, still surprised that Donald Trump would do a reality-based television show.

"It's going to be terrific," Trump replied with his usual self-confidence.

Wynn was not a big fan of reality shows. ("Who gives a damn about *Survivor?*")

But Donald Trump kept telling Wynn how smart Mark Burnett was. Wynn departed Trump Tower convinced that Trump's foray into reality television was risky business for him: "He stands to lose. I don't know that he stands to gain." It was hard enough to play someone else on television, Wynn thought, but for Trump to play himself—only a Jay Leno could get away with that.

Trump's close friend Regis Philbin was skeptical about the show at first as well. "I kept wondering, 'Is this going to be a success?' I was concerned for him."

To qualify as a contestant, someone had to meet the formal requirement of being legally able to work in the United States. He or she had to be at least 21 years old. When a casting call was announced for the show, some 215,000 applicants showed up in 16 cities across America, hoping to become one of the 16 contestants. Trump said later that when he learned of the number of applicants for the first series, "that's when I thought we might have a hit." Screening of the applicants took place around the country, where the hopeful showed up with videotapes, photos, and an ample dose of enthusiasm.

The program, which began airing January 8, 2004, earned spectacular ratings.

By February 2004, it was averaging about 19 million viewers a week on Thursday nights; it was holding its own against the mighty CBS hit *CSI.*

The Apprentice proved to be a television colossus, a huge ratings success, getting more popular each week as contestant after contestant faded away. "You're fired," the phrase that Trump used in the boardroom scenes to get rid of one contestant each week, became part of the American cultural lexicon. On *Saturday Night Live*, a Donald Trump imitator uttered, "You're fired" repeatedly, adding to the list of Americans who employed the phrase as the new national mantra.

With the success of the television program in 2004, Donald Trump gained a degree of stardom and won the kind of acceptance he had not known in earlier years. And it came not from those movers and shakers of the real-estate and casino hotel industries, and certainly not from the cynical parts of the media who still wondered what he was all about, but from millions of television watchers, from the public at large. *The Apprentice* made him feel famous and popular and starlike—and, quite frankly, he savored every moment of the experience.

The Apprentice became the number one new show of the television season among total viewers and among adults age 18–49. An average of 20.7 million people watched each week, and 40.1 million watched all or some of the April 15, 2004, finale. Excluding a single run of a reality series (the first *Joe Millionaire*), *The Apprentice* was the top-rated new series on any network in five years for the 18–49 adult category. It was also NBC's number one series of the season and NBC's number one new series in five years.

Significantly, the April 15 telecast marked NBC's highest adults 18–49 rating on any night or in any time period since October 3, 2002, and equaled the network's adults 18–49 category highest rating in the Thursday 9–11 PM time slot since November 16, 2000, excluding Olympic telecasts.

Trump was ecstatic. He was astonished at what was happening. "Well," he told Larry King on February 27, 2004, "now we really have a system where I go into the board room, I rant and rave like a lunatic to these kids, and I leave and I go off and build my buildings. And then it gets good ratings, and they pay me. I mean, can you believe this?"

He could not.

By way of acknowledging that he could not believe he had a hit on his hands, he asked family and friends for their opinions of the show. One of the people he called regularly was his oldest son, Donald Trump Jr. He wanted to be sure that he had watched the latest episode. "Watching his program was like homework," said Donald Trump Jr. "But I enjoyed it. I talk to my father every day. He knows he'll see me at 7 AM. at the office. I get the pop quiz. What did you think of that? He's checking to see if I actually watched." The son chose not to give his father advice: "It's his baby. I don't want to be perceived as taking that away from him."

Understandably, Trump could not stop talking about having the highest-rated show on television.

He delighted in getting a phone call from Hollywood producer Harvey Weinstein, who told him, "You know you're the number one star in Hollywood." Nothing could have made Trump happier than to hear such a comment.

"What are you talking about?" he asked Weinstein. Even Trump could not believe his ears.

"When you have the number one television program, you're the number one star," Weinstein said.

As if the point needed further explanation, Trump noted, "If you think of it, the *Friends* show had six people. I'm one person. And my show is

> *"In the history of business, nothing like this has ever happened."*

an hour. Theirs was a half an hour. It's been an amazing run. We've had fun. And it has been fun. In the history of business, nothing like this has ever happened."

Trump remembered appearing at a network publicity gathering before the season began and wondering which of the programs being promoted would survive. His did. Others did not.

There was a moment for Trump in the spring of 2004 when he realized what being a television star meant. He had just had dinner at 21 with his fiancée, Melania Knauss. They strolled home up Fifth Avenue to the Trump Tower. As they walked up Fifth, drivers and numerous passersby spotted Trump and began shouting:

"Trump, you're fired."

"Trump, you suck.'

"Way to go, Donald."

Despite Trump's fears that women would not watch the show, that people would stay away because of the Enron and other business scandals in the news, just the opposite happened. Trump was happily shocked: "It became the hottest show on television. It became the number one show on television. I think it's my biggest surprise."

Part of the surprise was how much time it took to do the show.

Mark Burnett had promised him that he would need Trump only three hours a week.

But the 3 hours a week quickly turned into 30.

Trump never griped about the longer hours. He loved every minute of it.

Suddenly, he was learning a whole new field. When the show climbed the chart in demographics, the all-important 18–49 age group that advertisers focus on, Trump had to get used to new terms. "I didn't know what demographics was four weeks ago," he explained.

The success of the show went far beyond the ratings. It became a part of American culture, largely on the strength of a phrase that Trump used once, then twice, and a third time: "You're fired." By the time he had used it a few times, Americans found that the phrase grew on them. They liked the way Trump said it, and they began repeating it, mantra-like, to friends over and over.

The now-famous one-liner, "You're fired," had little thought behind it. When a board-room scene went on for quite some time, Trump suddenly blurted out, "David, you're fired."

The drama of that moment struck everyone in the room as a kind of defining point for the show. "Those two words are very beautiful," Trump said. "They're very definite. You can't come back and say, 'Well, let's talk it over.' It's like over....You know, I'm not even so sure that the show would have been a huge success had we not done that."

> "Those two words are very beautiful," Trump said. "They're very definite. You can't come back and say, 'Well, let's talk it over.'"

Later, when it was clear that *The Apprentice* was making television history, everyone had an explanation for the show's success.

Some noted how different it was from all the other television reality shows, many of which put people in real-life situations of fear, danger, excitement, and romance. But none of them had delved into the world of business. And none had the colorful personality of Donald Trump. The program had plenty of human drama, one of the main components for a successful television show, but it also had the charisma and the charm and the wit of Donald Trump. "That is what made it work," said Jeff Zucker. "It's hard to imagine anyone else in that role."

The Apprentice essentially asked an appealing question: Who would survive in the jungle of Manhattan? "People like watching a train wreck at times," said Mark Burnett. "People like rubbernecking on the freeway." On *The Apprentice*, they watched the train wrecks in living color.

Some liked the dramatic elements of the show. Everyone praised Donald Trump for being its lynchpin. Ultimately, the show's success seemed to depend less on it being about business than about the pursuit of the American dream. "The pursuit of the American dream is a universal pursuit," said Jeff Zucker, savoring the show's success in the summer of 2004. "And [*The Apprentice*] was really about making it big in the Big Apple with the big guy."

Once doubtful that Trump could pull it off, Steve Wynn was completely won over. "Donald turned that TV show into a phenomenon. He had kids selling lemonade. Who gives a shit? It was about him. If anybody thinks that's easy, go try it."

Won over also was Regis Philbin: "He really stepped up and he got the hang of it right away. He hit a home run. He saw how important the show was. It was pretty heady."

The show did wonders for the careers of not just *The Apprentice* winner Bill Rancic. He was given $250,000 a year to work for Trump and was put in charge of the construction of a new building in Chicago. He also wrote a book and did speaking engagements during that busy year as the first apprentice.

Runner-up Kwame Jackson signed a multibillion-dollar real-estate deal in Maryland to develop 550 acres into commercial and residential property. He said at the news conference announcing the deal that he heard from Trump that "real estate can be one of the most successful vehicles for the production of wealth." At least he was listening, Trump noted.

One of the two board-room judges, Carolyn Kepcher, wrote a best-selling book, which appeared in October 2004. Others associated with *The Apprentice* had books published: contestant Amy Henry and George Ross, the second board-room judge.

Trump was such a smash hit that the original plan of replacing him with someone else after the first series was quickly scuttled.

Midway through the season, Mark Burnett looked at the ratings and "saw how well Trump had adapted to the process: I was the first person to say, 'Let's not look for someone else. Let's see how long Donald wants to do this for.' We saw that Donald was having a good time with it; it was more about fun and less about work. When Donald is having fun, he wants to do more. Clearly, he's not doing it for the money."

The ratings and Donald Trump's obviously crucial connection to the show now made him seem like the perfect match. But it was his unique blend of character traits that made him seem like the only business figure right for the starring role.

Those same character traits that had seemed so negative—the self-promotion, the showiness, the flaunting of his wealth, the constant purchases of a rich man's toys—could, under the right circumstances, work to his advantage if someone were looking for a man with such traits. Donald Trump was many things, but he was not gray, obscure, or dull, like most other business personalities. He was flamboyant, controversial, brash, and savvy; he had great stage presence, and he loved the klieg lights. That made him a perfect fit for Mark Burnett's television project.

Here was a business figure who actually loved the limelight, as was apparent every time he walked onto the board-room set. He had the natural talents of an actor. And he had an ego to match, as evidenced by the pride he took in the unique position he attained as *The Apprentice* host. He saw his own uniqueness and quickly boasted about it: "In the history of business, there's never been a businessman who has gone on to be the number one star on television. "

The selection of Donald Trump proved to be an act of genius. It was almost unimaginable that any other American business leader would have had the charisma, the outsized television personality, and the chutzpah to pull off what Trump did. His hosting the show became a chief factor in its success.

THE LAST BIG MOGUL

Mark Burnett called it the Donald Trump factor, that special blend of business and entertainment savvy that got through to audiences: "It's *Lifestyles of the Rich & Famous*, inside Trump's world and seeing the inside world of a genuine mogul, the last big mogul."

Donald Trump blended business and entertainment skills in ways that no other business figure of the time could. He had business acumen and a Hollywood look, and when he walked into the mock board room and sat down, he became Donald Trump the entertainer. His son, Donald Trump Jr., liked to tell his father that he had missed his calling: He should have been an actor. But then again, his father had been employing the skills of an actor his entire career, just not on stage.

Carolyn Kepcher, the board-room judge who sat on Trump's left during the board-room scenes, observed that Trump was quick on his feet and did not need more than a few words from the producers before he was ready to perform. "He can do it in one take. The producers are quite amazed." NBC president Bob Wright was equally lavish in his praise: "He has very good instincts for this sort of thing. They're better than any actor or performer that I've met."

The traits that Donald Trump possesses gave him perfect pitch for the acting he did on *The Apprentice*. Hollywood executive Alex Yemenidjian noticed, "He has this combination of self-confidence and a sense of narcissism so that he believes that all eyes should be on him. That's not a criticism. His belief in his stage presence is very strong. He plays within himself—he's not going to get up there and be something that he's not."

Many of his friends saw an "entertainer" in Trump; they saw an actor as well. They said they would be reluctant to mention these things to him. They know that he wants to be known for his building, not for his acting skills. Still, they know how much he enjoys being center stage. As one friend noted, "He hasn't seen a camera or a microphone that he didn't like."

Indeed, Trump was the perfect match as host of *The Apprentice*. To Mark Burnett, he was the right person for the show because he got high ratings whenever he appeared on television; to Regis Philbin, Trump was just the right person for the job because "he had the look, the charisma, the reputation." Kirk Kerkorian admitted that he could not see himself doing such a show "because I don't have the talent." Bob Wright said Trump was perfect because he had that in-your-face quality and he was comfortable with his celebrity. "Donald is comfortable promoting his own ice," said Wright, but a Jack Welch would not be comfortable promoting 'Jack's ice.'" It helped Trump enormously that the show could enlist as stage props his buildings, his apartments, and his golf clubs. "Other business leaders just don't bring that to the table," said Wright.

One big fan of Trump as the host of *The Apprentice* is Eliot Spitzer, the attorney general of the State of New York; he praised Donald Trump for "being good at every part of the show": "He is the decision-maker, the big dealmaker. He's perfect. The various strands of his persona are woven together perfectly in that show. You can't cast somebody for that part if it isn't a natural fit. If most CEOs were put into that role, the show would be on C-SPAN. When Trump does it, it gets the highest ratings because he has that flair and the capacity to connect with the general public—as the playful playboy billionaire. He merges all the pieces—the maximum of 'Access Hollywood' and 'The Squawk Box.'"

Jeff Zucker agreed that Trump was the perfect match: "He has the business mind and the personality and the sex appeal that's just an unbelievable combination that you don't find anywhere else. Even the best businessmen don't have the confidence that Donald Trump has that allows him to attack any situation brilliantly. The guy has more confidence than anybody I've ever met. I say that admiringly."

TOO QUIET, TOO NEUTRAL

It was inconceivable to imagine a Jack Welch or Bill Gates or Lou Gerstner presiding over *The Apprentice*. Though all three business leaders enjoyed wide recognition, they were too quiet, too neutral. Jack

Welch did not appear on television very much, thinking it a distraction from his business. Bill Gates preferred to make appearances at high-tech conferences. Lou Gerstner preferred to work behind the scenes at IBM. Trump himself expressed serious doubt that any other business figure could host such a show. "They would like to, but they couldn't do it."

To communications scholar Paul Levinson, audiences prefer a Donald Trump to a Jack Welch or Bill Gates or Lou Gerstner as the host of a reality show because of a "schizophrenia in our culture": "You're supposed to make money but not be a braggart. You're supposed to be modest. Donald Trump breaks that mold. He flaunts his success. That makes him very attractive. He doesn't apologize for his success."

Perhaps Las Vegas hotel owner Phil Ruffin summed up the reasons for Trump's success best when he said, "Everybody is intrigued by him. They want to know what his lifestyle is like. What does he do? He seems very unique. I've met a million businessmen who may be focused on business. They know their business. They're good at it. Trump can focus on many things. He has an opinion on everything. He's living as full a life as any human being can."

It was the strong reaction to Donald Trump, positive and negative, that compelled people to watch the show. "There are those who love Donald because of his stature and those who hate him because of his stature," said George Ross. "There are those who don't know whether to love or hate him. So they watch the show to find out more. Those who hate him decide he's not such a bad guy. Those who like him see that he's also funny. Those who love him love him even more."

However charismatic and charming Trump seemed, the show came in for some tough times from the critics, who argued that in the era of Enron and other scandal-ridden corporations, *The Apprentice* was sending the wrong kind of message about corporate leadership.

Deflecting such criticism, Trump retorted that the program was trying to teach something about leadership, competitiveness, winning—and there was nothing wrong with winning. Business, he suggested, was not simply about making money; perseverance was a big factor, for example.

One of the show's sharpest critics was Jeffrey Sonnenfeld, associate dean of the Yale School of Management, who thought the show "pretty vulgar": "It's deception, trickery, and sex peddling. The lesson is that leadership selection is developed in a process akin to musical chairs at a Hooter's restaurant."

Trump had to laugh at the trouble the critics had with sex in business. "[Sonnenfeld] says there's too much sex; it doesn't exist. Excuse me, it doesn't exist in building? I can tell you it exists, from personal knowledge—much personal knowledge."

The fact was that even Trump thought the women contestants exploited their sexuality too much in the early episodes of the show. By week four of that first season, he reprimanded the women for making the hawking look like hooking too much. He told them not to rely so much on short skirts and cleavage. They were depending on their looks much too much; they offered kisses and phone numbers as part of selling lemonade. "I was very proud of myself. I reprimanded the women. Can you imagine me, of all people, reprimanding the women for using too much sex? I was very proud of myself."

What about a point of the critics that *The Apprentice* candidates sold together as a team and then sold each other out?

Trump was not troubled. That kind of behavior happened in real life; people sold each other out all the time. He was not encouraging such behavior—just explaining it, he said.

Clearly, the show worked well to a large degree because of Trump's presence. Originally, he was not supposed to be such a looming presence; the show was not intended to center on the board room. But the ratings were higher when Trump conducted the board-room meetings. As a result, when the second season of *The Apprentice* aired in September 2004, the board-room scenes, starring Trump, became a much larger part of the show, and the business tasks, which took the most time in the first series, were relegated to a smaller portion of each program.

A CITY THAT EATS PEOPLE

Trump himself thought the show did well because it pitted brilliant young businesspeople against the City of New York—and often the Manhattan jungle came out on top. "It's a tough place," he told Larry King, "and the city has eaten these kids alive. And they're geniuses, but it's just eaten them up and spit them out, and it's been tough on them. We have doctors. We have Harvard MBAs who are doctors simultaneously. I mean, these are brilliant kids, and they get eaten up by the City of New York. And I think that's one of the magical moments of the show, and I think that's why the show does so well."

Another reason why the show succeeds, says Trump, is that he does not alter his decisions to get higher ratings. The decision on who gets fired has been entirely his. Mark Burnett never suggested that he fire one

person over another because it would be better television to keep someone longer on the show. Trump keeps people on the show—not firing
them—because he feels they are the best businesspeople—and viewers
seem to be reacting positively to that.

What was the real Donald Trump like? Was he like the Donald Trump
of *The Apprentice*?

It was a question that seemed constantly on people's minds. Those
who worked closely with Trump day after day felt he was often the
same—he exhibited the same toughness and the same gentility. They
had a vested interest in saying he was the same. On the show, Trump
came across in the most positive light, blending just the right amount of
toughness with gentility. Colleagues in real life did not want to explore
the possibility that Trump was more brutal or less kind in real life. They
might well have had their own examples. Let the world think he is as he
appears on television.

Whenever he appeared on the program, he was supremely in charge,
interrogating the losing team about why they failed, asking contestants
to evaluate the talents of each other, offering up an intimidating
presence that had some contestants clearly distracted and even overwhelmed. When it was time, he came to a decision with the same half-
apologetic expression of an executioner turning on the electricity; then,
pausing for dramatic effect, Trump let the newly expunged contestant
dangle in agony before uttering that now-famous phrase, "You're fired!"
"Please don't say it, Mr. Trump. Please don't say it," begged one contestant, asking for a last-minute reprieve, but it was too late. Trump
turned on the electricity. For the millions who were watching, that
moment seemed as dramatic as any of the soap operas or dramatic series
that monopolized television.

NO KICK OUT OF FIRING PEOPLE

As it turned out, however, in real life, Trump did not get a kick out of
firing people, as he seemed to do on television. In real life, he took
months, even years, before he got around to letting someone go. He
knew that whoever he fired would hate him for life. So he delayed the
execution.

There were people in real life whom he relished firing, those he caught
stealing from him. "When they're stealing money," he said, "I fire them
much more viciously than on the show. But generally speaking, I don't
fire people."

Mark Brown, the man in charge of Trump's casino hotels in Atlantic City, finds Trump different in real life from his television image. On the show, Trump comes across as a "tough tyrant who fires people left and right," Brown said. "But in real life, he actually knows who works hard and who doesn't. He can't put up with guys who don't work hard. Those are the ones who don't last. But you're only as good as your last results. He believes that there's a relationship between those who work hard and those who get good results, so he focuses on people who don't work hard, the guys who come in at 9:30 AM and go home at 5 PM."

Greg Cuneo, the head of HRH Construction and someone who works closely in business with Trump, laughs at the image that Donald Trump conveys on the television screen. "In business, he never fires anyone. He has a heart of gold. You've got to really fuck up before he fires you. If you're a wiseass or you fuck him, he'll fire you." At one of their jobs sites, Cuneo implored Trump to dismiss one employee who, in Cuneo's view, truly deserved the can. "He's not a wiseass," Trump said in explaining why he didn't want to let the man go. "We've got to get him through this."

No matter how his businesses were doing—and his casino hotels were clearly still having trouble—television audiences viewed Donald Trump as an incredibly successful businessman, smart and aggressive—and he was pleased with that. It had always bothered Trump that some thought him uneducated, and they were learning via *The Apprentice* to appreciate his intelligence: "I'm highly educated, which, until *The Apprentice*, most people didn't know. They thought I was a barbarian. But I'm highly educated."

Before the show, Trump felt that he was viewed among the public as too tough, "like a flame thrower," much tougher than he really is. The show softened his image, which he feels is far more accurate. Still, it was odd that the program softened his reputation even as he was firing someone week after week: "I was thought of like a really tough guy before the show and not a nice guy. Now people think I'm a tough guy, a strong guy but sort of a nice guy."

He was right. Once known for his excessive greed, for his womanizing, for his showy lifestyle, Trump became known for business qualities.

To George Ross, one of the two board-room judges and a senior Trump attorney, Donald Trump displayed human qualities on the show that somehow the public had never before witnessed. "Here we have a billionaire who is not really liked by many people because he's done what he [said] he was going to do. He appears brash or arrogant or abrasive but then appears on television, and they see him as a human being. He can relate to people and situations. Now you put him in a room with 16 contestants who want to work with him, and the interaction is really dramatic."

Trump Organization CFO Allen Weiselberg also sensed that a different and gentler side of Trump came across on the program. "He had always been seen as a tough negotiator, but in the show—take the example of when the mother of Heidi [one of the contestants] had cancer, Trump asked Heidi to come back and talked to her about her mother. That's Donald. He's a caring person. He wasn't always perceived as that."

Trump's son Donald Jr. especially appreciated the new "kinder and gentler" reputation that his father was enjoying in the wake of the program. "The greatest thing that has come out of *The Apprentice*, being a family member, is that America sees Donald Trump as a human. He's not a Ken Lay [former chairman and CEO of Enron] or this horrible corporate guy that goes back to his cave at night. He's a person. He's a smart-ass. He can come back really quickly. He's a funny guy. He's not some android.

"As his son, the greatest thing for me is to see that people get to see that he's a great guy—fun-loving, humorous guy—he still works, but he's not just this stiff who sits there and says, 'Okay, you're fired—next.'"

One indication that Trump had no idea that *The Apprentice* would be a runaway hit was the amount of money he took for each show ($50,000) during the first series. With the astronomical ratings, Trump decided to renegotiate a much better deal for himself as the star of the second and third series.

He turned to a friend, Hollywood studio head Alex Yemenidjian, to draw on his expertise of the entertainment world and its financial side as a way of figuring out how much he should ask for.

SAY YOU'RE *FRIENDS*

"Say you're *Friends*," was Yemenidjian's advice.

Trump repeated this to NBC and got the response, "Okay, you'll get $1 million per show. That was what the cast of *Friends* received per person.

That was not what Trump wanted to hear. "I'm like six Friends," he told NBC executives.

Precisely how much he negotiated for himself, Trump kept to himself, but he did say that he was comfortable with people thinking he was getting $3 million per episode. "Let's put it this way: I make a lot of money with *The Apprentice*."

The future of *The Apprentice* seemed secure into the future. As early as February 2004, NBC signed Trump for a second series of *The Apprentice*.

There was every indication that the show would continue to do well for a number of seasons to come. For one thing, one million people applied for the second series of *The Apprentice*. Roughly the same number applied for the third series that was due to start in January 2005.

By the summer of 2004, the first series was being shown all over the world. It was, as Trump suggested, "the hottest show in Australia—number one in Norway also." It was beginning in England in September 2004.

Perhaps not surprisingly, the show was so successful that it spawned copycats.

Trump was confident that only *The Apprentice* would survive. Richard Branson was planning to do a reality show and so was Mark Cuban. So was ex-Trump wife Ivana.

No longer did any one talk of replacing Trump. "Maybe it would work with someone else," said Jeff Zucker, "and maybe it wouldn't, but we are not going to take any chances."

Trump had to feel really good when Jeff Zucker was quoted as saying, "Donald Trump and Mark Burnett are the most potent force in television today, and I'm thrilled to say that *The Apprentice* will have an appointment on NBC for many years to come."

In interviews on July 27, 2004, both Bob Wright and Jeff Zucker thought the second *The Apprentice* series would hold up well. "The problem, if they have one," said Wright, "is the shooting star problem. It's consuming so much energy going up. It could run out of gas. It's hard to keep the momentum at that pace when you're so vertical. You're in a world of very few examples. That's not a bad thing. You can't put a governor on the success of something like this. *The Apprentice* is such a rocket. Forty million people watched the last episode. That's Bill Cosby kind of numbers. No one got close to that until Roseanne."

Before anyone knew whether the second series of *The Apprentice* would outperform the first series, it is time for casting calls for the third season.

The date is July 30, 2004.

A line of candidates starts near the front entrance of Trump Tower and extends around the corner on 56th Street back to Madison Avenue. The people in line mirror America's young business set. As they stand in line, they fill out application forms and waivers. They dress nicely, as if they are going for a job interview—which, in fact, they are. The media begins to show up. Television crews and still photographers take shots of the crowd. Reporters interview candidates.

Why do they want to become the next *Apprentice*?

It's the obvious question.

The candidates give various answers: They want to work for a visionary like Donald Trump. They want to make a lot of money. They want to be famous. They want to do something productive with their lives.

No one says it's because they might come off as too star-struck, but one big reason they are there is that they simply want to be on television.

Most of them exude a superenthusiasm because they have heard that bubbling over with energy and enthusiasm is a prerequisite for becoming one of the final 18 candidates (two more than in the first season) that actually get on the show.

Interviews begin at 9:30 AM.

Carolyn Kepcher, one of the two boardroom judges, walks past the crowd lined around the building. She is instantly recognized, and shouts of "Hi, Carolyn" and "Good morning, Miss Kepcher" come from a now-hushed crowd. Television camera crews crowd around her, and she begins talking into microphones.

Groups of candidates are let into the building and escorted to the Garden Level near the waterfall. They sit, ten to a table, while a staff member from *The Apprentice* goes around the table, asking them for their names and backgrounds. The job interview has begun. After they talk for a while, the staff member asks each one who he or she would pick to be part of a team working on a business project.

The dynamics at tables differ. At some tables, the conversation is conduced in low, polite tones. At other tables, candidates shout at one another, each trying to show the staff that he or she has the zeal and inner drive to make it in the business world.

One of the candidates looks like he is trying out for *The Sopranos*. He is dressed completely in black: His tie, his shirt, and even his hair are jet black. Clearly, his takeaway from the first *The Apprentice* series is to be as arrogant as possible. Someone at his table suggests that arrogance might not win him a spot on the next series.

"Oh, yeah," he sneers. "Well, I'll be the one sitting at courtside and you'll still be hawking tickets outside."

A DRAMATIC ENTRANCE DOWN AN ELEVATOR

It is now 10:30 AM. The media has gathered at the foot of the escalator that leads down to the atrium, one floor above where the candidate interviews take place. Many of the media are entertainment reporters; only one business reporter has shown up (from CNBC). They seem largely uncritical of Trump, almost fawning. They act as if they cannot wait to see him emerge.

The word quickly spreads that Donald Trump is about to make his entrance—and entrance it is. Suddenly, he appears at the top of the elevator. He is dressed, as usual, in suit and tie. He is alone, no entourage. He seems to be making a statement. He wants his entrance to be as dramatic as possible, with the same degree of drama he exhibits when he walks into the mock board room of *The Apprentice*. He peers into the distance, as if he is surveying his armies. He lifts his head up high. Television lights shine on him. He seems to sense that television cameras are whirring below him. He waves as if he is a political candidate seeking votes. Reaching the ground floor, he moves along the line of candidates that stretches through the front door, and, like a politician, he shakes hands, chats here and there, and then heads outside. All that's missing are babies for him to kiss. But these young adults left their babies, if they had them, back home—this is, after all, a job interview.

He learns that the line is clear around the block. The news seems to thrill him. He shouts to a writer, "Did you walk around the block? Did you see how many are here?" He seems bowled over by the turnout.

Again, he walks along the line of candidates; journalists corral him and ask softball questions about *The Apprentice*. What will be new about the next season? Will the ratings be as high as before? What kind of qualities must the next *The Apprentice* possess? Trump gives a knowing smile and offers brief sound bytes without giving away next season's plot or too many of the specific traits that would make for a likely winner. One female reporter asks a question about the length of miniskirts acceptable on the show, and Trump fires off a quick answer while walking away from her, indicating that he is peeved by the question. It is, so it seems, the only negative question put to him all morning.

Watching Trump work the crowd, one gets a sense of how much he loves greeting people. He thrives on the attention he gets, but he seems to know that this is part of what his business is all about, and he sinks his teeth into it with a relish that few other business executives would display. One cannot imagine a Jack Welch or a Lee Scott or a Warren Buffett wading through a crowd of well-wishers as if they were politicians or rock stars. Nor can one imagine such business leaders attracting entertainment reporters as Trump does.

Trump returns inside and heads for the Garden Level, one floor below where candidates are seated around the tables being interviewed. He takes a seat at one of the tables. Probably none of the applicants at the table assumed they'd be interviewed by Donald Trump himself, but, if they are nonplussed by his showing up, they do not show it. They are supposed to exude self-confidence; hence, they keep their composure in his presence.

He asks them what schools they went to, what they do. He listens intently as they explain why they would like to work for him. His questions are not belligerent. At times, he makes a passing reference to his own business career. After departing a table, he huddles with staff from *The Apprentice* and together they make snap judgments on who they've just met. Carolyn Kepcher spends time at some tables, interviewing people. Sometimes, she sits at the same table with Trump. Between visits to tables, she explains that sometimes it's easier to pick the ones who won't get on the show than to select who should. It amazes her, she says, that some people wait in line, come for the interview, sit around the table, and say nothing. "They might as well not come," she says, acknowledging that the way to get noticed is to speak up.

After visiting a number of tables, Trump holds an informal news conference, making sure to pass the word that he is announcing this very day a "major" new condo/residential tower that he will build on the Las Vegas strip on the grounds of the New Frontier Hotel; it will not be a hotel or casino.

He makes the transition from television star to real-estate developer flawlessly. With television cameras whirring, with entertainment reporters happily jotting down his every word, Trump has indeed a captive audience—and he takes advantage, garnering the kind of free publicity for his building projects that he loves to get.

Trump stays about an hour and then leaves. The casting calls continue.

The Apprentice became a fixture of the American scene. Northern Illinois University announced that students could take a one-credit course based on the show in its College of Business. When Donald Trump found out about the course, he exclaimed that if he were 20 years old again, he'd take it.

On September 9, 2004, the second series of *The Apprentice* began. Despite the absence of *Friends* as a lead-in to *The Apprentice* and weak ratings for lead-ins, *Joey* and *Will and Grace*, Trump's program remained a sizeable hit.

Just about every major entertainment publication wrote lengthy stories about the 18 new contestants. They wrote less about Trump this time around. He seemed pleased that the focus was on the contestants. In real life, he was going through a rough time trying to restructure debts on his Atlantic City casino hotels. He was glad to have the media concentrate on the contestants.

AND THE WINNER IS...

Ten days later, he was in Los Angeles so that he could be in the audience when the winner of the Emmy for Best Reality Program for the previous year was announced. *The Apprentice* had been nominated, and within the Trump Organization, it was simply assumed that the program was a surefire winner. "We had the hottest show on television last year. Who else would get it?" asked one Trump staffer who appeared on the show.

But when it came time to announce the winner for that category, *The Amazing Race*, a CBS reality program, took the honors. Trump was stunned. He, too, had assumed that the Emmy was his, though he told everyone afterward that he had been the only one to predict that *The Apprentice* would not win. In his disappointment, he sought to disparage the Emmys, suggesting that its ratings were low, that it had no credibility. He felt he had been overlooked because of one very disturbing fact: "I was screwed because I'm not establishment."

It was a remarkable statement.

The host of America's most popular television show felt that he was not a member of the establishment. The 74th wealthiest person in America felt that he was an outsider, looking in, like a little boy who could only peek through a fence and watch the other children enjoy the candy. The man who had changed New York's skyline and Atlantic City's boardwalk believed that he was the victim of some nefarious plot.

It was déjà vu, and it was unpleasant. He was a household name, but he was still not taken seriously. He thought that with the popularity of *The Apprentice*, he had overcome all that. But now, it seemed he had not.

CHAPTER

10

HEIGHTENED DEMAND, PERSISTENT DEBT

The Apprentice catapulted Donald Trump into supercelebrity status that surprised and delighted him. He had been well known before, so that was not new. What *was* new was how many who now knew who he was actually thought he was nice. In the past, even Trump understood that he often had as much notoriety as popularity.

His friends proudly proclaimed him the best-known person in America, employing the same exaggeration used so routinely by Donald Trump.

Certainly, more people knew who George Bush was; more knew who John Kerry was. But these were politicians. One of them was President of the United States. The other one wanted to become President.

But Donald Trump, a man who did not head a major corporation, a man whose business empire had nearly collapsed 14 years earlier, was at the height of his popularity in the spring of 2004. *Fortune* magazine and *Newsweek* put him on their covers; that June, when 1,000 talk radio listeners were asked who they would like to see hosting a radio show, Trump headed the list (Bill Clinton was second, Colin Powell was third). Lee Scott could walk through many of the 3,500 Wal-Mart stores in America and fail to be recognized as the company CEO by his own employees; Warren Buffett could walk the canyons of Wall Street, and hardly anyone would stare at him. Donald Trump could not walk down Fifth Avenue in Manhattan or through his hotel casinos in Atlantic City without being surrounded and shouted at—by strangers.

Trump presided over a business empire that had a mere 20,000 employees and that had as one of its main components a money-losing casino hotel business. And Trump did not even make the magazine lists of the most powerful and influential business figures in the nation. Yet his was certainly one of the most widely recognized faces in America; his name had risen to "household name" status.

For him, the burning question was how to exploit entry into the celebrity stratosphere—what he could and *should* do with this newly won supercelebrity status.

It was not a moot question.

People who had never heard of the man suddenly wanted a piece of him. They wanted him to be in their commercials, to endorse their inventions, to speak to their organizations, to adopt their favorite charities, or to put his name on a variety of objects, from pillows to perfume. And they were willing to pay him millions of dollars. At $350,000 a pop, he claimed to be the highest-paid speaker in America. At $5 million a pop, he was certainly one of the highest-paid stars of television commercials. At $3 million an episode for *The Apprentice*, he was one of the highest-paid television performers.

One might ask legitimately why a billionaire would want or need to do any or all of these things. Donald Trump had no trouble answering the question. Of course, he didn't need the money in the way that someone needs money to pay the monthly bills. Trump did all these things because he thought he would be nuts to turn down offers that paid him so much money. He loved the idea of all that publicity, boasting, "I make a lot of money with exposure." And although he would not admit it, he loved being in the spotlight.

He did face one intriguing question: In the wake of the incredible success of *The Apprentice*, should he retreat into a shell for a while and perhaps increase the demand for him down the road?

Or should he take everything that was offered to him?

Two schools of thought existed on Donald Trump's near future.

The first school took the view that he should adopt a low profile. If he wanted the public to keep him on a pedestal, so this thinking went, he should retreat into a zone of privacy for a while—precisely how long was never specified. In that way, the public would not tire of him, and when he returned to the public sphere, his admirers would crave him all the more. Were he to vanish from public sight, he might also avoid the media's arrows as it tried to take him down a few notches. Any public relations expert would advise clients to disappear temporarily. Indeed, that is precisely what Howard Rubenstein cautioned his clients when they attained sudden fame: "When the decibel level goes up, let it come back down again."

TAKE A TIME OUT

Jeff Zucker, president of the NBC Universal Television Group, agreed. He admitted to being concerned that the public, exposed to Trump too much between the first and second *The Apprentice* series, might tire of him and the program. "It was a concern that everybody wants a piece of Donald, which I understand," he said. "Everybody wants to use him for themselves, and I just wanted him to go underground a little bit between the first and second cycle so the program remained as special when it came back on."

He told Trump as much.

Trump's sister, Judge Maryanne Barry, weighed in with similar advice: "I told him to take a time out."

But Donald Trump deflected the suggestion quickly. "He doesn't find the exposure oppressive," Judge Barry said. "He loves it. It's cute to me how much he's enjoying himself. He doesn't understand that concept of getting too much exposure."

> *Judge Maryanne Barry, weighed in with similar advice: "I told him to take a time out." But Donald Trump deflected the suggestion quickly. "He doesn't find the exposure oppressive."*

Cherishing her own privacy, Judge Barry asked her brother how he could stand the constant requests for autographs and other things. "Don't you want to be left alone?"

Clearly, he did not.

It is a well-known fact in the art world that paintings fade from too much light, from over-exposure. But Donald Trump did not believe that light could hurt him. Light would not cause him to fade—at least, not in the short term.

He believed that the second school of thought had it right: There was no such thing as over-exposure.

He remembered a time in the early 1990s all too well when his business empire appeared in jeopardy, when the phone did not ring, when the media wrote his business epitaph, when the only articles about him were derisive and dismissive. During that period, he had gone under cover automatically. He had been there. He knew what it was like.

Now that was all behind him. And he wanted to savor the moment, to do all that he could to ride on the wave of fame. He was, in Hollywood and television parlance, hot—hotter than any other business personality had ever been. And though he made a big point that he had never sought the celebrity, he liked all that celebrity status brought with it.

More conscious than anyone else that one day he would cool off, he knew the public would tire of him and move on to the next superstar icon.

When that day came, he would accept it.

But for now, he was going to exploit the moment.

> *"There's no such thing as over-exposure. There will be times when I'm not that newsworthy, when I will be undercover automatically."*

To Jeff Zucker, he said, "There's no such thing as over-exposure. There will be times when I'm not that newsworthy, when I will be undercover automatically. There will be a time when it ends. And then I won't be over-exposed anymore."

In the end, even Zucker understood that it was pointless to argue with Trump, admitting, "He's a big believer in the philosophy of giving the people what they want. It's not possible for Donald Trump to go underground."

Trump thought the whole debate over whether he should go under-cover was beside the point.

THEY WON'T EVEN CALL

He wanted to accept the invitations and collect every penny because he had the feeling that no matter how much effort he put into *The Apprentice*, once his ratings dropped, NBC executives would begin to think about canning him and the show. "Look, if I came up with a cure for cancer, but it didn't get ratings, they're not going to put it on televi-sion. That's how ruthless these guys are."

One day, Trump was telling Lorne Michaels, the creator and executive producer of *Saturday Night Live*, that he knew all television programs and their stars have a limited shelf life. The phone would ring. An NBC executive would be on the line telling him, "Donald, your ratings aren't good anymore. We're canceling the show."

Michaels agreed that all this would inevitably occur, save for one part of Trump's nightmarish scenario: "They won't even call."

For Donald Trump, the only question was not whether he should remain in the public spotlight—of course, he should—but what projects he should pursue.

It seemed as if he pretty much agreed to do everything he was asked. That was obviously not the case.

One night, he was on Jay Leno. One day, he appeared at a gathering of public relations executives. Another evening, he was appearing in a video with rapper Eminem. He also did television commercials and book signings, gave speeches, showed up for shootings of the third season of *The Apprentice*, and—oh, yes, he also ran his businesses.

He could have done much more if there was enough time in the day and he was willing. But he was against traveling huge distances. He was invited to give six speeches in Australia and New Zealand for millions of dollars. Then he balked. The would-be hosts pruned it down to just one speech, but he turned that down, too.

Within a certain radius from home, hoping to do as much as possible in New York and nearby places, he seemed game for whatever came up. Hence, in the course of 2004, he seemed to be everywhere, doing anything and everything. Because he did so much week after week, Trump gave the impression that he pretty much accepted whatever was offered to him. But the reality, he suggests, was far different.

He turned down 95 percent of all the proposals that came his way. He was, he noted, extremely selective in the interviews he agreed to do and turned down almost all of them. "Unless you're retarded, who wants to answer questions all day? I would rather be reading the newspaper or bullshitting. I don't like interviews." The fact is, Trump *does* do interviews—plenty of them—but many of them are three- or four-minute TV interviews with local stations or with entertainment program reporters. He will sit down for lengthy interviews, but mostly with reporters from the major media outlets.

He is in great demand as a public speaker as well, earning, he says, between $300,000 and $350,000 a speech. "I don't think anyone's higher," he noted. "I could speak three times a day every day of the year if I wanted to." He sometimes does speeches gratis, asking the sponsors to make a contribution to his favorite charity.

He decided, and perhaps it was more subconscious than not, that he need not do only those events that made him look like a serious business leader. It was okay—indeed, it was beneficial—to appear in less serious roles.

Trump had no trouble understanding how important it was for his reputation to show that he could let down his hair (figuratively) and that he could laugh at himself. Others had commented during and after the first season of The Apprentice how much more human Donald Trump seemed on television than what they had imagined. He saw that the public responded well to his seeming "human." And so in his public appearances, he became more self-deprecating, more human.

In his view, all the publicity meant more business for him. He saw his public exposure as one big free commercial for the Trump Organization. He was being given the chance to advertise himself and his products that otherwise might have cost him millions of dollars. Instead, he was being paid the millions. The more exposure he got, the more apartments he could sell and the more visitors he could get at his casinos. It was as simple as that. He was appearing in public before large audiences. That was all that mattered.

New opportunities were opening up for him.

His publishing house, Random House, wanted him to do book after book. ("I'm running out of ideas," he said in one candid moment. "What else am I going to say? They say they don't give a shit.")

The business deals that were offered to him were bigger. Financing was easier. He was selling memberships at his golf clubs faster than anyone had ever done before. It was the same with his apartments. Apartments at Trump Park Avenue were selling at a fast clip. Trump Place on the West Side was "the hottest job in New York," according to Trump. He was elated: "Now a lot of things come to me. I'm getting better deals than I got before, and they're more successful because of the exposure. It's become crazy. I'm getting more satisfaction, and I'm having a lot of fun." The heightened demand for his time—and his willingness to accede to so many demands—had, of course, the downside that he had to be on the run a lot. "If I could sit home and watch television, that would be almost like a great reward, but it doesn't happen that often. That's probably the negative." He still likes hanging around the office, so he meets his public commitments quite often by simply getting on the elevator at Trump Tower. But his new life is time-consuming. Still, he is willing to pay that price.

Donald Trump's most unconventional public activity was his remarkably smooth, highly professional performance as the host of Saturday

Night Live on April 3, 2004. The *SNL* host is typically someone with comedic talent; Trump, however, was never regarded as especially humorous. But on that night, when he delivered his monologue and appeared in several skits, he exhibited a droll sense of comedy that won him warm praise.

The very fact that he was willing to appear on the show and poke fun at himself for having such a giant ego left people charmed.

A number of Trump's friends wondered whether he could pull off hosting such a show. It was one thing to host one of those "birthday bashes" at the Trump Taj Mahal, where all he had to do was give out money and issue a few platitudes about how great the hotel was. But on *Saturday Night Live*, he had to deliver a lengthy monologue; he had to act, playing himself in different skits; and he had to be funny.

Steve Wynn was vacationing at his home in Sun Valley, Idaho. It was getting late. His friends had already gone to sleep. But he knew that Donald Trump was going to be on *Saturday Night Live* soon, and he was determined to stay up to watch. He was especially curious how Trump would handle the monologue. Would he be funny? Would he make fun of himself? Would some expletive fly out of his mouth? What would the television critics think of Trump's appearance?

Then the show began. For a moment, watching him on the screen, it was difficult to keep in mind that, for most of his career, Donald Trump had been a business figure, not an entertainer. But here he was hosting one of America's most famous comedy programs.

He went right into the opening monologue.

"It's great to be here at *Saturday Night Live*, but to tell you the truth, it's even better for *Saturday Night Live* that I'm here—because nobody's bigger than me. Nobody is better than me. I'm a ratings machine. I've got the number one television show, *The Apprentice*. And after just one season, I'm about to become the highest-paid television personality in America. And as everyone in this room knows, highest paid means best. Right?

"But television is really a hobby for me. I'm primarily occupied with my real-estate holdings; my best-selling books, and making love to women who have won prizes for their beauty—but not anymore because I have a great girlfriend." The audience snickered as if they didn't quite believe the part about the girlfriend.

"That's true," he emphasized, but more snickers followed. "I can't win. See, you can't win."

What was remarkable about the opening monologue—aside from Trump's very presence there—was the way he passed off the way he spoke every day to anyone who would listen: as comedy. The truth was, he did go around in real life saying that he was the biggest and the best, that he was a ratings machine, and that he was the highest-paid TV performer. The one thing he doesn't boast about, even in private, is that he is primarily occupied with making love to beautiful women. He is, after all, newly affianced.

The monologue over, Trump then played a janitor in one skit, replete in blue overalls, switching places with a Donald Trump character, a la *The Prince and the Pauper*. In another skit, he sang and "played" the piano (along with George Ross and Carolyn Kepcher look-alikes). In other skits, he watched as *SNL* actors parodied *The Apprentice* and mimicked Trump's famous "You're fired" catchphrase.

TRUMP'S HOUSE OF WINGS

The show-stealer, however, was Trump's parody of the branding of his name, this time selling buffalo chicken wings at Donald Trump's House of Wings. Dressing up in a yellow suit and yellow tie, he was joined by four dancers in yellow costumes designed as chicken wings, and together they sang and danced in praise of Trump's wings. No single image of Donald Trump better illustrated his willingness to do almost anything and behave in almost any manner to attain maximum exposure. To his credit, he seemed comfortable and relaxed, and he appeared to be having fun.

Steve Wynn was bowled over by Trump's performance.

"He did it. He did it better than the actors who come on most of the time. He was completely unself-conscious, totally believable and hysterically funny. When he played in the band, he had a deadpan delivery, a way of delivering comedy that was almost Jack Benny-ish, but he was playing Donald Trump. He was playing himself. That is extremely difficult to do."

To Donald Trump Jr., his father's performance on *SNL* helped to explain why his father felt there was no such thing as over-exposure. "He likes to be out there. He wants his name out there. He enjoys seeing it there. He feels it's a benefit for everything he does." Rather than being a negative, the excessive publicity made his father seem warmer, more human, he suggested. "Maybe it's excessive exposure, but it's kind of funny. *Saturday Night Live* was the funniest *SNL* in years. He really pulled it off as a non-actor type. He was flawless. There was only one skit that he wasn't in. I've never seen that in any *SNL*."

Trump kept finding new ways to gain exposure. In June 2004, he began doing radio broadcasts over the Clear Channel Premiere Radio Networks. It was a convenient use of his time. He was presented with scripts, which he read from his desk. The whole thing was over each day in a matter of minutes. By the fall, he was broadcasting over 400 stations. He wanted to talk about the war in Iraq and about nuclear weapons in North Korea, but the Clear Channel executives wanted lighter banter from Trump. "They didn't want to hear about nuclear weapons if they were going to play music in the morning," Trump said, by way of explaining why some of his broadcasts had to do with the latest antics of Britney Spears.

So, what listeners heard was a brew of Trumpisms that roamed from light subject to lighter subject.

Some examples:

On China and electronic pornography: "China has declared war on electronic porn. That means no nudity on the Internet...no sexy text messages...no racy radio talk shows...and no phone sex. It sounds to me like it might be a pretty boring country."

On Paris Hilton: "She's a lovely girl....The first time I saw Paris, she was 12 years old, and I looked at my friend and said, 'That is a beautiful girl.'"

A number of the broadcasts took listeners behind the scenes of *The Apprentice*, giving updates on first-season contestants and offering insights into the thinking behind the program.

I THOUGHT HE WAS DOING SO WELL

Just as he won praise for his appearance on *Saturday Night Live*, Trump won a great deal of plaudits for the Visa television commercial he did in early June. What people liked especially was his self-deprecating manner. Called "Rooftop," the ad featured Trump learning the hard way about the security his Visa Check Card afforded him. A gust of wind blew his Visa card out of his hand and over the roof of Trump Tower; he rushed to a dumpster below to retrieve the card.

As he made his way to the dumpster, a voice explained that Visa cardholders were not liable for fraudulent purchases made with their lost or stolen cards, no matter what the size of their bank account. But this information came too late to save Trump from a passerby who, watching him dig through the dumpster, declared, "And I thought he was doing so well."

(An odd footnote: NBC and Visa had a different commercial ready to go congratulating Smarty Jones on his historic Triple Crown victory right after the running of the Belmont Stakes in early June. The only trouble was that Birdstone won the Belmont, and NBC had to go to "Plan B," running a different commercial in the unlikely event that some other horse won the race; it ran the Trump commercial with him diving into the dumpster.)

Trump did a number of television commercials during 2004. Sometimes, the money was embarrassingly easy for him to earn. When a major company paid him a fortune to star in a 15-minute "commercial" for that company, he did not even have to show up in person; he taped his appearance in which he fired the company's rivals.

No matter how much money they paid him, Trump drew the line at some requests. When a company asked him to take part in a commercial in which he would grab a girl, he nixed the idea because, as he put it colorfully, it would have sent a message: Donald Trump saying "Fuck you to the world."

Even if reporters challenged him on doing the commercials, he could not resist doing them. It seemed so easy. On August 12, 2004, he took part in a television commercial for a product that the toy company Hasbro created called Trump—the Game. It was a revised version of a game that had appeared in stores in the 1980s. In the game, players circle the board making deals á là Donald Trump, and hopefully earn hundreds of millions of dollars.

Taking a break from the 90-minute shoot of the commercial, Trump raised his hand and stretched out his fingers to a visitor on the set to indicate "five." He was signaling that he was being paid $5 million to do this commercial. No one could turn down that kind of money, he told the visitor a few minutes later. His father would have thought he was crazy.

Watching Trump filming the commercial that morning, one gained a sense of the way he happily employed his entertainment and acting skills in quest of his business interests and in quest of his celebrity. Learning his lines and delivering them with ease, he seemed like the consummate actor. He rarely fluffed a line. He not only read the lines with ease, but he analyzed each word to make sure they were appropriate, that they sounded realistic. It was easy to forget that he was, first and foremost, a businessman. Yet, as he went through take after take, suggesting small changes in the script, employing just the right emotion and tone, he clearly seemed more an actor than a real-estate developer. To Trump, it did not seem important that others thought he had acting ability. He had never wanted to be an actor, so getting praise for his acting ability was much less important to him than being told that he was a great builder or that he knew how to run casino hotels.

He wanted to be known first and foremost as a great businessman. So, when doing the Trump—the Game commercial, he sometimes displayed a flash of impatience. After all, a few floors away, he and his staff were running billions of dollars' worth of businesses. He watched as the television crew employed their tape measures and their light-softening screens and their refrigerator-size cameras—and kept asking how much longer it would take. To a visitor, he said out of the crew's hearing that they were taking too long; they were doing a lot of takes because the more takes they did, the more money they earned.

But he waited it out, however impatient he became.

For he knew that millions of people would watch this commercial—it was going to air for the first time on September 9, on the opening show of the second season of *The Apprentice.*

Not everything was coming up roses for Donald Trump that summer of 2004.

It was ironic.

He was a household name, yet he could not keep the ghosts of the past from returning. He thought he had sent those ghosts packing when he restructured his debt on his Atlantic City properties back in the early 1990s.

But the ghosts had come back.

The debts on his Atlantic City properties remained. The problem for Trump was that he was still paying junk bond interest rates for his Atlantic City enterprises, 12 percent; in New York, he was paying 3 percent on new mortgages. Because of those heavy debts, there was never enough money to refurbish the hotels, which needed doing. The result was that his casino hotels remained a money-losing proposition even into the early 2000s.

In 2003, the Trump casino hotel company's pretax cash flow dropped to $255 million from $321 million in 2002. For the first six months of 2004, the cash flow was only $124 million, which was down from $132 million during the first six months of 2003.

According to his schedule of debt payments, Trump had to pay $73.1 million in May 2004 and another $73.1 million the following November.

Trump's personal stake in his casino hotel corporation—he controlled 56 percent of the company—was worth just $41 million in early 2004, down from more than half a billion dollars in 1996. The stock had been as high as $34 in 1996 but had fallen to $2.50 in early 2004. Trump was receiving an annual salary of $1.5 million from the corporation, which carried $1.8 billion in debt.

Trump's defenders sought to make the interesting case that the casino hotels were doing badly, but they would have done much worse without Donald Trump and his big brand name on the top of his establishments.

The situation he faced in the summer of 2004 was nowhere near as bleak as the one he had faced in the early 1990s: Now he did not face personal bankruptcy. Now he had no personal guarantees on the debt. Now he had plenty of money at his disposal to pay off the debts, if he chose to do so.

Trump did not seem overly agitated. His usual ebullient self, he mentioned frequently that he was putting together one of his best deals ever and that his casinos hotels would rise from the ashes and prove hotter than ever. He had good reason not to feel worried. In the early 1990s, he could not know whether the banks would support him in the end. But this time around, he seemed confident that his sudden spike in popularity would insulate him from further financial woes.

Because he did not seem to be in a panic, no one else was, either. For one thing, this time, no one seemed to be suffering very much from the Trump casinos' financial difficulties.

To be sure, there was rising urgency in the early months of 2004 on the part of Trump and his financial advisers to solve the debt payment problem of Atlantic City. They did not want to wait until the pressure for a solution mounted and deadlines got too tight. By 2006, Trump had to pay back $1.3 billion of the $1.8 billion in debt.

Knowing that deadline, Trump began trying to solve his debt problems as early as 2001. Given the terrorist attack on the World Trade Center in Manhattan on September 11 of that year, Trump's challenge was great. With New York the largest reservoir of visitors to Trump's casinos, customer traffic to Atlantic City went into a tailspin.

Plans to restructure the heavy debt payments began in earnest by 2002 as gamblers began returning to Atlantic City that year. Conversations with lenders ensued but took an on-again, off-again air because the deadline still seemed a long way off. The talks intensified in early 2004, and by the summer, Trump was able to announce that he had a prepackaged bankruptcy arrangement in place that would resolve his Atlantic City debts once and for all.

It was crucial for him to convince the media that, just as he had described his earlier financial difficulty as a blip, this, too, was just a blip, and he would get through it better than ever. But some in the media were not willing to go along with Trump's argument that, in the long run, he was ensuring the success of the casino hotels. They felt that, by entering into the "prepack," as it was dubbed in the business world, he was sullying his name and thus tainting the Trump brand, making it unlikely that he would be able to eliminate his huge debt as quickly as he hoped.

A DIFFICULT DAY

August 10, 2004, was a difficult day for Donald Trump.

That was the day that Trump's public corporation indicated that it planned to file for bankruptcy protection by the end of September. By doing so, it could acquire new financing that would reduce the $1.8 billion debt and allow for critically important hotel renovation.

Trump was to be bailed out by DLJ Merchant Banking Partners, an arm of Credit Suisse First Boston. Credit Suisse would own more than two-thirds of the company. This would mark the second time Trump casinos filed for bankruptcy court protection.

DLJ planned to invest $345 million in the newly reorganized company. With that infusion of cash, Trump's properties in Atlantic City could add rooms and expand beyond the town limits. "We want to go into other jurisdictions," said Trump Hotel & Casino Resorts president and CEO Mark Brown. "We are unable to do that. It's frustrating for us."

As part of the bankruptcy agreement, Trump was originally to relinquish his CEO position, to reduce his equity stake from 56 to 25 percent, and to invest $55 million in cash in the hotels. The debt of Trump Hotels & Casino Resorts would fall from $1.8 billion to $1.25 billion. With the interest rate on the newly issued debt only 7 percent instead of the previous 12 percent on the current bond issue, annual interest costs would fall from $215 million to only $100 million.

In return for the lenders giving him additional breathing space, Trump granted the one thing the bankers wanted: his name. He put into the deal a royalty-free "perpetual and exclusive worldwide trademark license"—that is, the right to use the Trump name, effectively valued at $100 million.

The good news for Donald Trump was that he had some solution in the offing. He really had no other choice, in his view, but to take the route of the prepackaged bankruptcy. But the bad news was that the announcement was likely to raise again the old questions of just how competent he was as a business figure. When the questions were raised in the early 1990s, there was no television program portraying him as a business titan whose genius had brought him fame and fortune. But now there was, and to the millions of people who watched *The Apprentice*, it might seem the least bit incongruous to learn that the emperor had no clothes—or very little, at least.

After all, Trump had cast himself as a superbusinessman on *The Apprentice*, firing contestants each week for poor performance in the workplace and dispensing advice on how to succeed in business.

What business titan declared bankruptcy, prepackaged or not? What business personality touted himself as a business genius once a week on television and then all but announced that he was not going to meet his financial responsibilities in the real world? It could be jarring to many, to say the least. Trump knew this but sensed he had little choice except to go ahead with the prepack.

No matter how optimistic Trump sounded—no, he wasn't going under; he wasn't going to suffer another financial setback—it was an embarrassing day for him.

The story was all over the media.

It was déjà vu: Donald Trump seemed to be in serious trouble. Could this be true? Hadn't he been in trouble 14 years ago and emerged stronger than ever?

Did any of this make sense?

To many people, it did not. Was there not some kind of shield or immunity for the man with the most popular show on television? How had he let disaster knock at his door once again, when things seemingly were going so well?

Surely, he would have wanted to avoid the negative publicity that would inevitably flow from such a decision.

The one way to avoid the embarrassment of entering bankruptcy, prepackaged or not, was to make the debt payment. Trump could certainly afford the payment.

But he did not want to throw good money after bad.

And once Trump decided that he did not want to make the debt payment, the only alternative was the prepack.

By taking the prepack route, Trump avoided a situation in which any single bondholder could object to a change in the terms of the debt payment and, thus, keep the restructuring from happening. By entering the corporation into bankruptcy, Trump did not need 100 percent approval of all bondholders for the changes in payment.

All of this seemed to allow Trump to emerge with a sweet deal in his hands. To get that sweet deal, Trump would have to suffer through a few days—or even weeks—of bad publicity to give his casino hotels a chance to emerge in better financial shape. According to a Trump attorney, "People would think he was nuts to pay $150 million a year out of his own pocket just so the thing would stay out of bankruptcy, when he could otherwise achieve all his financial objectives but take this hit for a few weeks."

For one reason or another, the media made it sound as if Trump could not afford to make the $146.2 million debt payments. That was not the case. Yet the *New York Times* wrote on September 23, 2004: "Trump Hotels has a $73.1 million debt payment coming due in November, and the company's financial coffers have been so severely strained that casino analysts and bondholders have questioned whether the company will have the resources to make that payment." In the same story was this line: "The company had to delay a similar payment in May for 30 days while it scrambled to put together the money that it needed." Trump was bemused by the fact that the media focussed so heavily on the casino hotels when they made up less than one percent of his net worth.

Despite the uncertainty hanging over his head created by his financial difficulties in Atlantic City, the media and others continued to turn to Trump, offering him more and more exposure. The questions he never asked himself: Was all of this exposure good for him or bad? And how long would it take before the public tired of him?

CHAPTER

11

No Such Thing as Over-Exposure

In the fall of 2004, two recurring themes surrounded Donald Trump's whirlwind existence: The world did not seem able to get enough of him, and like a nagging toothache, his Atlantic City financial difficulties remained a continuing annoyance.

Whatever financial problems lurked in the background, Donald Trump stood poised that fall to exploit the growing demand to get a piece of him at every possible turn.

In September, *Trump World* hit the newsstands, a slick, glossy bimonthly magazine that Trump was launching. It promised a peek into the lifestyles of the rich and famous, insider material on *The Apprentice*, and stories about how to live a luxurious way of life.

Michael Jacobson had been in the magazine publishing business when, on a visit to the Trump Marina casino hotel in Atlantic City in November 2001, he noticed that there were no magazines in the hotel rooms. A magazine called *Trump Style* existed but had not been published for the previous 18 months. Jacobson thought of producing a new Trump-sponsored magazine. A month later, he was pitching the idea to Donald Trump. *Trump World* was launched in November 2002 with a circulation of 100,000—50,000 for hotel rooms and 50,000 mailed directly to high-end casino customers. By the end of 2003, Jacobson had taken the magazine national, issuing it six times a year, two more than his earlier version. The first edition of the national magazine appeared in the fall of 2004 and had a 200,000 circulation. On the cover were the 18 contestants on the second series of *The Apprentice.*

In late September, Trump appeared at the Times Square Toys 'R' Us store to help promote a 12-inch doll made in his likeness (he approved of the hair but thought the doll needed a new suit). The doll sold for $26.99 and spouted a number of Trump-like phrases in Trump's own voice, such as "Stay focused," "Think big," and "I should fire myself just for having you around."

Trump launched a signature line of power suits sold in department stores for $577 a suit, along with blazers bearing Trump family crest buttons. In addition, he applied to trademark the name Trump University, which one day could offer online business and real-estate courses.

Meanwhile, the news on the restructuring front was one day good, the next bad. In late September, the restructuring plan that Trump was putting together with Credit Suisse First Boston fell apart. Once again, the media jumped onto the story, making it sound as if Donald Trump's financial world was having a meltdown.

It was not.

Trump's public corporation announced that it planned to seek a new restructuring arrangement directly with bondholders. He still believed that he would come out in fine shape.

Still, the Atlantic City properties were frustrating for Trump. He strongly believed that if only he spent more time there, he could guarantee the properties would look more attractive to customers. "If I were down in Atlantic City and really lived there, I would save millions and millions of dollars." But, alas, he conceded, "I can't be there. I just can't be there." He would not say it, but he clearly preferred living in Manhattan. "The one thing is I can't be everywhere. I can't do everything. So you have to say, 'What are you going to do? And what aren't you going to do?' And you rely on other people." But when the new deal is approved, Trump said he looked forward to spending a good deal of time in Atlantic City in order to build a great company.

That fall, Trump seemed to have Atlantic City and his financial difficulties on his mind relatively little. Every day, he seemed to be engaged in one promotional event after another. On October 11, he left his apartment in Trump Tower at 8:30 PM, took his limousine over to a heliport along the Hudson River, and flew 45 minutes in his helicopter to West Chester, Pennsylvania, where he was scheduled to appear on the QVC shopping channel to promote his latest book, *Trump: Think Like a Billionaire.*

Despite a very heavy schedule, he was delighted to appear on QVC, aware of what a great marketing vehicle it was: he was especially impressed with the QVC President, Darlene Daggett.

Previously that fall, he had appeared on the channel and sold 36,000 copies of his book in 20 minutes. The QVC executives invited him back for a second appearance because of the wild success of his first book sale on the channel. Emerging from the helicopter and arriving at the 30-acre QVC "campus," Trump was greeted by QVC executives, who escorted him into the building. Within seconds of meeting one executive, Trump pulled a "Trump candy bar" out of his pocket and suggested that she embrace the product. A discussion ensued on how best to market the candy bar. To those watching Trump in action that evening, it seemed like one more marvelous example of how the man simply could not stop selling—himself or his products.

A number of the contestants from the second season of *The Apprentice* were on hand at QVC and sat behind Trump as he promoted his book on television from 10 to 11 PM. QVC had played a role in one of the episodes of *The Apprentice*—hence, the presence of the contestants on the set.

Trump went to work plugging his book, explaining why he wrote the book, what it had to say. Meanwhile, he was able to watch a counter on a monitor in front of him, reflecting the growing number of sales of his book registered through automated phone calls into the shopping channel. He had even better luck this second visit than at the first appearance, selling 37,000 copies of the book in 30 minutes.

Four days later, on October 15, came one of the most talked-about New York events of the year—and Donald Trump was smack in the center. On this Friday afternoon, Trump was sitting on a dais at the New York Hilton as the target of the annual Friars Club roast. A private fraternity of sorts for entertainers, the Friars selects one celebrity each year to rake over the coals—all in good humor, although the humor can turn pretty brutal. After agreeing to appear, Trump spent several months wondering how scathing the attacks on him would be. He had a vivid memory of being present at a previous Friars roast when *Playboy* magazine founder Hugh Hefner was roasted. "It was brutal," Trump said over and over again.

Accordingly, Trump's agreement to take part in his own roast begged the question: Why would he willingly sit through such a barrage of criticism—and in public? The only answer: Donald Trump's willingness to endure almost anything to get public attention. As he says repeatedly, there is no such thing as over-exposure.

In the case of the Friars roast, however, the price for such exposure was high: At no other time in his career would so many nasty things be said about Trump in one afternoon—and the comments were coming from people who claimed to be his friends. Yes, it was all in fun. Still, Trump was nervous as he walked into the ballroom at noon.

HIGH SCHOOL WITH HER GRANDPARENTS

Regis Philbin, who counts himself as a close friend of Trump, began his emcee chores by telling Trump, "These people are trained professional killers. They want to say things in public to you that they've been saying behind your back for years. "

On the dais was a star-studded group that included the Rev. Al Sharpton, John McEnroe, Katie Couric, Stone Phillips, Jeff Zucker, Mike Wallace, Cheryl Tiegs, Richard Belzer, Jerry Ohrbach, Victoria Gotti, and Michael Spinks.

NBC's Jeff Zucker got a chance to lace into Trump: "Donald, I got the invitation for the wedding, but I can't make it. But I'll catch the next one."

Alluding to his network's faltering ratings this season, Zucker saluted Trump and *The Apprentice* as "the only thing that stands between NBC and a total collapse." NBC did not face total collapse; it was simply Jeff Zucker mocking Donald Trump's fondness for truthful hyperbole.

Zucker took a swipe at Trump's predilection for young women: "Donald has his dating down pat. There's the picking of the ring, the meeting of the parents, the meeting of the grandparents, and then the realization that he went to high school with the grandparents."

When the event was all over, Trump undoubtedly felt pleased, suffering few scars from the roasters. He was only sorry that his fiancée, Melania, sitting in the audience, had to hear all these jokes—some of which were directed at her—and all the profanity. Trump spoke only briefly toward the end, urging the crowd, "Go home, go to work, and watch your language."

Trump need not have been nervous in advance of the event. Though the comedians inside the ballroom *did* make fun of many aspects of his life—his hair, his fortune, his womanizing—he emerged from the experience with some of his best media. The *New York Times*, for example, led its story the next day this way: "There are probably very few social experiences in life more daunting than being the subject of a Friars Club roast, a slash-and-burn salute that involves sitting still while a bunch of foul-mouthed comedians lob off-color remarks about your career, your looks, your spouse (or spouses), your lack of sexual prowess and even— God forbid—your hair.

> "So some credit should be paid to Donald J. Trump, who smiled and laughed along yesterday afternoon as he sat for two and a half hours in a ballroom of the New York Hilton, while a series of comics, celebrities, and so-called friends absolutely savaged everything...."

Nearly two weeks later, while flying one morning from New York to Chicago, he looked back on the Friars roast with mixed feelings. "I thought the roast was funny and it was important, but if I had to do it over again, I wouldn't do it." Though he had sat through some rather brutal ones in the past, he was still taken aback at the profane insults thrown at some of the celebrities present that afternoon. He had been talking to Katie Couric, the NBC *Today* show co-anchor, just before the roast. She had told Trump how glad she was to be at this, her first Friars roast. Then, seconds after the roast began, one of the comedians lashed out at her for no apparent reason, calling her a name unprintable in most places. "And that," said Trump, recollecting that painful moment for him and for her, "was only the beginning."

What truly riled Trump, however, was the promise that the Friars had made—so it had seemed to him—that there would be no media coverage of the event. It turned out that numerous stories appeared the next day, offering up quite a number of the jokes that were said during the roast— without using any of the profanity. To Trump, it was fine for a comedian to tell a joke at the roast; everyone knew it was all in good, clean fun (well, maybe not so clean). But when the same joke appeared in print the next day, it sounded less humorous and more realistic. Still, for Trump, there was something positive about the experience: "The good side was that I was able to make fun of myself, and people respected that."

Going from one project to the next, watching and listening for the latest proposal to enlist his name as part of some product, Donald Trump seemed determined this time around not to let all these out-of-office pursuits distract him from his businesses.

> "I am the most effi-
> cient human being
> I've ever known..."

The demand for his time was high, but he managed to do many events within the confines of Trump Tower. "I am the most efficient human being I've ever known or known of," he said. Doing one of those television commercials, he noted, is only an elevator ride away for him. And when there's downtime during a shoot of a commercial, as there inevitably is, he's only a cell-phone call away from his office. He had several "board rooms" created as sets to be used in the filming of these events. "So I have a pretty efficient setup. You can bring the cameras in. I do it. It takes me five minutes."

He did not adopt all proposals. When somone proposed licensing his name to sell upscale caskets, he balked. "I'm not into caskets," he said dismissively. Still, Trump is eager to do all the self-promotional events possible.

For one thing, it's all free publicity. The National Football League had asked him to do an introduction to the Super Bowl. They were ready to pay him a healthy sum of money. "If I had to pay for that introduction, it would cost me $2.5 million. If I took an ad, it would cost me millions of dollars and it wouldn't be as good because the audience go to the kitchen during the ad and comes back later to watch the rest of the show."

Helping Donald Trump stay focused—apart from his determination to remain holed up at Trump Tower as much as possible—was the fact that the real-estate market in New York was flourishing.

He was putting up nine buildings: in Chicago, Miami, Las Vegas, New York, and elsewhere. He was building two golf courses: one in Los Angeles, California, and the other in Bedminster, New Jersey.

Trump Tower Las Vegas, due to open toward the end of 2007, represented Trump's first foray into a city he has tried to become part of for years. "Vegas will welcome him with open arms," said Phil Ruffin, on whose property the Trump building will rise. Ruffin is the owner of the New Frontier casino hotel in Las Vegas and an equal partner with Donald Trump in the new Trump Tower Las Vegas. Ruffin said that putting Donald Trump on the land improves the value of the rest of the land. Trump and Ruffin are considering building a second tower also on the New Frontier property because the first one sold so quickly.

It might be surprising that Trump's first Las Vegas initiative will not be a casino hotel, but indications are that he hopes to build one in the near future. Early in 2004, he obtained his Nevada gambling license. Of course, building a new casino hotel is expensive ($1.5 billion is Phil Ruffin's estimate); purchasing an existing one is only slightly less costly ($900 million). Owning a casino hotel in Las Vegas has to be tempting to Trump because all hotels on the "strip" are profitable.

For his part, Steve Wynn, who is building his Wynn Las Vegas casino hotel across the street from the New Frontier casino hotel and the future site of the Trump Tower Las Vegas, happily embraced Donald Trump's arrival in Las Vegas. "You'll do great here," he told Trump. "There are enough colorless executives to fill up a barrel."

Wynn said Las Vegas "thrives on what Donald Trump has: glitz, hyperbole. Las Vegas is a one great big hyperbolic explosion. It was made to order for Donald Trump. Atlantic City is a grindy kind of place. Las Vegas is where he should have been." Wynn did not exclude Trump from entering the casino hotel business in Las Vegas: "Maybe it could reinvigorate the Trump hotels."

Wynn believes that Trump became a better builder and developer after what he termed a less than successful experience in Atlantic City: "Donald never built anything that he conceived. Each of his hotels in Atlantic City was an acquisition, which is part of the problem. He would now know what to do. None of the Atlantic City hotels are from his design. With respect to the Taj, he was fooling with another guy's bad plan. None of them represented Trump's really good sensibility. Each of those buildings was built by someone else. I'm confident if he built one from scratch, you'd see a legitimate product that would have a lot of sex appeal. So you can't judge him by the New Jersey properties."

Though he has consistently dismissed the notion that he still harbors thoughts of running for office, Trump was not shy about putting forward his ideas on foreign policy during the presidential election season summer of 2004. He strongly diverged from the Bush Administration policy toward Iraq, questioning whether the United States could democratize Iraq. The more likely scenario, he insisted, after the United States departed the country, was an Iraq that would pose a far graver threat to the outside world than Saddam Hussein's Iraq. "C'mon, two minutes after we leave, there's going to be a revolution, and the meanest, toughest, smartest, most vicious guy will take over," he said in an *Esquire* magazine interview. "And he'll have weapons of mass destruction, which Saddam didn't have."

Donald Trump sometimes questioned whether his various pursuits—his business projects, his exercises in marketing and branding, his new venture in television and all the super celebrity it brought him—were truly worth all the effort. He sometimes sounded fatalistic toward the whole exercise of showing up for work every day: A person lives for a certain number of years, whether one is Donald Trump or not, and then dies—and that is that. So what is all the fuss?

In the end, though he never said it, one imagined that Donald Trump did much of what he did for the sake of his four children. He displayed little overt pride in the fact that some of them planned to enter the family business, the Trump Organization. But in his recounting of what the children were doing in the fall of 2004 and what they planned to do, he seemed quite pleased that some were coming on board.

Donald Trump Jr. was already a senior member of his team. In the fall of 2004, he had become one of the most senior of the executives in the Trump Organization. His engagement to Vanessa Haydon became public in early October.

It is hard to say what the Trump Organization will look like in 20 or 30 years, for it is far too early to tell which of the Trump family members will emerge as the leading force or forces in the company. Clearly, Donald Jr. has a leg up on his siblings because he has risen to senior executive status at the young age of 26. He likes to point out how he's different from his father. He's an outdoorsman. He's not at all interested in promoting himself or attracting publicity for himself. He and his father have an easygoing relationship during business hours. Donald Jr. is so close to the action, so involved in some of the most important decisions, that it would not be surprising for the father sometimes to get annoyed at the son if and when things go wrong. But watching them interact, one has the impression that the father knows that the last thing he wants to do is embarrass his son in front of others.

Like Donald Jr., Ivanka, Trump's oldest daughter, graduated from the Wharton School at the University of Pennsylvania. As a teenager, she developed a very successful career in modeling and appeared on the cover of the May 1997 issue of *Seventeen*. That same year, she hosted the Miss Teen USA Pageant (which her father owns); she cut short her modeling career to attend college. In the fall of 2004, she was working for a New York real-estate firm, Rattner Real Estate, to get her feet wet in the profession before joining the Trump Organization. She felt guilty, her father said, about going to work for her father directly from college.

Trump's younger son, Eric, was a business major in his senior year at Georgetown University in Washington, D.C.; he was planning to join the Trump Organization after graduation.

Tiffany, the one child Trump had with second wife Marla Maples, was born in October 1993 and attended a private school in California.

Donald Trump escorted a visitor into his office on Tuesday morning, October 26. He immediately launched into an explanation of why he was going to turn the Atlantic City casino hotels around. Indeed, five days earlier, he had announced what he called a "comprehensive recapitalization plan" that was supported by the overwhelming majority of bondholders. The plan was designed to restructure the $1.8 billion in debt, to give Trump's public company breathing space, and to pave the way for the eventual refurbishing and expansion of his casino enterprises.

A news release from Trump Hotels & Casino Resorts, Inc., described the company as "positioned to capitalize on [the] world-renowned Trump brand and become [a] major player in [the] gaming industry." The announcement went on to note that, as part of the plan, Trump was to remain chairman and CEO; he would invest $71.4 million into the recapitalized company.

He would remain the single largest individual stockholder of the company, with 27 percent of the company's common stock (down from 56 percent). The plan called for a $400 million reduction in the company's debt, with a reduced interest rate of 8.5 percent, saving $98 million in annual interest expenses. The plan permitted working capital of up to $500 million, which would permit the company to refurbish and expand the existing properties.

Just as August 10, 2004 had been perhaps the darkest day of the year for Trump, October 21 was certainly one of the brightest. He saw very little downside in the new preliminary agreement he had reached with bondholders. He was now ready to move forward for the first time with the prospect of creating competitive enterprises in Atlantic City that would be much less of a financial burden.

The *New York Times* story on October 21 all but made up for the bad publicity Trump had endured back in August. Now, the *Times* carried the news that Donald Trump's casino hotel corporation had reached a deal to avoid bankruptcy.

The restructuring agreement came less than two weeks before the date of a large bond payment. The restructuring plan would be completed by February 2005.

One might have thought that Trump had enough on his plate. But behind the scenes, he was wheeling and dealing, eager to purchase more properties. In public, all he would say about Las Vegas was that he had no plans at the moment to build or acquire a casino hotel. But he left the impression that if the right deal came along, he might pursue it. He doubted however that such a deal would materialize.

All these thoughts and plans were swirling around in his mind as he boarded his 727 jet with the name Trump emblazoned on its body on a Thursday morning in late October 2004. For Trump to make a business trip beyond the East Coast was proving quite the occasion; he liked to use the plane more to visit Mar-a-Lago. But months of planning and preparation for his 90-story $800 million luxury tower in Chicago had brought him and his team of executives to this celebratory day and the start of demolition of the *Chicago Sun-Times* building in the center of the Windy City. Trump had whipped up the idea of beginning the demolition of the *Sun-Times* building as a reason for calling a news conference. It was clever. For no more expense than, as Trump said, "the cost of the fuel of my plane," he wound up getting massive publicity for himself and for the Chicago property. Trump wanted to pump as much energy and enthusiasm into his first Chicago building as possible to set the stage for further Trump-led forays into the city.

Not Around the Corner

But Chicago was not around the corner from New York City, and to get there—even with a limousine and a private jet—Trump would have to devote much of a day away from the office. He employed two cell phones to keep himself in touch with the office; one he carried himself, and the second his bodyguard carried—and he occasionally handed it back to Trump in the limo. Trump wanted to know from his executive assistants who had called the office when he wasn't there. Sometimes, he returned calls. Often, he simply wanted to know who was dialing in to his office.

A word about the way Donald Trump travels: In an age when, upon reaching an airport, the average American citizen has to undergo time-consuming and unpleasant security checks, those accompanying Trump on his plane on this October morning are asked to show up at the original Marine Air Terminal at LaGuardia Airport just 30 minutes before take-off. A few minutes before the plane is scheduled to depart, they are escorted to the waiting plane without a security check. Trump arrives by limo separately. He undergoes no security check, either.

Normally, with his arrival on the plane, the pilot would start moving the plane, but not today. Traffic is too heavy, and everyone waits in the plane for a half-hour before takeoff. Flying time is around two hours. Trump mingles with his guests constantly; occasionally, he sits in his favorite window seat up front with a Diet Coke lodged in a round slot next to him. Occasionally, he loosens his tie (something he never does in his office), takes off his shoes, and props up his legs on the wooden table in front of him. Behind him is a private bedroom and bathroom. Along with the paintings on the wall, the wood paneling, the gold bathroom faucets, the comfortable couches, and attractive lamps, there are other reminders that this is not the way the ordinary person travels. The pilots make no announcements.

Guests on the plane are free to roam up to the cockpit and chat with the pilots. If someone wants to know flight details, an electronic board ticks off the plane's height, time of arrival, and local Chicago time. A breakfast buffet of bagels, coffee, and Danish is offered at the back of the plane. There are no airline attendants. One of the pilots doubles as the fellow who cleans up the plates and cups. None of this luxury escapes Donald Trump. Several times during the flight, he turns to a guest to say, "This is a good way to travel, right?"

At various times during the flight, Trump plants himself on a seat in the part of his plane where his guests are sitting. They talk about sports and business and the Chicago event and the media and anything that comes to mind. The subject gets around to prenuptial agreements, something Trump believes in with great fervor.

Along for the ride on the plane are several executives from the mortgage company financing the Chicago tower, as well as a number of Trump senior executives, including Donald Trump Jr.; Donald Jr.'s fiancée, Vanessa Haydon; and a TV crew from *The Apprentice* who doze on the plane but manage to capture nearly every moment of Donald Trump's adventures while on the ground. They appear to have free rein to film whatever they like, including some very private moments in equally private meetings.

Somehow, Trump has found out that a massive media turnout is expected at the Chicago event. He expects huge crowds, too. The plane lands at Midway Airport at the southern tip of Chicago. Trump is whisked away in a limousine.

Trump notes that while he supported President George Bush for re-election, he felt that a President-elect John Kerry would have asked Trump to become involved in a Kerry administration. As Trump tells it, Kerry spoke to Trump admiringly of his negotiating skills, and raised the prospect that he might appoint him as his Middle East representative. "You know how to negotiate. You'd be the best person to settle the Arab-Israeli conflict," Kerry told Trump, according to Donald Trump. Thinking about the prospect of becoming the American Middle East envoy, Trump then volunteered, "It would take me two weeks to get an agreement." Of course, Kerry's loss on November 2, 2004, precluded Trump's appointment.

A few minutes later, the limousine pulled up in front of an office building in downtown Chicago, and Trump was taken to the offices of a major contractor on the project. He is scheduled to lead a "buy-out" session with the contractor's executives to close a deal on a portion of the building. The bidding for the building's caissons is in the $16 million range, and Trump is confident he can close the deal at $13 million. With the building expected to cost $800 million, this represents a seemingly small but not insignificant chunk of the entire cost.

Trump and the others gathered around a conference table. Trump sat at one end of the table, with Donald Jr. to his right. What then happened offered a rare insight into how things can suddenly go very, very wrong in a business deal. It was rare for it to happen to Donald Trump—and it was perhaps even rarer that anyone from the outside was present to report on such events.

BIZARRE FEATURE

In a bizarre feature of these events, a camera crew from *The Apprentice* kept its cameras rolling and its microphone firmly planted near Donald Trump every second of the way. No one asked the crew to turn off their cameras or move their microphones. A writer seated off to the side of the conference room watched in growing fascination, and no one asked him to forget what he saw and heard. One could imagine Donald Trump thinking to himself later that perhaps being exposed so much to the media had its drawbacks from time to time. This was certainly one of those moments.

The meeting began, as most of these buy-out sessions do, with Trump chatting with his advisers on what the bidding is all about, who they want to close with, and how much they can shave off the lowest bid.

Trump has done this countless times before, and more often than not, he concludes the negotiations to his satisfaction, getting the bidder he wants at the right price.

He personally dials the first bidder. They exchange pleasantries. Trump, in his usual line at this point, tells the bidder, "I want to give you this job, but your price is too high. What's your best offer?"

At this point, the bidder, knowing he is talking to Donald Trump and knowing that he won't get the job unless he budges from his price, budges—but this doesn't happen this time.

Instead, there is dead silence at the other end of the line. Trump is waiting. So are the others around the table. Why isn't the man speaking? Doesn't he know what he's supposed to do? Finally, Trump asks the man, "So what's your best offer?" Shockingly, the man replies, "I can't go any lower."

Trump is baffled. He can't recall the last time this has happened.

He hangs up, telling the man he will get back to him.

He calls a second bidder. The same exchange of pleasantries takes place, and then it's time for dealing. The man blurts out that he knows all the bids, so he knows he's the lowest bid. And he has no plan to budge from that price.

The faces of everyone seated around the conference table turn various shades of red in embarrassment. The executives look at each other. "What did he say?" "He knows our bids?" "How did that happen?" It now appeared that both men to whom Trump had spoken knew of their bids. "Had they spoken to each other?" That was deemed unlikely. But now, the Trump team knew why neither had budged or was likely to budge.

Trump starts asking the same questions. He can't believe this has happened. Who could have sent these men such information? Was it intentional? Was it a mistake? Trump assumes from the start it's a mistake. No one was talking corporate or industrial espionage. Still, the matter was highly serious. The mistake was costing Trump, so he thought, at least $1 million in savings that he could have squeezed out of one of the bidders before closing on this deal.

One executive from the contracting firm promised that he would get to the bottom of it. A second executive raced from the room to try to find out what had happened. The room became tense. Trump stayed calm. But without raising his voice, he told one executive that this had happened only once to him in the past, and he had fired the man for the misdeed. He wasn't going to fire this executive, but he wanted him to know, Trump said, how serious this was.

The second executive came back in the room with the explanation that an intern had sent out the wrong papers. It was indeed a mistake.

The atmosphere that began in such celebratory tones—they were all going off to the demolition party in 30 minutes—had turned sour, and a pall of uncertainty and frustration and disappointment filled the room.

The talk turned to how to rescue this situation. Trump wanted to get one of the bidders down to $15.5 million. Getting one down to $13 million was now out of the question.

It was agreed quickly that Trump should not call the first bidder back today to try to negotiate. The first bidder was in far too strong a position. The other executives had to massage him a bit more before they could try to get him to lower his price.

(Later, back on the plane, Trump's executives concluded that the contracting company should be penalized by being paid a smaller fee. It had cost Trump at least a million dollars, they estimated; the company should get $500,000 less in fees. Trump went along.) Trump ended up getting a substantial amount off the contract. After Trump did not call the winning bidder back in late October, the bidder called Trump repeatedly, enabling Donald Trump to get the price down to what he wanted originally.

It struck some in the room that, unlike in the board-room scenes in *The Apprentice*, in which Donald Trump rips apart the business strategies and assumptions of various contestants and then fires one of them each week, in this conference room in Chicago, with this $16 million contract up for grabs, this was no reality program—this was real life, and they were all playing with real money.

And the tables were truly turned on Trump. Instead of putting contestants on the show and embarrassingly showing them their faults, then firing one of them each week, this time, he was the victim of just such an embarrassing business initiative. It was truly ironic that the television cameras of *The Apprentice* were busy filming this entire scene. One is hard put to imagine it ever getting on the show.

In real life, Donald Trump was far more sympathetic to the executive or executives at fault than he might have been on *The Apprentice*. He was not willing to fire anyone on the spot. He sensed that someone had made a mistake, and while mistakes should not happen, no one should lose a job over such an error. They would not go unpunished, however; their pay would be docked.

With that embarrassing incident behind them, the Trump executives moved on to the demolition party. Walking to the site of the party, Trump passed hundreds of people who had gathered to watch him, talk to him, and give him something. He signed autographs on $1 and $5 bills. He signed copies of his books. He shook hands. He waved. One woman yelled out, "Richest man in the world." Trump said, more to himself than to her, "Tell that to Bill Gates." Many people shouted at him. Some said simply, "Hey Donald, you're fired." Some said, "Hi, Mr. Trump." No one was disrespectful. No one misbehaved. The media jostled for position to interview Trump, sandwiched in between the well-wishers and members of Trump's visiting party.

"Hey Donald, you're fired."

The man who emceed the demolition party events was Bill Rancic, the man who had won *The Apprentice* the previous April and was now helping to build the Chicago property.

Arriving at the *Chicago Sun-Times* building, Trump held a news conference in front of 15 television cameras, 30 still photographers, and a bunch of print reporters. He was not asked any questions. He said simply that he planned to build one of the greatest buildings in the world and he loved doing it in Chicago, one of his favorite places. The TV journalists sought him out separately, and he acquiesced, holding mini news conferences with various TV reporters as he walked to the site where the demolition was to take place. Hard hats were distributed to members of Trump's party. He did not take one. There was some talk that Trump would get into the tractor and do the demolishing himself; but he stood off to the side of the tractor and watched as it tore apart the covering over the front door of the building. (Later, back on the plane, Trump asked his executives a number of times how long it would take to demolish the whole building. Estimates were either January or February 2005. "That long?" Trump asked. He clearly wanted to get started putting up the 90-story tower.)

It was a quiet October evening, and Donald Trump was relaxing on a couch in the living room of his apartment at Trump Tower. A visitor had been invited at 7:30 PM for some conversation with Trump. A few minutes earlier, Melania Knauss had opened the door and greeted the visitor warmly. By now, it was an open secret that she would marry Donald Trump in early 2005.

Trump appeared a moment later wearing an overcoat, prepared for the visit he would soon make to Pennsylvania.

The three stood around in the lobby and chatted about an event that Trump planned to attend the next evening: a New York Yankees baseball game at Yankee Stadium in the Bronx. Trump has the best seats in the house: in the box of Yankees owner George Steinbrenner. He was asked, was he a Yankees fan? "I'm a George Steinbrenner fan," he replied. Trump began to explain to Melania why she would enjoy the game.

"Have you seen the apartment?" Trump asked the visitor.

It was the visitor's first time, so Donald and Melania escorted him into the dining room, which looked like it sat 20 or so people comfortably. "We hardly use it," Trump said, leaving open the question of why it was underused. Later, he confessed that he had been out 23 nights in a row—and that seemed like a partial explanation.

Trump sat down on the couch and began chatting with the visitor.

"You know about *Trump Tower*?" he blurted out. At first, the question seemed odd. Of course, the visitor knew about the skyscraper. But Trump was talking about a television soap opera to be called *Trump Tower* and modeled partially after the highly popular *Dynasty* that had been on television years earlier.

Trump then explained with great enthusiasm how he had agreed to produce the weekly television show for NBC. "Every network wanted it," he said proudly. "I won't be in it. I don't have time. I'd love to be in it." The show would have a Donald Trump character. "I want to pick a really good-looking guy," he said, not naming any particular actor. The character would not have the name Donald Trump, but was to have the last name Cabot.

Trump preferred the name John Barron, told the producers of his preference, and his word seemed decisive.

With his incredibly successful appearances on *The Apprentice*, much speculation arose over whether Trump would find another post-*Apprentice* television vehicle for himself.

"Did he want to do another TV program?" his visitor asked. "NBC has been great to me. Every network has contacted me about doing some kind of show. I can't tell you what I will do. What I can say is it's very infectious." (He meant, one assumes, seductive.)

His thoughts quickly turned to the "*Apprentice* wannabees," those business leaders such as Mark Cuban and Richard Branson, who began their own television reality shows in the wake of the success of *The Apprentice*. Trump just snorted at the competition, "Everyone who's rich wants to do a show. They'll all fail. Ninety-five percent of all shows fail."

Trump returned to the success he's had with his own show. "It's a very seductive thing. I thought I was well known before, but this has gotten ridiculous. It could be that I'll do something else (on television) or I'll continue doing *The Apprentice.*"

A visitor to Donald Trump's office in early December 2004 found even more evidence that he was not lying low and was still gearing up Trump brand marketing initiatives with the speed of light. For one thing, he was dressed in one of his "Donald J. Trump" suits, proudly showing off his name on an inside jacket label. For another, bottles of his new "Donald Trump, the Fragrance" sat on his desk. He offered them to visitors, even spraying a bit of the scent on a visitor's hand. His mood remained ebullient. He had just received the good news from Random House that his *How to Think Like a Billionaire* book had already sold 150,000 copies in its opening two months, and his *How to Get Rich* book had sold 300,000 since it was published early in 2004.

He was even upbeat with respect to his troubled casino hotels. Two weeks earlier, his casino hotels corporation had filed for bankruptcy. The news stories played up the fact that Trump had won a $500 million line of credit from Morgan Stanley, a major reason why Trump insists that he will come through this bankruptcy in greater shape than ever. But just in case the hotel casino turn-around takes longer than he hopes for, he reminds people that the casino hotels represent less than 1 percent of his net worth.

Among the happier developments for Trump was the rapid disintegration of Richard Branson's *Rebel Billionaire* reality television program, a clear-cut competitor to *The Apprentice.* To Trump's delight, the Branson program had so far posted weak ratings, with 5.4 million viewers compared to 15.8 million for *The Apprentice* one week in late November 2004. Trump wrote Branson after seeing his near-fatal ratings: "Now that I have watched your show, I wish you came to me and asked my advice. I would have told you not to bother. You have no television persona. Do not use me to promote your rapidly sinking show." Branson wrote back in conciliatory terms (so Trump interpreted his letter), ending his letter: "Perhaps you could reread what I have said to date and decide whether it's worth us remaining as friends—or alternatively, you adding me to your list of enemies!"

On December 16, 2004, Trump pulled out all the stops to make the finale of the second *Apprentice* season a huge ratings success. The show, staged at Lincoln Center in Manhattan, was extended to three hours and was shown live. The final two contestants, Jennifer Massey, 30, a Harvard Law School graduate and San Francisco attorney, and Kelly Perdew, 37, a West Point graduate and software executive, competed one-on-one in the finale for the grand prize of earning $250,000 a year as Trump's second *Apprentice.* Trump chose Perdew. Asked whether he wanted to work for the Trump Organization in Las Vegas or New York, Perdew chose New York as his home base in order to be closer to his new boss.

The finale easily won the night in total viewers as well as the 18-49 demographic. However, an average of "only" 16.9 million viewers watched the second *Apprentice* finale, 40 percent below the 28 million who watched the first season's finale. Despite those lower ratings, the show provided NBC with its highest non-sports rating on a Thursday since the finale of *Frasier* in May 2004. Nearly 20 million people were watching as Trump closed in on his decision to choose Perdew.

The good news for Trump was that the second *Apprentice* finale was strong enough to beat back its competitors on the other networks, which included *CSI* on CBS and The *O.C.* on Fox.

The third season of *The Apprentice* was due to begin January 20, 2005. NBC made clear that *Apprentice 4*, with Trump was decided upon.

Two days later, on January 22nd, Trump was set to marry Melania Knauss in Palm Beach, Florida. When two networks asked in December if they could televise the ceremony live, Trump at first scoffed at the idea. Then, reconsidering, he realized what a ratings bonanza a televised wedding could be, and began leaning toward allowing the cameras in.

It seemed that Donald Trump had a never-ending set of choices to make, and they are all good. The only question is how many he can fit into his days and nights. But underlying the great demand for Trump's time and for the benefits that come from getting him involved in a project is the question of just how long his superstardom will last.

Is he on some spiral that keeps going higher and higher? Or will he be suddenly—or even slowly—pulled back to Earth to join all the other mortals?

This was not a question he wished to ask of himself.

For now, there seems to be no downside to all this attention. Every once in a while, Trump and his colleagues suddenly became aware of the possible cost of too much over-exposure. That scene in the Chicago meeting filmed for *The Apprentice* was one such moment, catching Donald Trump as he watched his colleagues make a very embarrassing mistake at his potential expense—and then correcting it.

Yet, for the most part, Trump sees the klieg lights only in positive terms. His look of giddy pleasure at the amount of attention he is getting says it all. He savors having so many choices to make that put him in the public spotlight. If he could, one imagines, he would not make a choice at all. He would do everything.

After all, in Donald Trump's world, there is no such thing as over-exposure.

ACKNOWLEDGMENTS

As the reader can tell from the Preface, this book has had its twists and turns.

Helping to guide me through those twists and turns was Tim Moore, my editor at Financial Times Prentice Hall, and I want to thank him for the steady, solid support he gave to me throughout this project. It's been a pleasure working with him. I also want to express my gratitude to Russ Hall, who edited the manuscript with his usual deft eye. Both Tim and Russ were always there with kind words about my work, something authors always like to hear.

My thanks as well to others at Financial Times Prentice Hall: John Pierce, Martin Litkowski, Logan Campbell, Kristy Hart, Gina Kanouse, and Krista Hansing. I'm also especially grateful to Lisa Berkowitz and Laura Robinson.

I also want to thank a number of people who facilitated the research in various ways: Ben Borowsky, Jim Dowd, Norma Foerderer, Rhona Graff, Robin Himmler, Suzanne Lupovici, Meredith McIver, and Renee SaintJean.

I am very grateful to Joe Weinert for providing continuous help with the Atlantic City part of the Donald Trump story. Joe was there to answer my e-mails on a continuing basis. My two interviews with him in Atlantic City were especially insightful.

When Donald Trump decided to cooperate with the project, I was able to interview him a number of times starting in early June 2004.

Mr. Trump also arranged for me to attend various private meetings related to his building projects; to travel with him to a building site in Manhattan and watch him inspect it; to journey with him on his helicopter for a book promotion event at QVC, the shopping channel; and to fly with him on his private jet to a "demolition party" for the building of his Chicago property. I also spent time at a casting call for the third season of *The Apprentice* and at the filming of one of the episodes for that third season.

I want to express my gratitude to those who agreed to be interviewed. They are Scott Allen, Kurt Anderson, Tom Auriemma, Tom Barrack, Maryanne Barry, Ben Borowsky, Elizabeth Jane Browde, Mark A. Brown, Mark Burnett, Matthew F. Calamari, Lou Cappelli, Ben Cohen, Ashley Cooper, Greg Cuneo, Frank Fahrenkopf, Steven T. Florio, Norma Foerderer, David M. Friedman, Eric Gillin, Roberta Brandes Gratz, Albert N. Greco, Alan C. Greenberg; Jaime Handwerker, Peter Haynes, Dan Heneghan, Rick Hilton, Abe Hirschfeld, Michael Jacobson, Richard Kahan, Jane Holtz Kay, Natalie L. Keith, Caroline Kepcher, Kirk Kerkorian, Larry Klatzkin, Dan Klores, Sarah Kovner, Robert Kraft, James S. Kunen, Richard Laermer, Richard S. Lefrak, Saul F. Leonard, Milton Leontiades, Paul Levinson, Pamela Liebman, Larry Light, Howard M. Lorber, Ruth Messinger, Larry Mullin, John Myers, Peter Newcomb, Regis Philbin, Michael Pollock, Charles Reiss, Larry Reibstein, Alan A. Rockoff, Marvin Roffman, Nelson Rose, George H. Ross, Howard J. Rubenstein, Phil G. Ruffin, Phil Satre, Richard Schaffer, Jerry Schoenfeld, Elliott D. Sclar, Lisa Silhanek, Steven Spinola, Eliot Spitzer, Andrew M. Susser, Donald Trump Jr., Sid Vaikunta, Jeffrey S. Vasser, Joe Weinert, Allen Weisselberg, Fred Wilpon, Steven C. Witkoff, Bob Wright, Steve Wynn, Alex Yemenidjian, Andrew Zarnett, and Jeff Zucker.

A number of people made this project considerably easier for me, and I wish to thank them: Richard Winkler, Michael and Bobbi Winick, Frankie and Russ Meppen, Debbie Slater, Malcolm Frame, Bernard Sterling, Barry Feldman, Jean Max, Marcus and Eva Eliason, Herb and Mary Stewart Krosney, Mel and Anat Laytner, Marco Greenberg, James Jampel, David Straus and Lynne Breslau, Stacy Perman, Beth Comstock, Anna Perez, and Ed Rock.

Finally, my greatest supporter throughout my entire book career—and during this project—has been my wife, Elinor. Using her skills as a professional editor, she took her usual tough stance on her read-through of an early draft of the manuscript, helping me to clarify numerous points. But I thank her most of all for helping me simply to enjoy our lives together as I traveled thousands of miles and devoted many hours to a project that had one of my tightest book project deadlines.

To the others in my immediate family: my oldest daughter, Miriam, and her husband, Shimon, and their three children: Edo, Maya, and Shai; to my younger daughter, Rachel; and to my son, Adam—I say thank you for being there with such love and good cheer during those moments when I sought relaxation and escape from the research and the writing.

In a sense, the most important person in every book that I write is always the same, and I have always tried to single her out in every acknowledgment that I write for one of my books. But this time, I want to truly single her out—and her alone.

I dedicate this book to my wife, Elinor Slater.

ENDNOTES

PREFACE

"Be advised that...," e-mail from Jason D. Greenblatt to Robert Slater, 8 April 2004.

"The book...," e-mail from Robert Slater to Meredith McIver, 23 March 2004.

"...what an amazing...," Donald Trump, interview with author, 18 May 2004. All other Donald Trump quotes in the book are from my interviews with him on 3 June 2004, 27 July 2004, 18 August 2004, 21 September 2004, 22 September 2004, 11 October 2004, 28 October 2004, and December 2, 2004, unless otherwise indicated.

CHAPTER 1

"Truthful hyperbole...," *Trump: The Art of the Deal,* Donald J. Trump with Tony Schwartz (New York: Warner Books, 1987), p. 58.

"She cost me...," Donald Trump speech to Couture Diamond Conference, 13 October 2004, Plaza Hotel, New York.

"He wants...," ibid.

"I've never seen...," Lou Cappelli, interview with author, 30 July 2004. All other Lou Cappelli quotes in the book are from my interviews with him, unless otherwise indicated.

"If you don't tell people...," *Trump: How to Get Rich,* Donald J. Trump with Meredith McIver (New York: Random House, 2004), p. xiii.

"Billionaire authors are...," ibid., p. xiv.

CHAPTER 2

"You're great...," Eliot Spitzer, interview with author, 9 August 2004. All other Eliot Spitzer quotes in the book are from my interview with him, unless otherwise indicated.

"You've got to try...," Bob Kraft, interview with author, 29 September 2004.

"I hear his voice...," Meredith McIver, interview with author, 11 October 2004.

"He never takes...," Mark Brown, interview with author, 7 June 2004. All other Mark Brown quotes in the book are from my interview with him, unless otherwise indicated.

"He's a machine...," Donald Trump Jr., interview with author, 13 August 2004. All other Donald Trump Jr. quotes in the book are from my interview with him, unless otherwise indicated.

"Total focus...," *Trump: The Art of the Deal,* p. 47.

"Controlled neurosis...," ibid., p. 47.

"It's his money...," Matthew F. Calamari, interview with author, 14 October 2004.

"Oh, I won't have an hour...," Norma Foerderer, interview with author, 29 July 2004. All other Norma Foerderer quotes in the book are from my interview with her, unless otherwise indicated.

"He can't sit still...," Dan Klores, interview with author, 3 August 2004. All other Dan Klores quotes in the book are from my interview with him, unless otherwise indicated.

"One day, Pam Liebman...," Pam Liebman, interview with author, 1 June 2004, All other Pam Liebman quotes in the book are from my interview with her, unless otherwise indicated.

"I do it to do it," *Trump: The Art of the Deal,* p. 1.

"We call it Trump-it-is..., " Greg Cuneo, interview with author, 16 August 2004. All other Greg Cuneo quotes in the book are from my interview with him, unless otherwise indicated.

"All right, I'll be out...," incident recounted by Pam Liebman and Ashley Cooper; Ashley Cooper, interview with author, 27 July 2004.

"Take two rooms...," incident recounted by Alex Yemenidjian, interview with author, 2 August 2004.

"Richard, they're putting...," anecdote told to the author by Richard Lefrak, interview with author, 28 July 2004. All other Richard Lefrak quotes in the book are from my interview with him, unless otherwise indicated.

"Donald takes out...," David Friedman, interview with author, 2 June 2004. All other David Friedman quotes in the book are from my interview with him, unless otherwise indicated.

CHAPTER 3

"When the lights went...," *The Trumps*: *Three Generations That Built an Empire*, Gwenda Blair (New York: Touchstone, 2000), p. 227–228.

"He had guts...," Maryanne Trump Berry, interview with author, 29 July 2004. All other Maryanne Berry quotes in the book are from my interview with her, unless otherwise indicated.

"Nobody knows where...," *Donald Trump: Master of the Deal*, A&E Biography, 2001.

"...the toughest situation...," "Donald Trump Interview," *Playboy*, March 1990.

"Because of his brother's...," Donald Trump on *Larry King Live*, CNN, 8 October 1999.

"He was a strong...," "Donald Trump Interview."

"...humble, modest...," Tom Barrack, interview with author, 6 April 2004. All other Tom Barrack quotes in the book are from my interview with him, unless otherwise indicated.

"He built typical...," Allen Weisselberg, interview with author, 28 July 2004. All other Allen Weisselberg quotes in the book are from my interview with him, unless otherwise indicated.

"Get in, get it done...," *Trump: The Art of the Deal*, p. 65.

"...very assertive, aggressive...," ibid., p. 71.

"I never respected...," *Donald Trump: Master of the Deal*.

"We used to call him...," ibid.

"You said the wrong thing...," ibid.

"he was perfectly built...," Regis Philbin, interview with author, 27 July 2004. All other Regis Philbin quotes in the book are from my interview with him, unless otherwise indicated.

"There's something about...," "Donald Trump Interview."

"He wanted to crawl...," George H. Ross, interview with author, 28 July 2004. All other George H. Ross quotes in the book are from my interview with him, unless otherwise indicated.

"Don't go to Manhattan...," Donald Trump quoted his father on *Larry King Live*, CNN, 8 October 1999.

"And being piloted around...," Cindy Adams, quoted in *Donald Trump: Master of the Deal*.

"A lot of people thought...," Richard Kahan, interview with author, 8 June 2004. All other Richard Kahan quotes in the book are from my interview with him, unless otherwise indicated.

CHAPTER 4

"I believe in doing...," *Trump: The Art of the Comeback*, Donald J. Trump with Kate Bohner (New York: Random House, 1997), p. 154.

"I was out to build...," *Trump: The Art of the Deal*, p. 47.

"It turned out...," Jerry Schoenfeld, interview with author, 14 April 2004. All other Jerry Schoenfeld quotes in the book are from my interview with him, unless otherwise indicated.

"Before he was able to promote...," Howard Lorber, interview with author, 2 June 2004. All other Howard Lorber quotes in the book are from my interview with him, unless otherwise indicated.

"...thought he was crazy...," George Ross, interview with author, 28 July 2004.

"The idea that Donald Trump...," Saul Leonard, interview with author, 27 April 2004. All other Saul Leonard quotes in the book are from my interview with him, unless otherwise indicated.

"You can't con people...," *Trump: The Art of the Deal*, p. 60.

"As Edward Gordon...," *Donald Trump: Deal Maker*, A&E Biography, 1994.

"He turned it into...," Steve Spinola, interview with author, 2 June 2004. All other Steve Spinola quotes in the book are from my interview with him, unless otherwise indicated.

"He made a good deal...," Roberta Brandes Gratz, interview with author, 1 June 2004. All other Roberta Brandes Gratz quotes in the book are from my interview with her, unless otherwise indicated.

"He wants to tear..." Roberta Brandes Gratz, "Invasion of the Monster Buildings," *New York*, 11 June 1979, p. 40–44.

"Whole damn mountain...," "Donald Trump Interview."

"We ran a news conference...," Howard Rubenstein, interview with author, 11 June 2004. All Howard Rubenstein quotes in the book are from my interview with him, unless otherwise indicated.

"Every building casts a shadow," "Donald Trump Interview."

"It was gargantuan in size...," planning official who asked not to be identified, interview with author, 12 April 2004.

"The most revolutionary...," Roberta Brandes Gratz, "Unique Partnership Forged Riverside Oasis," *New York Daily News*, 2 April 2001.

"I found myself...," Sarah Kovner, interview with author, 10 June 2004. All other Sarah Kovner quotes in the book are from my interview with her, unless otherwise indicated.

CHAPTER 5

"Donald Trump was viewed...," Michael Pollock, interview with author, 8 June, 2004. All other Michael Pollock quotes in the book are from my interview with him, unless otherwise indicated.

"As long as my name...," Phil Satre, interview with author, 21 May 2004. All other Phil Sartre quotes in the book are from my interview with him, unless otherwise indicated.

"I had never....," Steve Wynn, interview with author, 4 August 2004. All other Steve Wynn quotes in the book are from my interview with him, unless otherwise indicated.

"Roffman recounted his tale..." Marvin Roffman, interview with author, 19 April 2004. All other Marvin Roffman quotes in the book are from my interview with him, unless otherwise indicated.

"When this property opens...," quoted in *Take Charge of Your Finance Future*, Marvin Roffman (New York: Birch Lane Press, 1994), p. xiii.

"Dear Mr. Wilde...," quoted from the letter which hangs on the front wall of Marvin Roffman's office in Philadelphia; "I call it in the Donald decor," Roffman said. The letter is also quoted in full in *Take Charge of Your Financial Future*, ibid, p. xiv.

"Donald Trump was in his glory...," Joe Weinert, "'I Told You So!'", Trump Says of Mirage Deal," *The Press of Atlantic City*, 21 January 1998, page AI.

CHAPTER 6

"To be young...," "Donald Trump Interview."

"...thanks to hair coloring." Trump wrote: "I will also admit that I color my hair," *Trump: How to Get Rich*, p. 152.

"The most daunting...," ibid.

"In the late 1980s...," Alan Greenberg, interview with author, 26 July 2004. All other Alan Greenberg quotes in the book are from my interview with him, unless otherwise indicated.

"He confused brains...," John Myers, interview with author, 29 July 2004. All other John Myers quotes in the book are from my interview with him, unless otherwise indicated.

"For me, you see...," *Trump: Surviving at the Top*, Donald J. Trump with Charles Leerhsen (New York: Random House, 1990), p. 6.

"...I know firsthand...," *Trump: The Art of the Comeback*, p. 149.

"If you set Donald...," *Donald Trump, Master of the Deal*.

"What Trump found...," Paul Levinson, interview with author, 13 April 2004. All other Paul Levinson quotes in the book are from my interview with him, unless otherwise indicated.

"By far the worst...," *Trump: The Art of the Comeback*, p. 4.

"Donald Trump. The name is...," Larry Light and Joseph Weber, "The Donald's Trump Card," *Business Week* 23, March 1992, p. 74–77.

CHAPTER 7

"Most CEOS are eager...." When I was researching a book on General Electric's Jack Welch, he wanted to make sure that I gave sufficient coverage to the people who ran his businesses and did not focus the book entirely on him. When I wrote a book about Cisco Systems' John Chambers, he preferred that the publisher not put his photo on the book cover.

"I could get him...," Natalie L. Keith, interview with author, 21 April 2004. All other Natalie L. Keith quotes in the book are from my interview with her, unless otherwise indicated.

"Sit down with him over...," "Donald Trump Interview."

"Honestly, Donald...," Ruth Messinger, interview with author, 11 June 2004. All other Ruth Messinger quotes in the book are from my interviews with him, unless otherwise indicated.

"There has always been a display...," "Donald Trump Interview."

"You wonder why...," Larry Light, interview with author, 11 June 2004. All other Larry Light quotes in the book are from my interview with him, unless otherwise indicated.

"*Forbes* put the figure at...," Richard L. Stern and John Connolly, "Manhattan's Favorite Guessing Game: How Rich Is Donald?" *Forbes*, 14 May 1990.

"Since then...," Peter Newcomb, interview with author, 9 June 2004. All other Peter Newcomb quotes in the book are from my interview with him, unless otherwise indicated.

"Most of those...," Larry Reibstein, interview with author, 9 June 2004. All other Larry Reibstein quotes in the book are from my interview with him, unless otherwise indicated.

"It wouldn't quite be...," "400: the Richest People in America," *Forbes* 30 September 2002, p. 144.

CHAPTER 8

"He has never missed...," Phil Ruffin, interview with author, 4 August 2004. All other Phil Ruffin quotes in the book are from my interview with him, unless otherwise indicated.

"You need to generate interest...," *Trump: The Art of the Deal*, p. 56.

"...magnetic...," Steve Witkoff, interview with author, 26 July 2004. All other Steve Witkoff quotes in the book are from my interview with him, unless otherwise indicated.

"Donald's style when it comes...," Tony Schwartz, quoted in *Donald Trump: Master of the Deal*.

"He could have been an unbelievably...," Albert N. Greco, interview with author, 14 April 2004.

"...a closer...," Kirk Kerkorian, interview with author, 2 August 2004.

"People may not...," *Trump: The Art of the Deal*, p. 58.

"He liked to schmooze...," Daniel Heneghan, interview with author, 20 April 2004. All other Daniel Heneghan quotes in the book are from my interview with him, unless otherwise indicated.

"He's not purporting...," Cindy Adams, quoted in *Donald Trump: Master of the Deal.*

"Sam Lefrak used his name...," Fred Wilpon, interview with author, 28 July 2004. All other Fred Wilpon quotes in the book are from my interview with him, unless otherwise indicated.

"How do we get these...," Larry Mullin, interview with author, 20 April 2004.

'I have a lot to lose...," Donald Trump, quoted on *Larry King Live*, CNN, 8 October 1999.

"His great strength...," Andrew Zarnett, interview with author, 3 June 2004.

CHAPTER 9

"That says a lot...," Mark Burnett, interview with author, 25 August 2004. All other Mark Burnett quotes are from my interview with him, unless otherwise indicated.

"Let's think about...," Robert Wright, interview with author, 27 July 2004.

"A lot of people...," Jeff Zucker, interview with author, 27 July 2004.

"You're going to be...," Rick Hilton, interview with author, 28 July 2004.

"Well...," *Larry King Live*, CNN, 27 February 2004.

"Those two words...," *Dateline*, NBC, 16 April 2004.

"It's Lifestyles of the Rich...," *The O'Reilly Factor*, Fox News Channel, 5 January 2004.

"He can do it...," Carolyn Kepcher, interview with author, 30 July 2004.

"...pretty vulgar..." Keith Naughton and Marc Peyser, "Donald Trump and *The Apprentice*: TV's Guilty Pleasure for a Nervous Economy," *Newsweek*, 1 March 2004, p. 48–57.

"[Sonnenfeld] says...," *Dateline*, NBC, 16 April 2004.

"I was very proud...," ibid.

"It's a tough place...," *Larry King Live*, CNN, 27 February 2004.

"When they're stealing...," ibid.

"I'm highly educated...," ibid.

"Like a flame thrower...," *Dateline*, NBC, 16 April 2004.

"Donald Trump and Mark Burnett are...," Knight Ridder/Tribune News Service, 6 February 2004.

CHAPTER 10

"Trump Hotels has a $73.1 million...," Timothy L. O'Brien, "Trump Hotels and Equity Firm Break Off Talks," *New York Times*, 23 September 2004, http://query.nytimes.com/gst/abstract.html?res= F00B1FFB3B5D0C708EDDA00894DC404482&incamp=archive:search.

CHAPTER 11

"Michael Jacobson has been...," Michael Jacobson, interview with author, 4 October 2004.

"There are probably...," Jesse McKinley, "Donald Trump Is Done to a Turn," *New York Times*, 16 October 2004: Section B, p. 7.

"C'mon. Two minutes after...," Donald J. Trump, "What It Feels Like to Be...," *Esquire*, August 2004, p. 72–75.

INDEX

A

accessibility to the media, 126-130
acting skills, 15
Adams, Cindy, 54, 107, 156
Ali, Muhammad, 151-152
The Amazing Race (television show), 192
Ammann, Othmar, 50
Anka, Paul, 67
Anniston, Jennifer, 16
The Apprentice (television show), xiii, xxiii-xxiv, 6-7, 10, 15, 19, 23, 29-30, 124, 150, 165, 169-192, 211-212, 219
    buy-out session in Chicago, 220-222
    casting call for, 188-191
    college course on, 191
    concept for, 171-173
    copycat shows, 224
    criticism of, 183-184
    Donald Trump as perfect host for, 181-183
    Donald Trump's payment for, 187-188
    effect on Donald Trump's reputation, 185-187
    Emmy nomination, 192
    initial doubts about, 174-176
    publicity from, 193-198
    ratings, 177, 225
    signed by NBC, 173-174
    success of, 176-181, 184-185, 188
Atlantic City casinos
    bankruptcy filing, 203-207, 210, 217-218, 225
    financial troubles of, 7
    marketing for, 161, 163
    using profits for Manhattan real estate, 80-82
attention, reasons for attracting, 3, 5. *See also* publicity
attention to detail, 37, 39
author, Donald Trump as, 7, 125-126

B

Ballmer, Steve, xiv
bankruptcy. *See also* foreclosure
    of Atlantic City casinos, 203-207, 210, 217-218, 225
    of Trump Taj Mahal, 115
Barrack, Tom, 46, 157
Barron, John, 224
Barry, Maryanne. *See* Trump, Maryanne (sister)
Barsky, Neil, 89
baseball ambitions, 49
Belzer, Richard, 212
Benanav, Johathan, 101
billionaire lifestyle, 100, 112-113
birthday party, 5-6
Bloomberg, Michael, 22
boardrooms in Trump Tower, 8, 19
Bogle, John, xiv
Bollenbach, Steve, 112
books. *See* publishing
brand recognition
    in avoiding foreclosure, 109
    importance to Donald Trump, 11-14
branding of Donald Trump's name, 145-166, 225-226
Branson, Richard, 174, 188, 224-225
Brown, Mark, 24, 33, 96, 127, 186, 205
Buffett, Warren, 10, 15, 135, 191, 193
building projects. *See* real estate dealings
Burnett, Mark, 165, 171-184, 188
burnishing egos, 13
Bush, George W., 193
business focus, loss of, 104-105
business leaders
    rankings in *Fortune*, 15
    uniqueness of Donald Trump, 15
business magazines, Donald Trump's attitude toward, 137-140
business strategies, 74
Business Week (magazine), 115, 138-139
buy-out sessions for Chicago building, 220-222. *See also* negotiation skills

C

Calamari, Matthew, 28, 36
Cappelli, Lou, 12, 32, 160
Carson, Johnny, 67
casino industry, 77-97
    Atlantic City casinos
        bankruptcy filing, 203-207, 210,
            217-218, 225
        financial troubles of, 7
        marketing for, 161, 163
        using profits for Manhattan real
            estate, 80-82
    Las Vegas, Donald Trump's plans for
        building in, 214-215, 218
    profit margin of casino hotels, 77,
        80-82, 96
Cassini, Igor, 53
casting call for The Apprentice, 188-191
celebrities, Donald Trump's friendships
    with, 20-22
celebrity of Donald Trump, 10-11,
    15-16, 25, 74, 111-112, 135-137,
    170-171, 226. See also branding of
    Donald Trump's name
Chambers, John, xiv, xviii
Chanel, Coco, 153
charisma, 149-151
Chicago, trip to, 218, 220-223
Chicago Sun-Times building,
    demolition of, 218, 223
children of Donald Trump, 20, 216-217.
    See also Trump, Donald Jr. (son);
    Trump, Eric (son); Trump, Ivanka
    (daughter); Trump, Tiffany (daughter)
Civic Alternative and Riverside South
    project, 71-73
civic groups, opposition to Riverside
    South project, 71-73
Clear Channel Premiere Radio
    Networks, 201
Clinton, Bill, 22, 193
clothing, signature line of, 210, 225
Cohen, Roy, 54
Cohn, Harry, 50
college course on The Apprentice, 191
cologne (Trump Cologne), 225
Columbus Day parade (1963), Donald
    Trump leading NYMA in, 50
commercials. See television commercials
Commodore Hotel project, 11, 59-62
    Donald Trump as rescuer, 62-63
    efficient execution of, 63, 65
connections, importance of, 53-55
contract reading, aversion to, 32
Cooper, Ashley, 38, 159

Couric, Katie, 22, 212-213
Credit Suisse First Boston, 205, 210
criticism of The Apprentice, 183-184
Crosby, James, 87
CSI (television show), 176
Cuban, Mark, 174, 188, 224
Cuneo, Greg, 35, 37, 186

D

debt payments. See also financing
    avoiding foreclosure, 106-113
    bailout by Fred Trump, 114
    bankruptcy filing of Atlantic
        City casinos, 203-207, 210,
        217-218, 225
    for casino hotels, 87, 96
    effect of 1989 recession, 102
    financial crisis, overcoming, 114, 116
    reduction of personal debt, 116
    on Taj casino hotel project, 88
Dell, Michael, 15
Delmonico Hotel, 25
demolition of Chicago Sun-Times
    building, 218, 223
Diana, Princess of Wales, 132-133
discipline at NYMA, 48-49
divorce
    from Ivana Trump, 100-101,
        105-106, 115, 132
    from Marla Maples, 219
DLJ Merchant Banking Partners, 205
Dobias, Theodore, 48
doll modeled after Donald Trump, 210
Dynasty (television show), 224

E

Economist (magazine), net worth
    rankings, 116
economy, effect of
    1989 recession, 102-104
    on Donald Trump's businesses, 101
efficiency
    of Donald Trump, 8-9, 213-214
    importance in Commodore Hotel
        project, 63, 65
ego burnishing, 13
Eminem, 197
Emmy nomination for The Apprentice,
    192
Enron, 187
Esquire (magazine), 216
Etess, Mark, 101
exaggeration. See "truthful hyperbole"

The Eye of the Storm: How John Chambers Steered Cisco Systems Through the Technology Collapse, xviii

F

finances
    Economist net worth rankings, 116
    Forbes net worth rankings, 5, 69, 99, 108, 141-143
    off-limits for discussion, 126
financial crisis, overcoming, 114, 116
financing. *See also* debt payments
    avoiding foreclosure, 106-113
    bailout by Fred Trump, 114
    bankruptcy filing of Atlantic City casinos, 203-207, 210, 217-218, 225
    for casino hotels, 80
    for Commodore Hotel project, 61-62
    effect of 1989 recession, 102-104
    for Hilton casino hotel purchase, 86
firing people, Donald Trump's attitude toward, 185. *See also* "You're fired" phrase
flattery, use of, 150-151
Florio, Steve, 153
focus, loss of, 104-105
Foerderer, Norma, 22, 30-31, 69, 120
Forbes (magazine), 137
    net worth rankings, 5, 69, 99, 108, 141-143
Forbes, Malcolm, 121
Fordham, 50
foreclosure, avoiding, 106-113
foreign policy, thoughts on, 215
Fortune (magazine), 131, 156, 193
    cover story on Donald Trump, 10
    powerful business leaders rankings, 15
Friars Club Roast, 163, 211-213
Friedman, David, 39, 158
Friends (television show), 16, 187
friendships with celebrities, 20-22

G

gatekeeper, 30-31
Gates, Bill, xiv, 4, 10, 15, 134-135, 145, 156, 165, 174, 183, 223
Gehry, Frank, 95
Gerstner, Lou, xiv, 135, 183
Goldwyn, Sam, 50
golf, Donald Trump's love for, 8
goods, importance in branding, 151-153
Gordon, Edward, 64

Gotti, Victoria, 212
Graff, Rhona, xix
Grand Hyatt project. *See* Commodore Hotel project
Gratz, Roberta Brandes, 65-66, 71-72
Greco, Albert N., 151
Greenberg, Alan, 102, 120-121
Greenberg, Hank, 15
Greenblatt, Jason D., xiii, xv
Griffin, Merv, 87

H

Hamill, Pete, 131
hand-shaking, aversion to, 23
Harrah, Bill, 79
Harrah's, partnership with, 83, 86
Hasbro television commercial, 202-203
Haydon, Vanessa, 216, 219
Hefner, Hugh, 211
Heidi (*The Apprentice* contestant), 187
helicopter crash, 101
Helmsley, Harry, 52, 101
Helmsley, Leona, 53, 101
Heneghan, Daniel, 154
Hilton, Barron, 84, 87, 175
Hilton, Conrad, 175
Hilton, Paris, 175, 201
Hilton, Rick, 175
Hilton Corporation, buying casino hotel from, 86-87
Holiday Inns, partnership with, 82
HRH Construction, 186
Hudson River project. *See* Riverside South project
Hutton, E. F., 25
Hyatt and Commodore Hotel project, 61
Hyde, Stephen F., 101

I-J

Iacocca, Lee A., 125
IBM, 183
ice-skating rink project, 68-69
Immelt, Jeff, 15
instinctive feel for marketing, 160-165
Iraq, thoughts on, 215
"Is That All There Is?" (song), 6

Jackson, Kwame, 180
Jacobson, Michael, 209
Jobs, Steve, 10, 135
Joe Millionaire (television show), 177
Johnson, Ned and Abby, 15
Johnson, Philip, 95
journalists. *See* media

K-L

Kahan, Richard, 54, 62-63, 65, 72
Keith, Natalie L., 127-128
Kepcher, Carolyn, 173, 180-181, 189, 191
Kerkorian, Kirk, 153, 182
Kerry, John, 193
King, Larry, 149, 177, 184. *See also*
    Larry King Live (television show)
Kissinger, Henry, 164
Klores, Dan, 32, 34, 68, 161, 163
Knauss, Melania, 4, 6, 164, 178, 212, 223
Koch, Ed, 70
Kraft, Bob, 21

landlords, 120
Larry King Live (television show), 121,
    134, 161, 163
Las Vegas
    Donald Trump's plans for building
        in, 214-215, 218
    Trump Tower in, 8
Lay, Ken, 187
Le Club, membership in, 53
Lefrak, Richard, 38, 67, 146, 150-151, 158
Lefrak, Sam, 158-159
Leno, Jay, 22, 176, 197
Leonard, Saul F., 61
Levinson, Paul, 111, 183
Lewis, Lennox, 135
Liberace, 67
Liebman, Pam, 32, 128, 149
lifestyle, billionaire lifestyle, 100, 112-113
Light, Larry, 137-139
litigation, threats of, xiii-xviii, 138-139
Lorber, Howard, 59, 109, 115, 135

M

MacLeod, Mary. *See* Trump, Mary (mother)
Manhattan, start of Donald Trump's
    real estate career, 51-52, 54-55
Maples, Marla, 4, 14, 101, 104-105, 114,
    122-123, 133, 217, 219
Mar-a-Lago, subdivision of, 113
marketing. *See* publicity
Mayer, Louis B., 50
McCarthy, Joseph, 54
McEnroe, John, 212
McIver, Meredith, xiv, 8, 23
media. *See also* publicity
    accessibility to, 126-130
    attitude toward Donald Trump, 9-10
    business leaders' attitude toward,
        119-120
    and Commodore Hotel project, 62-63

Donald Trump's attitude toward,
    120-121, 123, 137-140
focus on Donald Trump during 1989
    recession, 103
handling by Donald Trump, 12-13
sharing personal life with, 133-135
Messinger, Ruth, 73, 132
Meyer, Jim, 92
Michaels, Lorne, 196
micromanagement, 31-37, 39
Midas touch, 100, 104
Miller, Peter, 93
Moore, Tim, xvi
Mullin, Larry, 161-163
multitasking, 7-9, 23
Murdoch, Rupert, 15
Myers, John, 39, 104, 122-123, 148, 163

N

name recognition, 145-166, 225-226
naming of Trump Tower, 67
National Enquirer (magazine), 163
National Football League (NFL), Super
    Bowl introduction, 214
NBC, 202, 212-213, 224
    signing of *The Apprentice*, 173-174
negative publicity, 111, 120-121, 123,
    130-133
negotiation skills, 32-37
    buy-out session for Chicago build-
        ing, 220-222
net worth rankings, 5, 69, 99, 108, 116,
    141-143
New York Construction (magazine),
    127-128
New York Daily News (newspaper),
    19, 102
New York Military Academy (NYMA),
    48-50
New York Post (newspaper), 54, 123, 131
New York Times (newspaper), 115, 127,
    207, 213, 217
New York Yankees game, Donald
    Trump attending, 224
Newcomb, Peter, 141, 159
Newsweek (magazine), 10, 193
NFL (National Football League), Super
    Bowl introduction, 214
Nicklaus, Jack, 147
Northern Illinois University, college
    course on *The Apprentice*, 191
NYMA (New York Military Academy),
    48-50

O-P

office environment. *See* work environment
Ohrbach, Jerry, 212
open-door policy, 20-23
organized crime and casino industry, 78-79
Ovitz, Michael, xiv

Palm Beach Post (newspaper), 16
Palmisano, Sam, 15
Pearlstine, Norman, 92
Perot, Ross, 10, 135
personal debt, reduction of, 116
personal life, sharing with the media, 133-135
personality, force of, 149-151
Philbin, Regis, 22, 49, 67, 176, 180, 182, 212
Phillips, Stone, 212
phone. *See* telephone usage
Plaskin, Glenn, 128
Playboy (magazine), 99-100, 105, 121, 128, 134, 211
Pollock, Michael, 82, 129-130
popularity of Donald Trump. *See* celebrity of Donald Trump
Post, Marjorie Merriweather, 25
postive publicity, 111
Powell, Colin, 193
power suits, signature line of, 210, 225
powerful business leaders rankings in *Fortune*, 15
presidential campaign, 163-164
press conferences, first of Donald Trump's career, 59
Press of Atlantic City (newspaper), 129-130
Prince, Chuck, 15
Pritzker, Jay, 61
profit margin of casino hotels, 77, 80-82, 96
property visitations, 25-26, 28
public persona, 146-150
publicity. *See also* attention; media
    Donald Trump handling personally, 124
    from *The Apprentice*, 193-198
    importance to Donald Trump, 11-14
    instinctive feel for, 160-161, 163-165
    negative publicity, 111, 120-121, 123, 130-133
    positive publicity, 111
    tallest building project, 132
publishing, Donald Trump as author, 125-126

Q-R

QVC, appearance on, 210-211

radio broadcasts, 201
Rancic, Bill, 31, 180, 223
ratings of *The Apprentice*, 177, 225
reading contracts, aversion to, 32
real estate dealings, 31
    with casino hotel profits, 80-82
    Commodore Hotel project, 59-65
    effect of 1989 recession, 102-104
    influence of father on Donald Trump, 46, 48
    Riverside South project, 69-73
    start of Donald Trump's career, 51-59
    Trump Tower project, 65-66, 68
    Wollman ice-skating rink project, 68-69
Rebel Billionaire (television show), 225
recession in 1989, financial effect of, 102-104
Reibstein, Larry, 142
reputation of Donald Trump, effect of *The Apprentice* on, 185-187
rescuer, Donald Trump as, 62-63, 68
Resorts International, buying casino hotel from, 87-88
restructuring. *See* debt payments
Ribis, Nick, 82
richest person rankings. *See* net worth rankings
risks of using name for branding, 158-160
Riverside South project, 69-73
Rodriguez, Alex, 20
Roffman, Marvin, 89-93
Rose, Michael, 82
Ross, Diana, 83
Ross, George, 52, 60, 67, 69, 109, 153, 173, 180, 183, 186
Rubenstein, Howard, 68, 120-121, 129, 140, 153, 157, 195
Ruffin, Phil, 147, 183, 214

S

sales figures for Donald Trump's books, 225
Satre, Phil, 83, 97
Saturday Night Live (television show), 134, 163, 176, 196-201
Schoenfeld, Gerald, 58-59
Schwab, Charles, 125
Schwartz, Tony, 150
Schwarzenegger, Arnold, 20, 22

Scott, Edgar Jr., 91-92
Scott, Lee, xiv, 15, 191, 193
self-marketing. *See* branding of Donald
   Trump's name
Seventeen (magazine), 216
Sharpton, Al, 212
Shepard, Stephen B., 138
Sinatra, Frank, 121, 133, 147
Smarty Jones (horse), 202
Smith, Anna Nicole, 172
Smith, Liz, 105
Sonnenfeld, Jeffrey, 183
The Sopranos (television show), 189
Soros, George, xiv
Spears, Britney, 146, 201
Spielberg, Steven, 67
Spinks, Michael, 212
Spinola, Steven, 65
Spitzer, Eliot, 21, 65, 165, 182
statistics
   celebrity of Donald Trump, 10
   net worth rankings, 5, 69, 99, 108,
      116, 141-143
   powerful business leadesr rankings
      in *Fortune* magazine, 15
   ratings of *The Apprentice*, 177, 225
   sales figures for Donald Trump's
      books, 225
Steinbrenner, George, 224
Stewart, Martha, 147
subdivision of Mar-a-Lago, 113
substance, importance in branding,
   151-153
success of *The Apprentice*, 176-181,
   184-185, 188
Super Bowl introduction, 214
Survivor (television show), 171

T

Taj casino hotel project, 88-90, 115
tallest building project, publicity about,
   132. *See also* Riverside South project
Taylor, Lawrence, 20
technology, dislike of, 29
telephone usage, 24
television. *See also The Apprentice*
   (television show)
   contribution to Donald Trump's
      celebrity, 170-171
   Donald Trump's future plans for,
      224-225
   power for marketing purposes,
      161-164, 166
Television City project. *See* Riverside
   South project

television commercials, Donald Trump
   in, 8, 201-203
Tiegs, Cheryl, 212
Tiffany and naming of Trump Tower, 67
Today (television show), 213
travel, aversion to, 29
traveling with Donald Trump, 218-219
Trump Cologne, 225
Trump, Donald
   attention to detail, 37, 39
   author's interviews with, xix-xxiv
   baseball ambitions of, 49
   birth of, 44
   childhood of, 43-44, 46-47
   children of, 20, 216-217
   college education, 50-51
   competition in real estate with his
      father, 52-53
   daily schedule of, 19, 21
   divorce, 100-101, 105-106, 115,
      132, 219
   early success of, 69
   education at NYMA, 48-50
   Hollywood ambitions of, 50
   motivation of, 11-14, 33
   parental influence on, 43-44, 46, 48
   physical height of, 3, 149
   proximity to his office, 20-21
   rumored affair with Marla
      Maples, 105
   success during 1980s, 100-101
   uniqueness as business leader, 15
Trump, Donald Jr. (son), 4, 20, 24, 28,
   32, 34, 37, 177, 181, 187, 200, 216,
   219-220
Trump, Elizabeth (sister), 45
Trump, Eric (son), 20, 217
Trump Factor, 166
Trump, Fred (father), 43-46, 48, 52-53,
   58, 66, 114
Trump, Fred Jr. (brother), 45
Trump, Friedrich (grandfather), 44
*Trump: How to Get Rich: Big Deals
   from the Star of the Apprentice*,
   xiv, 6, 13, 23, 30, 126, 225
Trump, Ivana (first wife), 30, 65-66, 87,
   100-106, 115, 121, 132-133, 188
Trump, Ivanka (daughter), 20, 216
Trump, Mary (mother), 44-45
Trump, Maryanne (sister), 44-45, 48,
   149, 195
Trump Park Avenue, construction of,
   25-28
Trump Place project. *See* Riverside
   South project
Trump, Robert (brother), 45, 90

Trump Style (magazine), 209
Trump: Surviving at the Top, 105, 126
Trump Taj Mahal. *See* Taj casino
   hotel project
Trump: The Art of the Comeback,
   106, 126
Trump: The Art of the Deal, 33,
   125-126, 150, 154, 163, 171
Trump—the Game television
   commercial, 202-203
*Trump: The Way to the Top: The
   Best Business Advice I Ever
   Received*, 126
*Trump: Think Like a Billionaire:
   Everything You Need to Know
   About Success, Real Estate, and
   Life*, xxiv, 7, 23, 126, 210, 225
Trump, Tiffany (daughter), 20, 217
Trump Tower
   boardrooms in, 8, 19
   construction of, 65-68
   in Las Vegas, 8
Trump Tower (television show), 7, 224
Trump University, 210
Trump World (magazine), 209-210
"truthful hyperbole," 3-4, 128, 150-151,
   153-156, 158
Turner, Ted, 10, 135
21 (restaurant), 52, 54
Tyson, Mike, 135

U-V

U.S. foreign policy, thoughts on, 215
UDC (Urban Development Corporation)
   and Commodore Hotel project, 62

Verazanno Narrows Bridge, opening of, 50
Visa television commercial, 201-202
visiting property. *See* property visitations

W

Wal-Mart, 193
Wall Street Journal (newspaper), 19,
   89, 115
Wallace, Mike, 212
Washington, Denzel, 135
*The Way to the Top: The Best Business
   Advice I Ever Received*, 23
Weinert, Joe, 94-96, 129-130
Weinstein, Harvey, 16, 177
Weisselberg, Allen, 46, 53, 187
Welch, Jack, xiv, xix, xxii, 10, 134-135,
   145, 165, 182-183, 191
Welles, Chris, 138

Westpride, opposition to Riverside
   South project, 71
Wharton School of Business, 51
Wilde, Norman, 91
Wilpon, Fred, 159
Winfrey, Oprah, 147, 161
winning, value of, 49-50
Witkoff, Steve, 149
Wollman ice-skating rink project, 68-69
Woods, Tiger, 147
work environment, 28-29
work ethic, 24-25
workaholic, Donald Trump as, 28
world's tallest building project,
   publicity about, 132. *See also*
   Riverside South project
Wright, Robert, 173-174, 181-182, 188
Wynn, Elaine, 85
Wynn, Steve, 12, 78-79, 83-86, 93-96,
   156-157, 160, 175-176, 179,
   199-200, 215

X-Z

Yemenidjian, Alex, 38, 132-133, 150,
   181, 187
"You're fired" phrase
   origin of, 179
   popularity of, 176, 178

Zanuck, Darryl, 50
Zarnett, Andrew, 164
Ziegfeld, Flo, 50
Zucker, Jeff, 16, 174, 179, 182, 188,
   195-196, 212

Winning Habits
4 Secrets That Will Change the Rest of Your Life
BY DICK LYLES

"In *Winning Habits,* Dick gives us the secrets of a lifetime of fulfillment."

—Spencer Johnson, Author of the worldwide best seller *Who Moved My Cheese?*

Winning Habits is a powerful parable that identifies the four fundamental habits at the heart of success in business and in life—and shows exactly how readers can apply those habits in their own lives. The 4 secrets that will change the rest of readers' lives are: 1) Be first on, last off, and add extra value; 2) Never trade results for excuses; 3) Solve problems in advance; 4) Always make those around you look good.

ISBN 0131453580, © 2004, 128 pp., $19.95

The Power of Impossible Thinking
Transform the Business of Your Life and the Life of Your Business
BY JERRY WIND, COLIN CROOK, AND ROBERT GUNTHER

How often have we heard: "You can do anything once you set your mind to it," or "It's all in the way you look at it." This book helps readers unleash the straitjacket of your current thinking and unleash your potential with powerful new mental models so you can do the seemingly impossible! Jerry Wind and Colin Crook explain how your mental models stand between you and reality, distorting all your perceptions… and how they create both limits and opportunities. Wind and Crook tell why it's so hard to change mental models, and offer practical strategies for dismantling the "hardened missile silos" that are your old and obsolete models. With profiles on Howard Schultz, Oprah Winfrey, and Andy Grove the authors provide real examples of their ideas in action. Simply put, this is the first "hands-on" guide to enhancing your mental models: the key to breakthrough success in business—and in life.

ISBN 0131425021, © 2005, 336 pp., $24.95